Contents

'Foundations of an Ever Closer Union'

'FOUNDATIONS OF AN EVER CLOSER UNION'

An Irish Perspective on the Fifty Years since the Treaty of Rome

Edited by
Mark Callanan

LE CHÉILE
Ó 1957

ToGEthe®
SINCE 1957

DEPARTMENT OF FOREIGN AFFAIRS
AN ROINN GNOTHAI EACHTRACHA

First published in 2007
by the Institute of Public Administration
57–61 Lansdowne Road
Dublin 4
Ireland
www.ipa.ie

in association with
Department of Foreign Affairs and Department of the Taoiseach

ISBN: 978-1-904541-66-0

British Library cataloguing-in-publication data
A catalogue record for this book is available from the British Library

Cover design by Vermillion Graphic Design Consultants, Dublin
Typeset in Ireland by Computertype, Dublin
Printed in Ireland by Betaprint, Dublin

Foreword by An Taoiseach

The signing of the Treaty of Rome fifty years ago represents a key milestone in Europe's history. By putting in place a set of common policies and establishing a set of European institutions, the treaty laid the foundations of today's European Union. The process of integration was based on the pursuit of peace and prosperity by member states, convinced that more can be gained through cooperation and the sharing of sovereignty than by remaining isolated.

Their conviction has been justified by the success of the Union on myriad fronts, as evidenced by decades of enlargement and its continuing allure. It is not hard to understand why member states are equally convinced of the Union's necessity today: many of this century's most vital challenges, particularly those thrown up by climate change, can only be managed through effective international responses. There is no better vehicle available, here or elsewhere, than the European Union.

It is right that we mark the fiftieth anniversary of the Treaty of Rome in Ireland as we have much to celebrate. This book offers an insightful account of the effects that some of the key developments in the European Union have had on Ireland and across Europe. It also reflects on how, throughout our membership, Ireland has been able to shape our Union in areas such as CAP reform, development aid and the negotiation of EU treaties.

As many of the authors comment, the European Union has changed significantly over the past half-century. Ireland too has seen profound changes during the same period. Our participation in the European project has been part of the successful transformation of Irish society and the Irish economy. As we have done in our thirty-five years of membership, Ireland remains ready to play our part in ensuring that Europe meets the challenges which we face today, and will face in the future.

An Taoiseach, Bertie Ahern TD

Foreword by the Minister
for Foreign Affairs

The European treaties have served the people of Europe exceedingly well since the ideal of European integration was first elaborated in 1957. They have brought our diverse European societies into a unique partnership based on the possession of common values and the pursuit of shared objectives. They have provided a pathway to an unrivalled period of European peace and prosperity – arguably the longest period without war in our continent's long history. Among many other things, the treaties have made possible the creation of the European single market, the operation of the Common Agricultural Policy and the structural funds as well as the launch of the euro.

In this publication, *Foundations of an Ever Closer Union*, which has been produced to mark the fiftieth anniversary of the Treaties of Rome, a range of distinguished contributors offer a comprehensive Irish perspective on the process of European integration, which has proven to be so beneficial for Ireland. Active European engagement continues to be a vital priority as we seek to consolidate and build upon the significant national gains we have made during the years of our EU membership.

The essays that follow serve to underline the extent to which Europe has become a central part of the everyday lives of ministers, the Oireachtas, the civil service, our business community and indeed every single Irish citizen. 'Europe' is no longer a place we look to for inspiration or succour as we often did in past centuries. The Union that Europeans have created so painstakingly during the past half-century is an integral part of what we are as a modern nation.

Critics of European integration speak of 'Brussels' as if it were a separate entity to which member states cede sovereignty. In fact, the EU is a unique cooperative project dedicated to advancing the wellbeing of the people of Europe in which Ireland and the other member states are the joint stakeholders. It is we who determine what the European Union does. Its sole role is to serve the people of Europe by enabling our diverse nations to work together in areas where concerted European action makes sense and has proven its worth.

Ireland has been a particular beneficiary of European integration and our advancement within the Union is seen as a model by many of the newer member states. When we joined in 1973, as part of the first enlargement, we were easily the least developed state in what was then the European Economic Community. Access to European markets for Irish exporters and the financial support available under the Union's common policies combined to place our economic development on a dynamic footing.

Our membership, however, has brought us much more than economic benefit. Through its constant and generous support for the Peace Process, the EU has been a catalyst for positive political and economic developments on this island. European involvement has enabled Ireland to contribute to international peace and security in a manner consistent with our best national traditions.

The EU's fiftieth anniversary has a special resonance for Ireland above and beyond that which comes from the many gains we have made as members. This European anniversary also connects with a powerful turning point in Ireland's own economic history, one that was, arguably, the first step on our path to EU membership.

1957 was a very tough time to be in Ireland. The country was crippled by low growth, high unemployment and what Seán Lemass described as the 'appalling drain of emigration'. Years of economic isolation and protectionism had simply not delivered for the Irish people. This prompted radical new thinking about Ireland's future direction. Ideas that incubated in Ireland in the year in which the Treaty of Rome was signed triggered a momentous policy shift towards free trade and the creation of a more efficient, outward-looking economy. In that sense, the prosperity we enjoy today owes much to those far-seeing decisions taken here, and in other European capitals, fifty years ago.

The late 1950s was also a momentous time in the wider world, for that period witnessed the beginnings of the process of decolonisation in Africa as the era of the European empires receded and Europeans turned their attentions to resolving the problems of our own continent.

By any standard, European integration has been a remarkable success story. In 1957 there was no guarantee that this venture would flourish. Nothing like it had ever been tried before and the burden of history might have appeared to make success unlikely. All that has been achieved can, I think, be attributed to the fact that this has fundamentally been a pragmatic rather than a Utopian venture. The ideal of an 'ever closer union' has inspired us, but the accent of EU integration has always been on the delivery of economic and social benefit.

The abiding strength of the Union lies in the fact that the advancement of one member state does not occur at the expense of others. Indeed, we find time and again that one country's success works to the benefit of us all. Membership is not, of course, a sufficient condition for economic success. What the Union provides, however, is a positive framework within which growth and prosperity can be pursued.

The inclusion of a chapter examining Ireland's contribution to 'treaty-making' is particularly timely given the recent completion of the negotiations on the new Reform Treaty. After fifty years, the Union's decision-making arrangements inevitably require some adjustment in order to deal with new circumstances. This treaty represents the latest stage in the evolution of the Union. It is designed to make the EU more effective in its delivery of benefits to European citizens. It is a priority that it be ratified by the twenty-seven member states. In the years ahead, an effective European Union will be one of the important ways in which Europe can cope with the challenges of an increasingly competitive global economic environment. That is why the ratification of this treaty is vitally important for Ireland's future.

Minister for Foreign Affairs, Dermot Ahern TD

Acknowledgements

This book has been published to mark the fiftieth anniversary of the Treaty of Rome in Ireland in 2007. A number of different parties were involved in bringing the project to fruition.

The book is a collaborative venture which would not have been possible without the assistance of the contributing authors, who kindly gave up their valuable time to the publication. My gratitude is due to each of them for bringing their experience and expertise to print, as well as putting up with my frequent emails and telephone calls!

My very good thanks to Jennifer Armstrong who copy-edited the text and who once again brought her efficiency and professionalism to the task. The publications team at the IPA showed their usual patience in dealing with last-minute changes.

The financial contribution of the Department of the Taoiseach and the Department of Foreign Affairs towards the cost of producing this book is gratefully acknowledged. However, it should be noted that any opinions expressed in the book represent the views of the respective authors, and do not constitute the views or policies of government departments or of the Institute of Public Administration.

Mark Callanan

Contributors

Tom Arnold is Chief Executive Officer of Concern Worldwide. He was previously Chief Economist and Assistant Secretary General at the Department of Agriculture.

Dr Gavin Barrett is a Senior Lecturer and President's Research Fellow at the School of Law, University College Dublin, and a visiting scholar at the Institut des Hautes Études Européennes, Strasbourg.

Peter Brennan is Managing Director of EPS Consulting. He is a former Director of the Irish Business and Employers Confederation and previously worked at the Departments of Industry and Commerce and of Foreign Affairs.

Dr Mark Callanan is a Lecturer specialising in European governance and in local government at the Institute of Public Administration, Dublin.

Alan Dukes is Director General of the Institute of European Affairs, Dublin. A former TD and leader of Fine Gael, he has held a number of ministerial portfolios, including Finance, Justice, Agriculture, and Transport, Energy and Communications.

Anthony Foley is Senior Lecturer in Economics and Head of the Economics and Finance Group at Dublin City University Business School. He has published extensively on a range of issues, including the multinational and indigenous industrial sectors in Ireland.

Aoife Keogh is a doctoral researcher in the Department of History and Civilisation at the European University Institute (EUI), Florence.

Professor Dermot Keogh is Head of the History Department in University College Cork, and Emeritus Jean Monnet Professor in European Integration Studies.

Professor Brigid Laffan is Principal of the College of Human Sciences in University College Dublin, and Jean Monnet Professor of European Politics.

Dr Margaret Mary Malone is a Lecturer in European politics based in the Louvain Institute for Ireland in Europe, Leuven.

Dr Michael Mulreany is Assistant Director General at the Institute of Public Administration, Dublin. He has published extensively on a range of issues, including the single European market.

Professor Nicholas Rees is Vice-President for Research and Graduate Studies at the National College of Ireland, Dublin, and Emeritus Jean Monnet Professor of European Institutions and International Relations.

Dr Barry Vaughan is a Lecturer specialising in criminal justice at the Institute of Public Administration, Dublin.

Dr T. K. Whitaker is a former Secretary General of the Department of Finance. He has also served as Governor of the Irish Central Bank, Chancellor of the National University of Ireland, a Senator and a member of the Council of State.

Abbreviations

AFT	An Foras Talúntais
AIDS	Acquired Immune Deficiency Syndrome
AIFTA	Anglo-Irish Free Trade Agreement
BMW	Border, Midland and Western Region
CAP	Common Agricultural Policy
CBF	Coras Beostoic agus Feola
CFSP	Common Foreign and Security Policy
CIO	Committee on Industrial Organisation
COREPER	Committee of Permanent Representatives
CO_2	Carbon Dioxide
CSF	Community Support Framework
D/T	Department of the Taoiseach
EAFRD	European Agricultural Fund for Rural Development
EAGF	European Agricultural Guarantee Fund
EAGGF	European Agricultural Guidance and Guarantee Fund (also known as FEOGA)
EAW	European Arrest Warrant
EC	European Community
ECHR	European Convention on Human Rights
ECJ	European Court of Justice
ECOFIN	Economic and Financial Affairs Council
ECSC	European Coal and Steel Community
ECU	European Currency Unit
EEC	European Economic Community
EFTA	European Free Trade Association
EMS	European Monetary System
EMU	Economic and Monetary Union
EP	European Parliament
EPC	European Political Cooperation
ERDF	European Regional Development Fund
ERM	Exchange Rate Mechanism
ESDP	European Security and Defence Policy
ESF	European Social Fund
EU	European Union

EUMC	European Union Military Committee
Euratom	European Atomic Energy Community
Europol	European Police Office
FEOGA	Fonds Européen d'Orientation et de Garantie Agricole (also known as EAGGF)
FRONTEX	European Agency for the Management of Operational Cooperation at the External Borders
GAERC	General Affairs and External Relations Council
GATT	General Agreement on Tariffs and Trade
GDP	Gross Domestic Product
GNI	Gross National Income
GNP	Gross National Product
HIV	Human Immunodeficiency Virus
IAOS	Irish Agricultural Organisation Society
IBEC	Irish Business and Employers Confederation
ICMSA	Irish Creamery Milk Suppliers' Association
ICOS	Irish Co-operative Organisation Society
IRCHSS	Irish Research Council for the Humanities and Social Sciences
IFA	Irish Farmers' Association
IGC	Intergovernmental Conference
IMF	International Monetary Fund
IPEX	Interparliamentary EU Information Exchange
JHA	Justice and Home Affairs
LDR	Less-Developed Region
MEP	Member of the European Parliament
NAI	National Archives of Ireland
NATO	North Atlantic Treaty Organization
NDP	National Development Plan
NFA	National Farmers' Association
NGO	Non-Governmental Organisation
NUTS	Nomenclature des Unités Territoriales Statistiques (Nomenclature of Territorial Statistical Units)
OECD	Organisation for Economic Co-operation and Development
OEEC	Organisation for European Economic Co-operation
OSCE	Organization for Security and Co-operation in Europe
PANA	Peace and Neutrality Alliance
PSC	Political and Security Committee
QMV	Qualified Majority Voting
R&D	Research and Development
RABIT	Rapid Border Intervention Teams

RDP	Regional Development Programme
REPS	Rural Environment Protection Scheme
RTÉ	Radio Telefís Éireann
S&E	Southern and Eastern Region
SEA	Single European Act
SFP	Single Farm Payment
SHAPE	Supreme Headquarters Allied Powers Europe
SIS	Schengen Information System
SME	Small and Medium-Sized Enterprise
SOG	Senior Officials Group
TD	Teachta Dála (Member of Dáil Éireann)
TEU	Treaty on European Union
UA	Unit of Account
UCC	University College Cork
UK	United Kingdom
UN	United Nations
US	United States
VAT	Value Added Tax
WEU	Western European Union
WTO	World Trade Organization

1

The Treaty of Rome Fifty Years On

Mark Callanan

1957–2007 – Fifty Years of 'Ever Closer Union'

The Treaty of Rome establishing the European Economic Community (EEC), signed in 1957, referred to the determination of the leaders of six countries 'to lay the foundations of an ever closer union among the peoples of Europe'. In the fifty years since, what is today called the European Union (EU) has undergone enormous change.

Fifty years on from the Treaty of Rome, today's EU would in many ways be unrecognisable to the original 'founding fathers', such has been the extent of the transformation in both its membership and mandate over the past half-century. It now has a far wider membership, involving countries that in 1957 were firmly shackled behind the Iron Curtain. It also has a far more extensive mandate, spanning a wide range of areas of public policy.

This book has been compiled and published as part of the celebrations marking the fiftieth anniversary of the Treaty of Rome in Ireland in 2007. It brings together the perspectives of a number of practitioners and academics on developments that have taken place in the process of European integration over the past fifty years. These include chapters covering the early years of European integration and considering Ireland's relationship with the founding members, how developments in continental Europe helped influence changes in Irish economic policy in the 1950s and 1960s, the effects of evolving areas of European public policy and their impact in Ireland, and how Ireland at political and administrative levels has adjusted to the demands of membership.

Overview of book

The common thread running through this book is the Treaty of Rome as the foundation for the process of European integration, and each chapter gives an Irish perspective on a number of different dimensions of that process over the past fifty years. The Rome Treaty, signed in 1957, has been revised a number of times since, and the resulting collective text acts as the 'basic law' governing the operation and the mandate of the EU that exists today. Some of the areas examined by different chapters in this publication directly relate to provisions in the original treaty. In other cases, a more indirect route back to 1957 is discernible, where the Rome Treaty set a somewhat general foundation upon which subsequent treaties built.

For example, Dermot Keogh and Aoife Keogh in Chapter 2 trace the twists and turns in the early years of Ireland's relationship with 'the Six' – the six founding member states that signed the Treaty of Rome in 1957. Based on interviews and correspondence from the period, the chapter explains some of the preparations that were made for and the discussion that surrounded Irish accession, including the membership applications and disappointments of the 1960s, leading up to 1973 when Ireland became a member state in the first wave of enlargement, alongside the United Kingdom and Denmark.

Writing from the perspective of one centrally involved in the changes in Irish economic policy in the 1960s, and in the preparations for joining the EEC in the years before 1973, Ken Whitaker discusses in Chapter 3 the effect that early developments in free trade and integration in continental Europe had on the domestic debate over Irish economic development.

The Treaty of Rome set out a detailed timetable for the establishment of a customs union. The treaty also included somewhat more vague provisions which aspired towards what it called a 'common market' (including the free movement of goods, services, workers and capital), but which today is usually termed the internal market or single market. More detailed provisions on the single market were subsequently agreed upon with the signature in 1986 of the Single European Act. Michael Mulreany, Tony Foley and Margaret Mary Malone in Chapter 4 discuss how the single market project was revived in the 1980s, and some of the benefits that have accrued. They also examine current efforts at completing the single market in areas such as services, and some of the challenges and opportunities this will present.

As Peter Brennan in Chapter 5 notes, the Treaty of Rome referred to a general need to promote the 'harmonious development' of the different economies of the founding six members, and it also established a European Social Fund. In later years, these provisions were built upon to achieve a more developed European cohesion policy, which Ireland and other member states were able to benefit from. The chapter examines the original provisions of the Rome Treaty in this area, the Irish approach to negotiations on cohesion in the run-up to 1973, developments in the 1970s, and the changes instituted since a formal cohesion policy was provided for under the Single European Act in 1986.

The Treaty of Rome also contained a number of far more specific provisions and objectives for the establishment of a Common Agricultural Policy (CAP), which, as Tom Arnold points out in Chapter 6, has had profound effects on the shape and evolution of modern Irish and European agriculture. The chapter reviews the state of Irish agriculture before Ireland became part of the CAP system in 1973, the changes that resulted after 1973, and the effect of the subsequent reforms of the CAP since the 1990s. The chapter also examines the changing role of agriculture in the Irish economy and identifies some of the key political, administrative and institutional actors within Ireland and Europe who were instrumental in bringing about this change.

In contrast, the Rome Treaty was virtually silent on some of the other matters dealt with in this publication – these were areas of European cooperation that only emerged after the treaty was signed and ratified. In terms of external policies, while the Treaty of Rome stated that member states would 'coordinate their trade relations with third countries' under a Common Commercial Policy, and provided for arrangements for the collective conduct of trade negotiations, the practice of coordinating foreign policies developed informally only during the 1970s. This was later extended to include security and defence matters, and this area is addressed by Nicholas Rees in Chapter 7, which looks at Irish foreign policy before membership and how it has evolved in the context of EU membership, tracing some of the key policy and institutional changes.

Similarly, cooperation in the area of justice and home affairs, discussed by Barry Vaughan in Chapter 8, has now become one of the most active areas of policy-making at EU level, but at first only developed informally and outside of the treaty structures in the 1970s and 1980s. The chapter looks at the evolution of this policy area at European level from the 1970s onwards, including the treaty changes agreed at Maastricht and Amsterdam, and discusses some of the challenges that exist for this area of EU activity.

The Treaty of Rome also provided for the establishment of a set of institutions, and remains the basis for today's EU institutions, albeit subject to some reforms since then. Alan Dukes in Chapter 9 gives a fascinating insight into the work of the Council of Ministers, established by the Rome Treaty as a central decision-making institution. The chapter argues that EU business has now become part and parcel of the work of most ministers. As the author has held a number of ministerial portfolios, the chapter provides a unique window into the practicalities of the traditionally secretive business of the Council.

In Chapter 10, Brigid Laffan traces how, within the Irish administrative system, the approach to managing European dossiers has evolved from the early years of membership to the present day. Irish civil servants act as 'boundary managers' in the interface between Dublin and Brussels by tracking developments in Brussels, determining Irish preferences and approaches and representing Ireland's position within various committees and working groups that make up the 'Brussels maze'. The chapter also examines the work of the Irish Permanent Representation (including within COREPER and Council working groups) as an integral part of Ireland's management of EU business, and how, following later amendments to the Treaty of Rome, EU initiatives have become more important for a wider range of government departments. The Irish negotiating style and the approach to coordination between government departments is also assessed.

The Rome Treaty also provided for a system of law-making at European level in a number of specified policy areas, despite the fact that this is a role traditionally reserved for national parliaments. Gavin Barrett addresses the question of parliamentary scrutiny of the executive in relation to EU policy-making in Chapter 11. New arrangements have been put in place following the 'no' vote in the 2001 referendum on the Nice Treaty and the chapter outlines some of these innovations, as well as discussing how further improvements could be made.

Whilst Ireland was not present during the negotiations and signing of the Treaty of Rome in 1957, it has been closely involved in the negotiation of subsequent treaties that have amended the original 1957 text. Mark Callanan in Chapter 12 assesses the Irish contribution to the 'treaty-making' process, from the Single European Act to the recent negotiations over the Constitutional Treaty and the subsequent Reform Treaty.

This book has been designed to allow readers to dip in and out of individual chapters as they please, in the expectation that most will choose this option rather than reading it through on any one occasion. For this reason, an effort has been made to make each chapter as self-contained as possible. Inevitably, this led to some limited overlap in content between chapters, although an attempt has been made to minimise this through cross-references to other chapters where appropriate.

This book does not and could not purport to be a fully comprehensive assessment of EU developments over the past fifty years from an Irish perspective, and a somewhat selective approach had to be taken in choosing which issues to address. To keep the publication within manageable proportions, a number of notable developments are only briefly referred to in this book. While the book covers some key developments in a number of EU policy areas, space has not allowed consideration of the significant impact that, say, EU environmental policy or EU employment law and social policy has had on Ireland. The book examines the effect of European integration on the Oireachtas, and the role of ministers in the Council of Ministers, but there is no chapter devoted to the considerable input that the European Parliament now makes to EU legislation.

A note on names and terms used

The process of European integration is based on a convoluted set of treaties, and different titles have been used to describe the association of European states since World War II, from EEC to EC to EU. Three different 'European Communities' were established in the 1950s. The first of these, the European Coal and Steel Community (ECSC) was established under the Treaty of Paris signed in 1951. Two treaties signed in Rome in 1957 created the other two: the European Atomic Energy Community (Euratom), and the most important of the three, the European Economic Community (EEC).

The European Union (EU) was created by the Treaty on European Union signed in 1992 (often referred to as the Maastricht Treaty). Under the Maastricht Treaty, the EEC was renamed the European Community (EC). The three Communities became component parts of the EU as part of the first pillar of the Union, along with cooperation in areas of foreign and security policy (the second pillar) and justice and home affairs (the third pillar). At the time of publication in 2007, a new Reform Treaty (signed in Lisbon) had just been agreed upon. If ratified, the Reform Treaty will give the EU a single legal personality, and will replace references to EC and European Community in earlier treaties with EU and European Union.

Until then, from a legal point of view, it is strictly speaking more correct to refer to European Community or EC law or policies in many cases. However, the term EU has become much more commonplace in recent years in public discourse. For ease of convenience for the reader, the term EU is generally used in this book for more contemporary references, although EC, EEC and Community are all used for more historical references where this is considered appropriate.

2

Ireland and European Integration: From the Treaty of Rome to Membership

Dermot Keogh and Aoife Keogh

Introduction

This chapter, drawing on the files of the Departments of the Taoiseach and of External Affairs (renamed Foreign Affairs in the 1970s) and interviews with Irish participants, will first examine the background to Ireland's shift in policy from protectionism towards free trade at the end of the 1950s. It will then trace the Irish policy-making and decision-making processes from the time of application in mid-1961 to de Gaulle's veto of British membership in January 1963. It will also examine the renewed application for membership in 1967 and conclude with observations on Ireland's engagement with the European Union.

A small group of politicians and senior civil servants were responsible for the drafting and management of the application for membership and for the subsequent round of discussions which eventually resulted in a positive decision to allow Ireland to enter negotiations on membership.[1] The Irish Permanent Representation to the Commission was not established until 1963. Up to that point the Ambassador to Belgium, Francis Biggar, had the responsibility of playing a dual diplomatic role.[2] He was assisted by

---

[1] The names which feature most frequently in this chapter are the following: Seán Lemass (1899–1971), Taoiseach and leader of the Fianna Fáil government; Frank Aiken (1898–1983), Minister for External Relations; Dr Ken Whitaker (1916–), Secretary, Department of Finance; Cornelius Cremin (1908–1987), Secretary, Department of External Affairs; Hugh McCann (1916–1981), Ambassador to the Court of St James (United Kingdom); Denis McDonald (1910–1986), Ambassador to Paris; Brian Gallagher (1909–1968), Ambassador to the Netherlands up to 1962 and then Ambassador to Germany; and Thomas J. Kiernan (1897–1967), Ambassador to the United States.

[2] The Irish government had acquired a building to house the Permanent Representation in 1962. It remained unoccupied until 1963 when Biggar took over the position as Permanent Representative to the EEC. The failure to open the Permanent Representation earlier may be attributed to administrative infighting over which government department would have the responsibility. Source: Conversation in July 1996 with Noel Dorr, former Secretary of the Department of Foreign Affairs.

Eamonn Gallagher, Department of External Affairs. Donal O'Sullivan, seconded from the Department of Industry and Commerce, also played an important role in the 1961/62 application process.[3] Ireland's civil service generally was poorly prepared to cope with the new challenges thrown up by the decision to 'go into' Europe. There were exceptions, the Secretary of the Department of Finance, T. K. Whitaker, and the Secretary of the Department of External Affairs, Cornelius Cremin, being among the most prominent.[4]

Historical background: From protectionism towards free trade

Between 1945 and 1950 Ireland retained its policy of neutrality. There was a view expressed by Irish diplomats serving in Europe, particularly Joseph Walshe at the Holy See, that a third world war was imminent. In such an uncertain and unpredictable international environment, it was unlikely that Ireland would abandon its position of attempting to stand back from entangling alliances and radical new regional departures. Ireland was prepared to take as much as might be sent its way from Marshall Aid and from international support in general for post-war reconstruction. But the idea of getting engaged in alliances which might involve a mutual defence commitment was not attractive. That, fundamentally, may have been the reason behind the country's refusal to join the North Atlantic Treaty Organization (NATO) in 1949. That isolationist impulse was also evident when Ireland confronted the desire on the continent for the dismantling of the nation-state through the establishment of a federal Europe.

The federalist movement may have had a few followers in Ireland, but there was no enthusiasm in government circles, at the level of the cabinet or senior civil servants, for such a radical integration plan. Neither Éamon de Valera nor the leadership of the Inter-Party Government saw much future for Ireland in a unionist approach to integration as exemplified by Winston Churchill. De Valera, at the Council of Europe, encouraged integration on the continent, but he did not feel that Ireland had any role to play at that time in the process. He felt that historical factors prevented

---

[3] The Irish government, which first considered joining the EEC in 1960, did not transfer additional staff abroad in anticipation of the need to prepare the ground in the capitals of the six member states (the Six) for the formal application when it was submitted on 31 July 1961. Neither did any of the Irish embassies in the EEC, including Brussels, receive any additional staff to help deal with the obstacles which arose in relation to entry to the negotiations.
[4] One of the authors of this chapter (Dermot Keogh) had the good fortune to know Con Cremin well during his retirement and interviewed him a number of times during the 1980s. Dermot Keogh also interviewed Dr Ken Whitaker in July 1996.

Ireland from being able to participate in a project like the European Coal and Steel Community.

Irish economic policy, rooted in protectionism, ran counter to what Jean Monnet sought and worked for during his lifetime. It took nearly a decade, through the depressed years of the 1950s, before the principles and rationale underpinning protectionism would be challenged. The signing of the Treaty of Rome, and the emergence of the European Economic Community (EEC), did not force a major rethink in Irish foreign policy. Ireland was still looking towards Britain for markets. The continent did not appear relevant.

The 1950s was a decade characterised in Ireland by high unemployment and mass emigration (Keogh, 1994). In 1957, the worst year of emigration during the decade, the net loss of population was 54,000 people. The total loss for the decade from 1951 to 1961 was 400,000 people. By 1961 the population had declined to 2.8 million, a drop of 5 per cent on the figure at the foundation of the state in 1922. Unemployment peaked in 1957 when there were 78,000 people out of work (see Walsh, 1979, pp. 28–29). Ireland was wholly dependent on the British market with 81 per cent of its exports going there in 1956. (That figure had dropped to 66 per cent by 1969.) Ireland's dismal economic record stood in contrast to the relative prosperity in neighbouring Britain, in Scandinavia and in the Six.

But, as Girvin (1989) has shown, all the major government departments were slow to move away from the comfort of the old orthodoxies. Confronted by the emergence of the European Free Trade Association (EFTA), the dilemma of the Irish civil servants and politicians was evident and they continued to opt for 'the primacy of traditional policy' (Girvin, 1989). The more heterodox among the civil servants had struck a 'damned if we do and damned if we don't' policy stance. But that was to postpone the inevitable. Outside government circles, between 1957 and 1959, influential economists, including Professor Patrick Lynch in University College Dublin and W. J. Louden Ryan in Trinity College Dublin, signalled the need for a change in policy. In the intimate world of Dublin's minuscule policy-making elite, the thinking in academic, business and agribusiness circles had an influence on senior civil servants, and the impetus for change came from within what would have been commonly regarded as the citadel of conservatism – the Department of Finance.[5]

---

[5] The interaction between civil servants, academics and the business community in Ireland in the late 1950s and early 1960s is an area yet to be explored by historians. Both Lynch and Ryan were, according to Fanning (1978), consulted by Whitaker in the drafting of *Economic Development* (1958).

Ken Whitaker, appointed Secretary of the Department of Finance at the age of forty in 1956, has been duly credited with leading the drive for change in economic policy in the years leading up to the application for full membership of the EEC in 1961 (Lee, 1990). But the significance of that policy decision is better understood in the context of the rearguard hostility to a departure from protectionism which was very evident within the Department of Industry and Commerce and elsewhere. Walsh (1979) correctly argues that 'the formal end of the era of protectionism in Ireland was signalled by its first application for membership' of the EEC (pp. 28–29). Files in the Department of Finance, which were not available to Professor Walsh when he wrote the above, confirm that view.[6]

The Minister for Industry and Commerce, Seán Lemass, authorised the publication on 21 November 1958 of the 250-page study *Economic Development*, prepared by Whitaker, which noted that, 'After 35 years of native government people are asking whether we can achieve an acceptable degree of economic progress. The common talk among parents in the towns, as well as in rural Ireland, is of their children having to emigrate as soon as their education is completed in order to secure a reasonable standard of living' (p. 5). Completed six months before, many of the ideas in the study were adopted by the government White Paper, *Programme for Economic Expansion* (Government of Ireland, 1958) which had already been published on 11 November. Both documents had a significant influence on the changing of the fundamental orthodoxies of Irish economic thinking.[7]

Lemass, who had chaired the cabinet committee which had finalised the text of the White Paper, became Taoiseach in June 1959. The implementation of those ideas became his first priority in an Ireland which in the early 1960s was beginning to show some signs of recovery from the malaise and torpor of the 1950s. The establishment of an Irish television station in 1961 did much to expose the society to self-analysis, to self-criticism and to seeing the state of the nation in a comparative European and wider international context (Savage, 1996; for a general discussion on Irish society, see Keogh, 1994, pp. 243–294).

The new economic strategy was to increase Irish agricultural production and look for markets in the higher-priced continental food market. The plan was also to attract foreign capital for investment in employment-intensive, manufacturing export industries (Breen *et al.*, 1990). The shift

---

[6] See, in particular, personal file in possession of Ken Whitaker which he kindly allowed Dermot Keogh to consult in July 1996.
[7] This view is not universally accepted. Whitaker himself has traced the process (Whitaker, 1983).

towards swift trade liberalisation was not that easily achieved against what Whitaker described on 27 November 1959 as 'the diehard Industry and Commerce contention that joining EFTA (and presumably any other free trade area) would be of no economic benefit to this country'.[8] Lemass came to share Whitaker's desire to move away from what the latter had termed 'unprogressive isolation'.[9] Whitaker had developed his ideas on the matter on 14 December 1959 in a memorandum entitled 'Reasons for Reducing Protection' (see Whitaker, 2006, pp. 51–57). This internal debate was taking place in the context of the wider discussion about possible Irish membership of EFTA, which the British strongly encouraged.[10] The Secretary of the Department of Industry and Commerce, J. C. B. MacCarthy, was less than impressed with Whitaker's line of argument, and he told him on 22 December:

> I feel, however, that I ought to say at this stage in relation to your memorandum on the desirability of reducing protection that I cannot accept the views set out in it other than as a, if you will not mind my putting it that way, somewhat idealistic approach which is not, as I am sure you will agree, backed by anything more than faith in the operation of the economic laws which are expounded.[11]

Whitaker did very much mind, and he wrote on 23 December to MacCarthy:

> Before we enter the season of goodwill I feel I should make a short comment on your letter of 22nd December, which rather unfairly tries to force me into accepting, as applying to our memorandum 'Reasons for Reducing Protection', either of two denigratory epithets, 'provocative' or 'doctrinaire'. I hope that on reconsideration you will treat this reasoned document not as putting forward an 'idealistic' approach but for reasons given in it and elaborated in the letter I sent Cremin yesterday as containing, in my view, the essence of realism. ... We both of us know people who are more Catholic than the Pope; should

---

[8] Whitaker to Charlie Murray (Department of the Taoiseach), 27 November 1959 (see also Whitaker, 2006, p. 31). The personal file from which this minute has been taken was kindly loaned to Dermot Keogh by Ken Whitaker and is referred to in future as the 'Whitaker file'.

[9] Whitaker to Maurice Moynihan, Secretary, Department of the Taoiseach, 27 November 1959 (Whitaker file).

[10] See Cremin's minute, 27 October 1959, of meeting between the Taoiseach and the Secretaries of Finance and of External Affairs, and the Deputy Secretaries of Industry and Commerce and of Agriculture (Whitaker file).

[11] MacCarthy to Whitaker, 22 December 1959 (Whitaker file) (see also Whitaker, 2006, p. 68).

Industry and Commerce not guard against being more protectionist than the Federation of Irish Industries?[12]

Whitaker had won the support of Lemass who was not an easy or enthusiastic convert to a free trade policy. Both men were enthusiastically supported by the Irish Council of the European Movement, which included among its active and influential membership the future Foreign Minister and Taoiseach, Garret FitzGerald (Hederman, 1983). Domestic pressure mounted to join the EEC, as Lemass revealed on 13 October 1962 in a conversation with French Foreign Minister Maurice Couve de Murville:

> In this connection, he [Lemass] recalled the existence already in 1960 of some pressure on the Government by economic interests to join the Six, adding that it became quite clear from the way in which Mr [R.] Maudling [minister who had managed the free trade area talks] reacted to a reference to this fact, during discussions in London in February of that year, that such a move on our part would be interpreted by the British in a way which would have had serious repercussions on our trade relations with them.[13]

The orthodoxies of protectionism had become deeply entrenched in the civil service, particularly in the upper echelons of the Department of Industry and Commerce, of which, paradoxically, Lemass was minister until his appointment as Taoiseach in 1959.[14] But by the latter years of the 1950s, the protectionist policy was under challenge. The Irish Council of the European Movement hosted events in Dublin which encouraged Irish government, industry and agriculture to look more favourably on the advent of the EEC.

Ireland's decision to apply for full membership of the EEC on 31 July 1961 was symbolic of the significant domestic political victory which the Taoiseach and a section of the civil service had enjoyed over the traditionalists in the ruling Fianna Fáil party and in the civil service (for an insight into how European developments influenced that domestic debate,

---

[12] Whitaker to MacCarthy, 23 December 1959 (Whitaker file) (see also Whitaker, 2006, p. 70).

[13] Cremin, draft minute, 5 November 1962, Department of the Taoiseach (cited henceforth as D/T), S17246 S/62, National Archives Institute, Bishop Street, Dublin (referred to henceforth as NAI). This exchange occurred during talks in London which ended with the signing of a trade agreement in 1960 (this was replaced by the Anglo-Irish Free Trade Agreement, which was signed on 14 December 1965).

[14] For general background to the history of that department, see Daly (1992). For one of the best overviews of the period, see Girvin (1989, pp. 169–201). See also Lee (1989, pp. 329–410).

see Chapter 3). The latter were still wedded to the idea of protectionism – a policy which had been pursued since Éamon de Valera first came to power in 1932. When de Valera retired from politics in 1959 at the age of seventy-seven, Fianna Fáil had been in office for twenty-one of those twenty-seven years. De Valera's departure did not so much precipitate the change from protectionism to free trade as facilitate the acceleration of a process which had been initiated by the untenable nature of the status quo. There was great surprise in Dublin when it was rumoured in early 1961 that Britain might apply for full EEC membership. Dublin now had no choice but to seek full membership. Britain influenced the timing of the Irish decision, but the ideological battle to opt for free trade had been long since won.

Ireland's application for membership, July 1961 to January 1962

The Irish government decided, following the submission of its letter of application to join the EEC on 31 July 1961, to send an explanatory *aide-mémoire* to each of the governments of the Six.[15] Drafted by Cremin, it concentrated very much on the economic dimension of the Irish application. This tactic resulted only in confusing and complicating the Irish position and Lemass had to instruct Irish diplomats on 14 August to state that the *aide-mémoire* was not part of the Irish application. Professor Ludwig Erhard, the German Vice-Chancellor, Minister for Economics and President of the Council of Ministers, had sent a query to Dublin as to whether the *aide-mémoire* formed part of Ireland's formal application.[16] Lemass replied in the negative on 19 August. Erhard then informed the Taoiseach that the Irish application would be placed before the Council of Ministers at their next meeting.

The Council met on 25, 26 and 27 September 1961 and agreed the United Kingdom and Denmark should be allowed to proceed to the negotiation stage. In the case of Ireland, the Council decided to wait upon the opinion of the Commission which would be ready by mid-October. Although never published, it is reported to have referred to the need to study whether Ireland, in view of her 'special circumstances', would be in a position to fulfil the economic and political commitments of member states under the Treaty of Rome.

---

[15] A White Paper on Ireland and the EEC was published in early July (Government of Ireland, 1961).

[16] Subsequently, Irish officials were to feel that the absence of any reference to the country's commitment to the political dimension of the EEC had been a mistake which they were obliged to correct throughout the latter part of 1961 (see Maher, 1986).

Following the Council, Erhard told Lemass in a letter on 24 October that the member states of the Six wished to have an 'exchange of views' with him in Brussels to discuss 'the special problems' raised by the application (Maher, 1986, p. 142). More experienced observers of EEC politics might not have reacted negatively to that proposal. But so concerned had Lemass already become at the reports from Irish embassies about the 'special problems' of the Irish case that he had sent Whitaker and Cremin on a tour of the capitals between 5 and 13 September 1961. Although they were very well received, they concluded that the political dimension of the Irish application was a source of much speculation.[17] Would Ireland play her role in a future Political Community and in a Defence Community if and when they came into existence? Here was the negative legacy of the policy of neutrality. Even more alarmingly, both men also gathered from a senior official in the Foreign Ministry in Bonn that the most Dublin could hope for was associate membership.[18]

As a consequence of their report, Irish diplomatic efforts in the second half of 1961 were directed towards assuaging the fears of European and American politicians and administrators concerning the country's economic preparedness and its good faith in regard to the longer-term objectives for the establishment of a Political Community and ultimately a European defence commitment.[19] Meanwhile, great care was paid in the intervening weeks to the drafting of a text for Lemass's speech on 18 January 1962 in Brussels. Sensitised by his recent trip to the capitals of the Six, Whitaker told Lemass in a memorandum that 'it would be economic disaster for us to be outside the community if Britain is in it'. He was especially keen to avoid any suggestion that, if joining NATO were insisted upon as a condition of membership, Ireland would not withdraw its application: 'Nobody has yet told us that this is a condition … On the other hand, nobody so loves us as to want us in the EEC on our own terms' (Whitaker, 1993). Whitaker's memorandum did have an influence and led to a number of significant changes in the text of Lemass's speech.[20]

---

[17] Whitaker recalled one anecdote about visiting Luxembourg where they were well received by a friend known to him from the World Bank. 'So glad to see you again and I remember your wonderful Scotch'. When Whitaker reminded him that it must have been 'Irish' he said he was only using the term 'Scotch' in the general sense.

[18] Whitaker interview, Dublin, July 1996.

[19] Lemass, in a speech to the Cork Chamber of Commerce on 11 November, spoke of the great economic progress enjoyed by Ireland in recent years and welcomed the immediate political obligations of membership of the Community being authoritatively defined. Although not a member of NATO, Lemass said that Ireland was not unwilling to participate in the movement for European integration (Maher, 1986).

[20] Whitaker, who made no claim to have been responsible for the changes, did mention one change in particular which was made to the text in relation to neutrality.

The Taoiseach, keen to counteract the view that Ireland was only half-hearted about its application, told the Brussels' meeting:

> While Ireland did not accede to the North Atlantic Treaty, we have always agreed with the general aim of the Treaty. The fact that we did not accede to it was due to the special circumstances and does not qualify in any way our acceptance of the ideal of European unity and of the conception, embodied in the Treaty of Rome and the Bonn Declaration of 18 July last, of the duties, obligations and responsibilities which European unity would impose (quoted in Maher, 1986, pp. 375–376).

Lemass covered all the major areas in his presentation. The overall impact was favourable according to Ambassador Biggar who spoke about the visit to officials in the Dutch, Swedish and Norwegian delegations. However, Ambassador McDonald in Paris was not able to ascertain with any degree of precision the reaction of the French who had taken over the Council presidency in January.[21] Senior officials in Dublin knew that doubts lingered among the Six and in the Commission about the weak state of the Irish economy. There were also concerns over Ireland's non-membership of NATO.[22]

Domestic concern over NATO and 'political union'

Domestic reaction to the Irish application had been broadly very positive. Lemass received praise from his Fianna Fáil colleagues and the opposition Fine Gael party broadly agreed with the government's EEC strategy. The Labour Party and a number of independent backbenchers were more agnostic; questions were asked in Dáil Éireann about the country's neutral status in the light of the application for membership of the EEC. Were the political dimension of the EEC to become the subject of internal political controversy, there would be a danger that such news would only reinforce doubts already expressed in a number of the European capitals over the bona fides of the Irish case. With the undoubted private promptings of the Taoiseach, the Minister for Lands Micheál Ó Moráin made a speech on 5 February 1962 in Claremorris, County Mayo, in the course of which he said:

---

[21] Biggar to Cremin, 30 January 1962 [dated 1961 in error] and Ambassador McDonald, 31 January 1962, D/T, S17246A/62, NAI.

[22] But the picture was not entirely bleak. The Economic Counsellor at the Irish Embassy in Brussels, Donal O'Sullivan, heard from Van Costen of the Netherlands' mission that the feeling in The Hague was 'it will now be difficult for any member government to justify opposition to your being accepted as full members'. O'Sullivan to Cremin, 29 January 1962, D/T, S17246A/62, NAI.

It had been made quite clear by the Taoiseach on different occasions that a policy of neutrality here in the present world division between communism and freedom was never laid down by us or indeed ever envisaged by our people. Neutrality in this context is not a policy to which we would even wish to appear committed … Our whole history and cultural tradition and outlook has been bound up with that of Europe for past ages. We have, I believe, a full part to play in this day and age in the integration and development of a United States of Europe, and towards this end it may be necessary for us to share any political decisions for the common good.[23]

Perhaps the minister exceeded his brief? But the speech only brought further unwelcome publicity and fuelled domestic controversy over the future of Irish neutrality. That did not please Whitaker who, on 10 February, told his counterpart in the Department of the Taoiseach, Nicholas Nolan, that if the political dimension of the EEC became the subject of internal controversy it would not escape the notice of Brussels. He suggested that, in order to counter any further speculation, Lemass should table a motion that Dáil Éireann approved of his statement in Brussels.[24] Whitaker was told that the idea would be put to the Taoiseach.[25] But that did not happen.

Lemass, facing hostile questioning in Dáil Éireann on 14 February on the political and defence dimensions of the Irish application, stated:

I say in this regard that it would be highly undesirable that remarks made here should give the impression in Europe that there is a public opinion in this country which regards membership of NATO as something discreditable. The view of the Government in that regard has been made clear. We think the existence of NATO is necessary for the preservation of peace and for the defence of the countries of Western Europe, including this country. Although we are not members of NATO, we are in full agreement with its aims.[26]

Seeking to ensure that an unambiguous message would reach Brussels, Lemass took many opportunities to stress the message cited immediately above. But as the survival of the government depended upon the vote of a single independent, Lemass had also to ensure that he pacified backbenchers in Dáil Éireann.

[23] Speech delivered in Conway's Hotel, Claremorris on 5 February 1962, D/T, S17246A/62, NAI.
[24] See minute on file D/T, S17246A/62, NAI.
[25] Whitaker to Nolan, 10 February 1962, D/T, S17246A/62, NAI.
[26] Dáil Debates, vol. 193, cols. 6–8, 14 February 1962.

The secretaries general of the government departments involved in the application – the Taoiseach's office, Agriculture, Finance, Industry and Commerce and External Affairs – met on the same day as the parliamentary session.[27] Cremin, of External Affairs, tabled a recent report from the Irish Ambassador in Paris: Ambassador McDonald had spoken to the Director of the Economic Division, Olivier Wormser, at the Quai d'Orsay and 'according to the impression he formed,' said Cremin, 'Mr Wormser's attitude to our application was negative'. That must have worried Cremin in particular. Cremin knew Wormser from the early 1950s when he had served as Irish Ambassador in France and would have agreed with Alain Peyrefitte's view of that distinguished official: '*Ce gaulliste de toujours et de premier rang n'a cessé de rendre les plus grands service a de Gaulle*' (Peyrefitte, 1994, pp. 434–435) (his powers of Cartesian analysis would become well known to the British negotiators). Cremin stressed to the meeting the ultimate uncertainty of the political implications of membership. Britain, he said, might enter the EEC without being 'allowed' to join the political union. Cremin continued:

> If one looked at the Bonn Declaration from that standpoint, it would be seen that, whereas it was interpreted to mean that if a country were to join the EEC it must be ready to join in the political union, it was not quite explicit on this point. These observations were, however, highly conjectural, arising out of press comment about the 'exclusiveness' of the second French draft [Fouchet Plan], and it would be imprudent to assume that willingness to participate in political union was not a prerequisite for membership of the Community.[28]

Whitaker, who worked closely with Cremin, sought the immediate preparation of a paper on the political implications of Irish membership of the EEC, not only in relation to NATO but it would also include matters such as the surrender of sovereignty to Community institutions. Cremin undertook to have a comprehensive document drafted on the political implications of membership.[29]

As senior officials in Dublin sought to interpret the politics of the EEC, the Irish government continued to receive bad news from the Ambassador

---

[27] It is worth noting two points here. The Secretary of the Department of Defence did not participate in the EEC interdepartmental committee discussions. There is no evidence that the views of the Minister for Defence were sought on the medium to long-term security and defence implications of Ireland's proposed membership of the EEC.

[28] Minutes of meeting of departmental secretaries, 14 February 1962, D/T, S17246A/62, NAI.

[29] Minutes of meeting of departmental secretaries, 14 February 1962, D/T, S17246A/62, NAI.

in Brussels during the last two weeks in February. Ambassador Biggar met the Secretary General of the Council of Ministers, M. Calmes, concerning the probable handling of the Irish application at the Council meeting on 5 March. Biggar, when told that the application was not formally on the agenda, spoke about the inconvenience of delay. Calmes undertook to speak to Couve de Murville, as France held the presidency of the Council.[30] Biggar's report together with one from the Paris embassy created a flurry of uncertainty in Dublin. Whitaker, in contrast, felt it was very important for the Irish to hold their nerve, as he told Cremin on 1 March, 'It is impolitic to rush them when they have other and more pressing preoccupations. If rushed, they may take up the position suggested by the most negatively minded member, this being the line of least resistance'.[31]

Whitaker suggested that it was better in the circumstances to maintain a 'dignified calm' and to take action through the Irish ambassadors in Brussels and Paris. He suggested that Couve de Murville be made aware that the Irish noted with disappointment that the question of Ireland's application had not been placed on the agenda for the Council meeting on 5 March, and it was to be hoped that that would not exclude the possibility of the Council dealing with it.

A meeting of departmental secretaries on the same day (1 March) agreed with Whitaker's suggestion that a tactful and moderately worded approach should be made as soon as possible by Ambassador McDonald to Couve de Murville, in his capacity as Chairman of the EEC Council of Ministers. This approach should take the form of a personal message from the Taoiseach to the effect that he had learned from the mission in Brussels that Ireland was not included in the formal agenda for the meeting of the Council, and that he was somewhat disappointed by this development as he had understood from the meeting of 18 January that Ireland's approach would be before the March meeting of the Council. Cremin was to inform McDonald in Paris of this decision. Ambassador Biggar in Brussels was also to approach Calmes to advise him of Dublin's overture to Couve de Murville.

At the same meeting Whitaker, worried by the divisions within Dáil Éireann on membership of NATO, told his fellow secretaries that they had to keep clear in their minds that, while membership of NATO may not be a *sine qua non* for entry into the EEC, Ireland would be committed to participate in the common defence arrangements and foreign policy of the

---

[30] Cremin's note on Biggar's report, 28 February 1962, D/T, S17246D, NAI.
[31] Whitaker to Cremin, 1 March 1962, D/T, S17246D, NAI.

Community. Whitaker stated that while European ministers would no doubt understand the political difficulties presented by a name or by certain formalities, he thought there was considerable danger that Ireland's present attitude would be understood in Community circles to mean that it could not join in any defence system with Britain.

Whitaker's emphasis clearly revealed his grasp of the EEC as a Community in the process of evolution; Ireland was not joining a static organisation. Therefore, in retrospect, it is important to point out Whitaker's ability to contextualise the NATO question which was not on the table but, even if only made semi-explicit, neither was it an abstract consideration.[32] As the session concluded, Whitaker returned to the suggestion that he had made at an earlier meeting; he felt that it was time to 'straighten these matters out by means of an objective, logical statement on the political implications of membership of the EEC'.[33]

That logical statement may have partially come from Lemass in the form of an interview on 15 March with Garret FitzGerald on Telefís Éireann's *Topic at Ten* programme. Lemass first stressed the need for full membership. He then went on to give full reassurance regarding the Irish position: 'Personally, I regard this coming together of Western European countries as the greatest, most hopeful event of this century, and enormous in its potential for good, not merely for the peoples of Europe but for the whole world'. When FitzGerald asked him about the coordination of foreign policy, defence and cultural matters, he replied: 'Yes, indeed, it is clear that without full and unreserved acceptance of these obligations, membership will not be conceded to any country'. FitzGerald then asked about the significance of NATO:

… we are not members of NATO, to explain that this did not mean that we are not in agreement with the general aims of NATO, but was due to special circumstances, and to stress that it implied no lack of enthusiasm or support for the idea of European unity. There is, however, no reason to think that our non-membership of NATO will be a decisive factor affecting our admission to the community.[34]

---

[32] The above lines are our interpretation of Whitaker's position.

[33] Minutes of meeting of departmental secretaries, 1 March 1962, D/T, S17246D, NAI.

[34] Transcript of Lemass's interview with FitzGerald, 15 March 1962, D/T, S17246D/62, NAI. A journalist colleague of FitzGerald's, Desmond Fisher, had interviewed Walter Hallstein around that time. While he declined to speak explicitly about Ireland and NATO, he did have the following observations to make. He said 'the nature of neutrality has changed'. He said that the art of diplomacy was not to act in a way that would win the next war but would rather ensure that there would be no war.

The message to Couve de Murville had been drafted on 2 March. Lemass approved the text and that evening it was delivered by McDonald to the Quai d'Orsay; Couve de Murville read the note down 'with a great show of concentration'. The ambassador noted that his attitude was 'friendly but non-committal' on balance, his manner 'was objective and perhaps encouraging rather than anything to the contrary'. Although Ireland was not on the agenda, McDonald was told that the Six would discuss a number of cases on 6 March, including Ireland, Spain and the neutrals which, Couve de Murville remarked, presented special problems. Asked about Denmark being in a special category, he said they were to have discussions with the Danes at the end of March. The ambassador asked if they were to be regarded as negotiations proper, but Couve de Murville 'pooh-poohed the idea a bit, saying that he did not know if he could call them negotiations'.

Couve de Murville went on to say, apropos of paragraph 4 of the Irish note, that perhaps the best thing would be for the Six to give something to the Irish government which could be passed on to the public after the discussions which were to take place on 6 March. The ambassador replied: 'I agreed, in so far as I could do so for myself, but I told him that I would like to check the point with Dublin and that I could do so immediately on returning to my office'. Couve de Murville agreed that, if the suggestion was agreeable to the Taoiseach, the ambassador would not have to do anything more. McDonald then asked, in a personal capacity, about his linking of Spain and Ireland and whether there was an association in the minister's mind between the two cases. Couve de Murville replied: '*il n'y a aucun rapport entre les deux cas*'.[35]

Cremin, on receipt of McDonald's report, wrote to Whitaker on 6 March that the Taoiseach regarded Couve de Murville's suggestion as 'reasonable' as did the other secretaries.[36] The outcome of the subsequent Council meeting was deemed to be satisfactory by senior Irish officials in Brussels. They were told, however, that the Council did not have sufficient information on the Irish case and a meeting on 11 May was suggested between Irish civil servants and the heads of the permanent representations.[37]

Ambassador Biggar also learned that things were going rather slowly with the British application, a finding supported by the Irish Ambassador in London, Hugh McCann, who reported on 9 March on an interview with

---

[35] McDonald to Cremin, 3 March 1962, D/T, S17246D/62, NAI.
[36] Cremin to Whitaker, 6 March 1962, D/T, S17246D, NAI.
[37] Biggar to Cremin, 13 March 1962, D/T, S17246D/62, NAI.

the British Minister for Agriculture, Christopher Soames, who brought up
the subject of the negotiations indirectly:

> He went on to add, however, that it was clear from his talk with Mr
> Pisani, the French Minister of Agriculture, that the French had greedy
> eyes set on the big food market in Britain. No doubt, the French would
> look on us as a source of competing agricultural surpluses and that they
> would probably wonder what they had to gain from our membership of
> the EEC.[38]

The Irish Ambassador in Bonn reported his conversation with the
German Secretary of State in charge of Economic Affairs at the Foreign
Office, Herr Lahr:

> To my disappointment, Herr Lahr spoke along the same lines as he had
> done when Messrs Whitaker and Cremin were here in September last.
> For instance, he repeated his thesis that it must still be decided what
> kind of connection – full membership or association – would really be
> in our interest.

Lahr, referring to the political aspects of the EEC, said that they had no
doubts about the Irish attitude in world affairs and they knew Ireland's
reasons for not joining NATO. But he said that the Irish application had not
been dealt with in any precise examination. He thought that, by the
summer, the Irish government would be able to get down to serious
discussions.[39]

Whitaker and other senior officials spent the first two weeks of April
1962 doing preparatory work on the Irish case. On 18 April Dublin
received a list of questions concerning economic aspects of its application
from Ambassador J. M. Boegner, Head of the French Permanent
Representation. On 4 May the departmental secretaries met to review the
final text of the answers.[40] On the day of the delegation's departure, 10
May, Lemass gave another strong pro-EEC speech to the Irish
Management Institute.

The press communiqué issued after the exchanges in Brussels on 11
May 1962 gave very little information to the Irish public on what had taken
place. It merely recorded that, under the presidency of Ambassador J. M.
Boegner, the Committee of Permanent Representatives of the member

---

[38] McCann to Cremin, 9 March 1962, D/T, S17246D/62, NAI.
[39] Irish Ambassador in Bonn to Cremin, 27 March 1962, D/T, S17246F/62, NAI.
[40] Meeting of departmental secretaries, 4 May 1962, D/T, S17246G/62, NAI.

states of the EEC met, in the presence of representatives of the
Commission, with a delegation of senior Irish officials led by Dr T. K.
Whitaker, Secretary of the Department of Finance. The meeting took place
in 'an atmosphere of frank cordiality and mutual understanding'.[41]

The delegation returned home confident that the questions had been
answered adequately.[42] An eighteen-page memorandum was prepared for
government, which reviewed the progress of the application to date,
providing details and an analysis of the consultations in Brussels on 11
May.[43]

Disappointments during summer 1962

There was to be no real movement on the Irish application until autumn
1962. But during the early part of the summer, Irish diplomats reported on
their high-level contacts in Britain, Germany and France. On 25 June the
new Irish Ambassador to Bonn, Brian Gallagher, was received by
Chancellor Adenauer. The latter started off by assuring the envoy that there
was a great amount of goodwill in Germany for Ireland. Regarding the new
applicants for membership, the Chancellor said that there were extremely
difficult negotiations in progress with the British at the present time, and
he thought that it would still take a long time before those difficulties could
be resolved. He felt that the connections between Britain and the overseas
countries of the Commonwealth, and especially with Canada, Australia
and New Zealand, were important and valuable, and he would not wish to
see them broken. It would no doubt be necessary to taper off gradually the
economic preferences. The position was also somewhat complicated by
reason of the fact that the issue was not only solely between Britain and the
Six. The United States also had a view in the matter. The Irish envoy
concluded: 'In dismissing me, the Chancellor reiterated that Ireland
enjoyed great goodwill in Germany and I could take it that this goodwill
would be carried over into the field which we had just been discussing'.[44]

In London, Ambassador McCann met the British Secretary of State for
Commonwealth Relations, Duncan Sandys, on 27 June 1962 for the
purpose of a 'general chat'. Sandys told McCann that he was still
reasonably optimistic about the successful outcome of the British
negotiations. He said that there appeared to be a general acceptance within
the Six that Britain would join the EEC. On the question of the time

[41] Text of communiqué, 12 May 1962, D/T, S17246G/62, NAI.
[42] Interview with Whitaker, July 1996.
[43] Text of memorandum, 24 May 1962, D/T, S17246G/62, NAI.
[44] Gallagher to Cremin, 25 June 1962, D/T, S17246K/62, NAI.

schedule, he said that while they were still aiming at getting an outline of the package by the end of July, he expected that they would have to 'stop the clock' at the end of July and then probably go on into the middle of August. He felt that the signature would take place at the beginning of the year, entering into force about the middle of 1963.[45]

On 29 June 1962 Ambassador McDonald reported to Cremin on a meeting with Prime Minister George Pompidou, who said that the British application had taken a good turn (*a pris une bonne tournure*) since the last conversation with Harold Macmillan. France had never really objected to the British entry into the common market, but, for a long time, had greatly doubted that it would be possible in view of the Commonwealth problem and the general orientation of British interests.[46] It was apparent from Macmillan's statement that there was a very serious desire in Britain to come into the Community and France would welcome that if it should prove possible. Pompidou said that it was difficult to state when the negotiations might be expected to end because most of the essentials had still to be resolved.[47]

The Committee of (departmental) Secretaries, having had access to both reports from Paris and London, met in Dublin on 3 July where Cremin stated that the permanent representatives had given a favourable opinion on the Irish application. Cremin would arrange to meet the ambassadors from the member states to convey to them the Irish hope that the Council would deal favourably with the application at its meeting on 23 July, and that Ireland would then proceed to negotiations proper on the same status as the UK and Denmark. He would emphasise to them that Dublin had refrained from pressing its case to date because the government was conscious of the preoccupations of the Council, but the point had now been reached where further delay in proceeding to the negotiation stage would occasion disappointment and misrepresentation in the public mind.

Cremin said that there were many indications that, if the British case were disposed of favourably, the Six would be ready to proceed speedily with the other applications. It would be wise to prepare for that eventuality by considering at that time possible 'fall back' positions, in the event of it being represented to Dublin that one or other of its desiderata constituted an obstacle to admission. Whitaker commented that, if the Council accepted the Irish application in principle, there would probably be a formal meeting at ministerial level to open the negotiations which would then proceed at deputy level, with a further meeting at ministerial level at

---

[45] McCann to Cremin, 27 June 1962, D/T, S17246K/62, NAI.
[46] McDonald to Cremin, 14 June 1962, D/T, S17246K/62, NAI.
[47] McDonald to Cremin, 29 June 1962, D/T, S17246K/62, NAI.

the end of the negotiations. He felt that it was unlikely that the government would be confronted by negotiations in September. More probably, he said, they would commence in October but, as the notice might be short, it would be desirable to be fully prepared.[48]

But disappointment was again in store for senior Irish officials. On 11 July 1962 Ambassador Biggar phoned the Dutch diplomat, J. Linthorst Homan, who confirmed that, contrary to expectations, the Irish application had not been placed on the agenda of the meeting of permanent representatives held the previous week, nor had the application been discussed outside the agenda. But Biggar was assured that it was definitely on the agenda for the meeting of 12 July and that the decision had been taken to put the Irish application on the agenda for the Council meeting of 24 July. Biggar also learned later from his sources, however, that the Irish application was unlikely to get a sympathetic hearing at that meeting.[49]

Donal O'Sullivan, based in the Irish embassy in Brussels, had a full account of the meeting of 12 July from a senior diplomat of the Netherlands' mission. He was told that when the Dutch Head of Mission had approached the chairman of the permanent representatives, Signor Venturini, he discovered that Ireland's case was not on the agenda. The item was then included on the insistence of the Dutch representative. At the meeting, Venturini prefaced the opening of the discussion on the Irish case somewhat along the following lines: 'Have we not some doubts about the Irish on economic and political grounds – they are not members of NATO'. The Dutch representative said the Irish application had reached the Council before that of the Danes and that of the Norwegians. The French representative read from a prepared note and took the line that, because of Ireland's economic dependence on the British market, there would be little point in proceeding with consideration of the Irish application until the situation in regard to the British negotiations was a good deal clearer than at present. He also mentioned the existence of some doubts in his delegation about Ireland's capacity to meet the full economic obligations of the Rome Treaty (the French at one stage suggested that the Irish case be referred back to the Commission for more detailed study). On the whole, the French delegate felt that it would be better to postpone discussion on the Irish case until after the summer recess. That suggestion was supported by Venturini, who said that the Six had not yet reached agreement in regard to neutral countries.

The German delegate said that while Bonn was fully satisfied that Ireland should be treated as a serious candidate under Article 237 of the

---

[48] Meeting of departmental secretaries, 3 July 1962, D/T, S17246K/62, NAI.
[49] See Biggar's reports for July, D/T, S17246L/62, NAI.

Rome Treaty (which provided that 'any European State may apply to become a member of the Community'), he would not object to the postponement of consideration of the Irish case until the autumn if that was the wish of the majority. The Dutch representative again intervened to urge that it was unrealistic to delay consideration of the Irish case because of Ireland's economic dependence on the British market.[50] With no real consensus at the meeting of the heads of the permanent representations, Ambassador Biggar reported to Iveagh House following the 24 July Council meeting on his interview with the President of the Council, Signor Colombo. The ambassador was told bluntly that the Council had no time to go into the Irish case in detail. It had instructed the permanent representatives to continue their study of the case and to report in the middle of September with a view to the consideration of the matter at an early meeting of the Council. Colombo added that that was in no sense an unfavourable reflection on the Irish case.[51]

Ambassador Biggar, attempting to convey the difficulties which procrastination would mean on domestic political opinion, said that the Council's failure to give a decision would be a great disappointment to the Irish government and could well have a disturbing effect on public opinion. He pointed out that the Irish application had been made a year before and stressed the difference in the status of the Irish application as compared with those of Denmark and Norway. Colombo said that he understood the Irish position perfectly and that everyone was full of sympathy for Dublin, but the view of the Council remained that the application had not yet been fully examined. He said that it was impossible for the Council to reconsider the matter before the summer. Biggar, attempting to salvage something from the situation, sought a reassurance that there was no fundamental objection to the application. Colombo, while not being able to speak for the Council, felt himself that that was the position.[52]

Lemass and senior officials met to review the situation. The matter was discussed in cabinet on 31 July 1962. There was consensus, at both cabinet and senior official levels, that action had to be taken to remove the doubts which lingered in the Commission and in the capitals of the Six regarding the political objections to the Irish application. It was decided immediately to seek an opportunity for Lemass to meet Walter Hallstein, President of the Commission.[53] Biggar, who had been asked to make an appointment, reported on 14 August that Hallstein's office had phoned stating that he

---

[50] O'Sullivan to Cremin, 18 July 1962, D/T, S17246L/62, NAI.
[51] Biggar to Cremin, 25 July 1962, D/T, S17246L/62, NAI.
[52] Biggar to Cremin, 25 July 1962, D/T, S17246L/62, NAI.
[53] See correspondence for August, D/T, S17246N/62, NAI.

was unable to accept an invitation to dine on 15 September at the embassy because he would not be in Brussels. The Taoiseach called Cremin to see him on 16 August, and wondered whether there would be any reasonable pretext for him (Lemass) being in Strasbourg at the same time as Hallstein was attending a meeting of the Council of Europe. Cremin explained that it would be possible for him to attend, if invited to do so, but that no invitation had been received. It would be necessary for the Taoiseach, if he were to be present, to speak. Lemass replied that a speech could be 'rather risky'. He also opposed the idea of sending a letter to Hallstein. Lemass, however, felt that something could be achieved by Biggar going to see Hallstein and giving him an *aide-mémoire* covering the points involved. Cremin expressed the view that that would be a possible compromise solution.[54]

Biggar's opinion was sought on the proposal. He argued by return on 22 August 1962 that the submission of an *aide-mémoire* might have 'unfavourable consequences'. That idea was temporarily shelved when another avenue for communicating the Irish position presented itself in early September.[55] At the invitation of the Irish Council of the European Movement, fifteen leading continental journalists arrived in Dublin to be briefed on the Irish application and to write about the changes in Irish society and politics. This initiative was undertaken with the full and active cooperation of the Irish government. Arriving on 3 September, they were given wide access to government ministers and to senior civil servants (see the *Irish Press*, 4 and 6 September 1962; *The Irish Times*, 6 September 1962). They attended a press conference given by Lemass on 5 September. Given the detailed nature of the replies, it is probable that the questions were submitted in advance. The Taoiseach used the opportunity to provide the most frank answers to the substantive questions which had preoccupied, if that is not too strong a term, senior EEC officials and leading politicians of the Six regarding Ireland's commitment to political union. Asked about Irish membership of NATO, Lemass replied:

We made our application for membership of the EEC in the light of the Bonn declaration which indicated that the applications were welcome from countries which accepted the political aims of the community and their proposed method for realising them. ... We do not wish, in the conflict between the free democracies and the communist empire, to be thought of as a neutral. We are not neutral and do not wish to be

---

[54] Cremin/Lemass meeting, 16 September 1962, D/T, S17246N/62, NAI.
[55] D/T, S17246N/62, NAI.

regarded as such, even though we have not got specific commitments of a military kind under any international agreement.

On the possible failure of the British application, Lemass replied:

> We did not make our application for membership of the European Community conditional on the success of the British application as Denmark and Norway have done. If the negotiations with Britain should fail we would, nevertheless, wish to pursue our application provided it was economically possible for us to do so. That would, of course turn upon the question of the relations that would, in such circumstances, exist between Britain and the European Community.

Despite the controversial nature of the remarks in a domestic Irish context, Lemass received strong support from the national dailies. An editorial in the *Irish Independent* on 6 September 1962, commenting on the fact that Ireland was not a member of NATO, stated:

> ... that should not be interpreted as implying that Ireland is a reluctant suitor. ... Our Government has accepted, without reservation, the principle of political unification expressed in the Bonn Declaration. It must be emphasised that this is commitment to a principle, not to details which are as yet unknown.

The visiting journalists were wined and dined and they returned to their respective countries where they wrote an article, and a series in some cases, about the Irish situation. These were republished in *The Irish Times* in the first two weeks of October. Ludwig Gelder of *Die Welt* wrote of Lemass's qualifying clause in his statement about joining without England 'provided that this is economically possible for us' that emphasis had to be laid on the 'provided that' as signifying a 'comprehensive neutralisation of the courageous main clause by the sub-ordinate clause'. But he added:

> The declaration of the Irish Premier may to this extent be regarded less as a real declaration of intent than as a gesture which nevertheless has political weight. For it lets it be known that the Irish art of politics is not purely a bread and butter matter. It is not only along the tracks of its biggest customer that Ireland, for better or for worse, directs its steps to Europe. Dublin regards adherence to the growing European Community not least as a political end in itself, and by no means only as a problem in mercantile arithmetic (Gelder, 1962).

That was precisely the message Lemass wished to direct towards Brussels and the capitals of the Six. The articles emphasised that the Irish were prepared to enter the EEC even if the British application failed. Secondly, the journalists stressed Lemass's positive attitude towards NATO and the defence of Europe. The text of the press conference was circulated widely to senior Commission officials and the Foreign Ministries of the Six throughout September. Ambassador Biggar reported that he had seen the Belgian Foreign Minister, Paul-Henri Spaak, on 18 September and had been told to see the Belgian Deputy Foreign Minister. The latter appeared to be impressed when he was shown the text of Lemass's press conference.[56] Ambassador McDonald called to the Quai d'Orsay on 19 September 1962 where he learned that the French had already read the reports of the press conference.

There was discussion in Dublin in mid-September about the idea of following up the distribution of the text of Lemass's press conference with the sending of an *aide-mémoire* to Hallstein, in anticipation of the Council meeting on 27 September. However, senior officials in the Departments of Finance and of Foreign Affairs successfully argued against such a *démarche* on the grounds that (a) it might revive old misgivings about Ireland's economic capacity and (b) Hallstein might take the line that any such document should be addressed to the governments of the member states. It was decided, instead, that Biggar would request an interview with Hallstein and simply speak from a prepared note.

Hallstein saw Biggar on 20 September when he spoke in general terms about the international situation. Hallstein was delighted at the recent success of General de Gaulle's visit to Germany between 4 and 9 September and of the meeting between de Gaulle and Adenauer (see Lacouture, 1991b). It demonstrated the desire for Franco-German reconciliation and their determination to avoid any possibility of a future war was far more deeply and sincerely felt than even the German press suspected. Hallstein regarded it as a veritable plebiscite for peace and friendship. Whatever about his euphoria over the German visit of de Gaulle, he was quite non-committal about the Irish situation.[57]

Only the very sanguine in Dublin would have expected anything significant to emerge from the meeting of the Council on 27 September 1962 on the Irish application. Irish diplomatic sources had been favourably impressed by the reaction in most of the capitals of the Six concerning the Irish application; but the French were identified in Dublin as being the major problem and that proved to be the case. Couve de Murville told his

---

[56] Biggar to Cremin, 19 September 1962, D/T, S17246O/62, NAI.
[57] Biggar to Cremin, 21 and 24 September 1962, D/T, S17246Q/62, NAI.

fellow ministers at the Council that he had no objection in principle to the Irish application but that he had to refer back to Paris for instructions. There was no alternative but to adjourn the item until the following meeting.[58]

Had Lemass and other senior politicians been more experienced in the ways of EEC affairs, there would have been less need to exhibit concern. Whitaker's strategy of 'dignified calm', outlined on 5 March, was a prudent one. But it was difficult to follow when the government needed a 'success' in Europe in order to forestall further domestic political criticism of its performance. Convinced that he could overcome the remaining doubts in the minds of the Foreign Ministers of the Six, should his trip to Brussels on 18 January not have an impact, Lemass now looked favourably on the suggestion of a tour of the European capitals. He was going to the opening of the Second Vatican Council on 11 October and saw that as an opportunity to extend his trip to visit the other capitals of the Six. It was a poor pretence.

Space does not allow a detailed explanation of Lemass's tour of a number of the capitals. He visited Brussels, Rome, Paris and Bonn. Upon his return to Dublin, Lemass knew that the Six would agree on the admission of Ireland to negotiations. But he was also aware that formal talks would not begin with Brussels until negotiations had first been concluded with Britain. In the final week in October, the Council agreed in Brussels to the opening of negotiations on the Irish application at a date to be fixed by agreement with Dublin and the governments of the Six. Lemass gave that news to Dáil Éireann on 30 October.[59] While he faced a series of questions from the opposition, the Taoiseach refused to give much detail about his trips to the capitals of the Six.[60] He remained, as ever, economical with his information.[61] Lemass recorded the goodwill shown to the Irish application by everyone with whom he had come in contact. However, because of the absolute priority which the Six had accorded the British application, it was 'thus unlikely that substantative negotiations with Dublin would begin for "some months"'. Failure of the British application would 'create an entirely new situation for all concerned and one about which it would be impossible to make any useful conjecture' at that time. When pressed by Dillon, Lemass speculated that British accession might occur on 1 January 1964.[62]

---

[58] Ambassador Lennon, The Hague, to Cremin, 1 October 1962, D/T, S17246Q/62, NAI.

[59] Dáil Debates, vol. 197, col. 3, 30 October 1962.

[60] Questions had been put down by the Leader of Fine Gael, James Dillon; by three members of the Labour Party, Patrick Corish, William Norton and Seán Dunne; and by Noel Browne and Jack McQuillan.

[61] Dáil Debates, vol. 197, col. 3, 30 October 1962.

[62] Dáil Debates, vol. 197, cols. 3–4, 30 October 1962.

A meeting of departmental secretaries reviewed the Irish position on 13 November. Cremin, addressing a number of the remaining problems, said that Britain was Ireland's main market, and he had gained the impression from the French Foreign Minister's remarks that he intended to write off the Six as a market for Irish exports. Cremin felt that viewpoint would come up again later. He also told his fellow secretaries that Adenauer had been extremely friendly, giving a dinner in honour of the Taoiseach and attending the dinner given by the Taoiseach. The reception accorded the Taoiseach in all the countries had been very friendly. Nowhere was there any indication that some form of preferential association was contemplated for Ireland. The only critical note was that sounded by Signor Cattani (Secretary General of the Italian Foreign Ministry) who, although well disposed, was inclined to look at matters from the Community viewpoint and seemed to say that Irish entry to the Community was not as simple a matter as his Italian colleagues appeared to think. Cremin added that he had heard from Dutch sources that Hallstein had said that it was not clear what would happen to other countries besides Britain. Cremin felt that that seemed to be a retreat from what he had previously said to the Taoiseach.

Having achieved their medium-term objective, it was a question of watching and awaiting the outcome of the British negotiations. In January 1963 de Gaulle's veto on British entry put Irish membership out of reach.

It would take another ten years before Ireland was accepted as a member of the EEC. Lemass, who was in declining health, resigned suddenly in 1966 at the age of sixty-seven. Taoiseach for only seven years, he did not live to witness Ireland's admission to the EEC. He retired from Dáil Éireann in 1969 and died in 1971. Whitaker wrote of him appreciatively some years later:

> One can, however, safely assert that this pragmatic nationalist, who had erected the high tariff wall in the 1930s to shelter Ireland's infant industry, would have been happy to see it razed to the ground in return for the benefits to Ireland of membership of the Community. He would have been gratified that many of the 'infants' were strong enough to make their way against Continental as well as British competitors (Whitaker, 1983, p. 77).

The Irish Times in an editorial described Seán Lemass at the time of his death as 'a mould breaker and a mould maker'. While he had found it hard to abandon the safe shores of protectionism, Lemass was not so rigid as to be unable to evaluate the opportunities which membership of the EEC offered Ireland. While the 1962 application had failed, it signalled the death knell of the policy of protectionism, marked the consolidation of

Monnet-style rational social and economic planning, and proved to be an irrevocable commitment to the achievement of Irish membership of the EEC. The political and administrative experience gained in handling the 1962 application finally demonstrated the prudence of the diplomacy of 'dignified calm', a diplomatic style more often aspired to than practised by Dublin during 1962. That earlier experience provided a new generation of diplomats and veterans alike with a valuable case study against which they could measure tactics and performance when, less than a decade later, they negotiated Irish entry into the EEC.

Jack Lynch and European integration

Lemass hand-picked Jack Lynch to succeed him. The outgoing Taoiseach had appointed Lynch as Minister for Industry and Commerce when he took over the leadership of the country in 1959. He then promoted Lynch to Minister for Finance in 1965 and, when he left office, he ensured that Lynch would become Taoiseach in December 1966. While Lynch was still Minister for Finance, Dublin had sought meetings at ministerial level with the Commission.[63] Those meetings took place on 20 September 1965. The Minister for External Affairs Frank Aiken attended, as did Lynch. The Commission was represented by Jean Rey (External Affairs), Sicco Mansholt (Agriculture) and Robert Marjolin (Economic and Financial Affairs). The Irish delegation sought to reaffirm Ireland's active and continued interest in full membership. The Irish government followed through with a series of ministerial meetings which began in January 1966 (Maher, 1986).

The central focus of the discussions was on the swift opening of negotiations with the EEC. Five of the six original members were still in favour of enlargement. France remained the obstacle. Lynch emphasised Ireland's wish to join as full members of the EEC simultaneously with Britain. He urged close contact between officials of the two countries and frequent personal contact at prime ministerial level. The meeting ended on a note of cautious and guarded optimism (Maher, 1986).

In July 1966 the Irish government accredited a separate mission to the three European Communities. Up to that point, the Irish Ambassador in Brussels had been assigned to Belgium, Luxembourg and the three European Communities.

---

[63] Aoife Keogh is the author of a forthcoming study on Ireland and the EEC in the 1966 to 1973 period, drawing on archive material from Dublin, London and Florence. This will be part of an IRCHSS series on Ireland and the EEC undertaken by a team of scholars led by members of the UCC History Department.

British Labour Prime Minister Harold Wilson reaffirmed, on 10 November 1966, the United Kingdom's intention to enter the EEC subject to safeguards. Wilson and Foreign Secretary George Brown made a tour of the capitals of the Six between January and March 1967. Wilson was impressed by the level of support that he encountered for British membership (Maher, 1986). Ireland's Department of External Affairs prepared an analysis of the tour. Dated 29 March 1967, it concluded: 'there is wide support for the view that the British Government will decide to request the reopening of negotiations and that the decision will be announced within the next month or so'.[64] Referring to the attitude of the French, the same document states frankly: 'The question of the continued existence and intensity of French political objections to Britain's membership remains an imponderable'. Nevertheless, it was concluded that Wilson seemed to be increasingly optimistic and to give the impression that progress had been achieved. The momentum generated by Wilson's tour of the capitals was unlikely to be lost. The department recommended arranging a meeting with the British as soon as possible.

Shortly after Lynch became Taoiseach, the government committed itself to publishing another White Paper on Ireland and the EEC in early 1967. The Committee of Secretaries of the relevant departments met in Dublin on 29 March 1967 to decide how the Irish government should proceed in preparation for Anglo-Irish discussions due to take place in April or early May 1967.[65] The Secretary of the Department of External Affairs, Hugh McCann, summarised the position of his department. A meeting between Wilson and Lynch was not likely to take place until the second half of April 1967 at the earliest. Doubt lingered as to whether the deadline of 1 July for the submission to the government of a comprehensive report on Irish admission to the EEC could be met because a number of the officers directly involved were working on the Kennedy Round and the negotiations on accession to the GATT (Maher, 1986).

The White Paper on the EEC was published in April 1967. The document was principally used as a way of informing the public on the EEC's legislative framework. It differed strongly in content and emphasis from the previous one published in July 1961. The earlier document had focused on trade and specifically Ireland's adhesion to the EEC (Maher,

---

[64] Government memorandum, D/T, 98/8/856, S18981B, NAI.

[65] Present at the meeting were the following: Department of Finance, T. K. Whitaker; Department of Industry and Commerce, J. C. B. MacCarthy; Department of Agriculture and Fisheries, J. C. Nagle; Department of External Affairs, H. J. McCann; Department of Agriculture and Fisheries, J. O'Mahony; Department of Finance, D. J. Maher; Department of Industry and Commerce, T. Dodfrey; and Department of Finance, P. Carthy. D/T, 98/8/856, S18981B, NAI.

1986; Fitzgerald, 2000). The 1967 White Paper covered the implications of EEC membership extensively. It described membership as 'boarding a moving train' (quoted in Maher, 1986, p. 208).

Meanwhile, the Department of External Affairs put forward a proposal to improve informal liaison between Dublin and London regarding EEC membership. This involved the setting up, at official level, of continuing contacts on EEC matters with regard, in particular, to technical questions. The matter was to be raised by the Taoiseach in talks with the British Prime Minister.[66] On 1 May 1967 the Taoiseach met the British Prime Minister in London.[67] The significance of those talks was underlined by the fact that the Irish delegation met the entire British cabinet. Wilson spoke about his recent tour of the six capitals of the EEC and of the six cabinet meetings that he had chaired since returning to London. He crushed rumours that there were deep divisions in his cabinet over EEC membership (Young, 2000 and 1984). He emphasised that a final decision on EEC membership had not been taken so his discussion with Lynch would, according to the Irish record of the exchanges, have 'to be on the hypothesis that a decision to apply would be made'. Wilson revealed to Lynch that a decision was likely to be taken the following day. Regarding negotiations, Wilson informed Lynch that it was 'almost certain that the British would decide on a completely fresh start'. In view of the previous negotiations, the Prime Minister doubted whether it was a good idea to work on the basis of reviving the dormant 1961 application (Maher, 1986). He recommended that the Irish should consider getting advice on the status of their existing application before settling the form of a new approach. He told Lynch that a formal application was likely to follow quickly upon the promised debate on the issue in parliament. He would like negotiations to begin with a minimum of delay, in advance of the August holiday season.[68]

---

[66] The matter had been raised by the Irish in the context of a meeting on 2 December 1966 during Anglo-Irish discussions. The British welcomed such discussions on technical matters but felt it was too early to establish machinery for that purpose. They proposed deferral until the results of the British exploratory talks were known. A memorandum prepared for a meeting of the secretaries entitled 'Liaison at official level with Britain on EEC matters' confirmed further that there was continuous contact between the embassies in that area. There was also no obstacle to ad hoc meetings of experts on points of interest or concern. More regular contacts could be arranged when the need arose. Meeting of secretaries, D/T, 98/8/856, S18981B, NAI.

[67] Those also in attendance were the Secretary of the Department of Finance, T. K. Whitaker; Assistant Secretary, Department of External Affairs, D. O'Sullivan; and on the British side, Commonwealth Secretary, Herbert Bowden; Minister of State, Foreign Office, F. Ulley; Joint Parliamentary Under-Secretary, Department of Economic Affairs, Peter Shore; Deputy Under-Secretary, Commonwealth Relations Office, Sir Arthur Snelling; Deputy Secretary, Ministry of Agriculture, Fisheries and Food, R. Wall; Cabinet Office, B. M. Thimont; and the Private Secretary in the Prime Minister's Office, D. H. Andrews. See D/T, 98/8/856, S18981B, NAI.

[68] Government report on meeting with Wilson, D/T, 98/8/856, S18981B, NAI.

Wilson stated that he did not wish to see a repetition of 1961/62, where talks were 'bogged down by matters of detail'; such matters could be dealt with after membership had been secured. Wilson told the Irish delegation that 'ratification could be a fairly long-drawn-out process'. He felt that the UK 'would need a year after admission to the Community before any stages of the agreement could take effect', and that 'massive legislation' would be required.[69]

Lynch and Wilson agreed that because of the similarity of the legislative systems in Britain and Ireland, close liaison between British and Irish officials would be of great advantage when the time arose.[70] Detailed discussion followed concerning the transitional arrangements the British would be seeking following entry. Wilson stated that British agriculture needed a transitional period in preparation for the implementation of the CAP. Wilson raised the question of the levies on food imports that they would be required to pay. Following his tour of the six capitals, Wilson felt that the leaders of the member states were aware that 'this would be inequitable for Britain'. There was further discussion on the issue of a transitional period for industry. Ireland and Britain differed on this aspect. Britain would require a transition period for its agricultural goods, while Ireland would need one for industrial goods. Both men agreed that there ought to be an early meeting of officials on both sides to discuss the matter in greater depth. Lynch stressed, at several points in the discussion, the need for the closest consultation between the two countries (Maher, 1986). That ought to be the case, particularly in the context of the recent Anglo-Irish Free Trade Agreement. According to the Irish note on the meeting, Ireland regarded that agreement 'as an interim arrangement pending the admission of both countries to the EEC' and Wilson fully accepted that point and 'expressed the understanding of the Irish view that our negotiations should, as far as possible, proceed *pari passu* with those of Britain'.[71]

When the Taoiseach stressed the importance of being able to count on full support from the British for simultaneous accession, Wilson stated that 'we could feel assured of this but, at the same time, Britain would not want to be tied too closely to others. They must avoid the risk of becoming bogged down'. He mentioned the cases of Norway and Portugal and did not wish to see them delay a decision unduly in the British case. But, he thought 'that this danger did not exist with us. Ireland's attitude towards the

---

[69] Government report on meeting with Wilson, D/T, 98/8/856, S18981B, NAI.

[70] These remarks took place in the context of a discussion on the harmonisation of industry. F. Mulley took the lead in the discussion at that point.

[71] Government report on meeting with Wilson, D/T, 98/8/856, S18981B, NAI.

Community was well known and everybody was aware that our objective was to accede at the same time as Britain'.[72]

Wilson acknowledged Lynch's concern over Ireland's special position of dependence on British markets and confirmed the point 'was fully recognised, not only in Europe but in Britain'.[73] Wilson inquired whether any problems existed as between Ireland and Northern Ireland in the context of EEC membership. Lynch gave the reassuring reply that the greater freedom of trading and equality of economic conditions which would result from the two countries 'being within the Common Market would undoubtedly be a considerable help in our relations with the North'. The Taoiseach said that he could see no problem on the economic side. Lynch asked Wilson whether he was now optimistic about Britain's chances of membership. The Prime Minister replied that he 'would not like to speculate on the ultimate prospects'. It was his opinion that de Gaulle would not be able to veto the British application but, 'at the same time, the French could resort to the tactic of playing the British along for some years'. Wilson was quite satisfied that the Five 'are very enthusiastic for British entry but, so far at any rate, the French have shown no enthusiasm'. The talks came to a conclusion with the Taoiseach again stressing the need for the closest consultation between the two governments. Lynch emphasised that that ought to be particularly the case as the negotiations proceeded.[74]

After a photo call at 10 Downing Street and dinner at Marlborough House, the British and Irish governments issued an agreed communiqué that stressed that the discussions had been 'cordial' and were a continuance of those that had taken place when the two leaders had met in December 1966. It was agreed that there would be continuing consultations between the two governments on relations with the EEC.[75]

The day after the conclusion of his talks with Lynch, Wilson made a significant speech strongly advocating reapplying for EEC membership (Maher, 1986, pp. 211–213). The House of Commons debated the proposal until it was agreed by majority vote on 10 May. The British government submitted its application for membership of Euratom, the European Coal and Steel Community (ECSC) and the EEC on 11 May 1967. The previous day, 10 May, the Irish government had made its application for membership of the three Communities. The Taoiseach wrote to the President of the Council of Ministers, Renaat Van Elslande, requesting the opening of negotiations on Ireland's application pursuant to Article 237 of

[72] Government report on meeting with Wilson, D/T, 98/8/856, S18981B, NAI.
[73] D/T, 98/8F/856, S18981B, NAI.
[74] Government report on meeting with Wilson, D/T, 98/8/856, S18981B, NAI.
[75] See text of communiqué, 1 May 1967, D/T, 98/8/856, S18981B, NAI.

the Treaty of Rome. Lynch assured Brussels that 'the Irish Government fully share ideals which inspired the parties to the Treaty and accept the aims of the Community as set out therein, as well as the action proposed to achieve those aims'.[76] The Irish application differed from that of the British by referring to Dublin's original application in 1961, drawing attention to the Council's decision in October 1962 to open negotiations with Ireland.[77] As stated above, Lynch's letter referred explicitly to the ECSC, EEC and Euratom as recommended by the Committee of Secretaries. In 1961 the Irish application had made reference only to membership of the EEC. This further demonstrated to Brussels Lynch's interest in all aspects of the European Communities, even if they were not to Ireland's immediate benefit.[78]

While Dublin awaited a reply, the Committee of Secretaries met in Dublin on 23 May 1967. Discussion centred on a proposed tour of the capitals by the Taoiseach to win support for Ireland's application for EEC entry. Whitaker advised the meeting that 'haste should be avoided in this matter', as he felt that 'precipitate action now could leave the Government in an embarrassing position if negotiations did not get under way'. That cool-headed reasoning contrasted starkly with Ireland's rushed application to join the EEC in the summer of 1961.[79] Whitaker suggested that the government should 'envisage a long-drawn-out process', the immediate aim being to arrange a meeting with the French government in June. The meetings with the other governments could 'extend into the months following'. He also told the meeting that 'if the French showed signs of not being co-operative, their attitude could be taken as indicative of an unfavourable outcome for the British application'. McCann, reinforcing that discussions should first be with the French, also thought it important that, as it came near to the time for discussions with the Six, Ireland 'should not be overtly in close contact with the British'. Ireland should demonstrate a certain degree of independence from Britain, he stressed.[80]

---

[76] Lynch to Van Elslande, 10 May 1967, D/T, 98/6/861, S8131E, NAI.

[77] The Irish government had worked extremely hard in 1961/62 to convince the EEC to open negotiations for EEC adhesion. They did not want to have to repeat this process in 1967. Despite Britain's plans to make a completely new application, Ireland simply wanted to reactivate its earlier application (see Maher, 1986).

[78] Ireland did not have any nuclear power and so would not benefit directly from admission to Euratom. The Irish government had considered this alternative energy in the 1950s but had not adopted it due to the cost of installation.

[79] The Irish government had learned from its rushed and unsuccessful application process between 1961 and 1963 to proceed with 'dignified calm' in 1967. Whitaker to Cremin, 1 March 1962, D/T, S17246D, NAI.

[80] Meeting of Committee of Secretaries, 23 May 1967, D/T, 98/6/857, S18081C, NAI.

The Council of Ministers replied on 6 June 1967, stating that it had decided 'to put in train the procedure envisaged by the Article of the Treaty'.[81] Having reactivated Ireland's application for EEC membership, the government's new priority was to ensure that formal negotiations would open as quickly as possible. Nobody wanted a repeat of what had happened during the 1961 to 1963 period. The Irish government laid down a careful strategy to persuade the Six to open negotiations to enable Ireland to achieve simultaneous accession with Britain (Maher, 1986). In spite of the international uncertainty following the war in the Middle East, the Department of External Affairs succeeded in organising the Taoiseach's tour of the Five, beginning in The Hague from 21 to 23 June. A visit to Bonn was to follow from 26 to 28 June. However, before departure, no news had been received from Paris regarding the Taoiseach's requested talks with de Gaulle and Pompidou.[82]

Cultivating support in the capitals

In light of the volatile international situation, the Irish government had settled upon a very low-key approach to the tour of the EEC capitals. Lynch and his advisers were conscious of the divisions between the EEC governments over the Six Day War. On the tour, Lynch was accompanied by Minister for Finance Charles Haughey and Secretaries General Whitaker (Finance) and McCann (External Affairs). The opening leg of the visit took place in the wake of Wilson/de Gaulle talks, which, according to what the Irish delegation learned in The Hague, had not changed the basic obstructionist French attitude towards enlargement. This situation was further confirmed in a detailed report from Brendan Dillon, the Irish Ambassador to Brussels.[83]

Whitaker's official minute of the Taoiseach's meeting in The Hague on 23 June 1967 revealed that de Gaulle had been stiff with Wilson and that, according to Dutch sources, Wilson appeared to have put too strong a construction on the outcome of the talks. Nothing had changed in the eyes of Irish government sources. It was thought by the Dutch that the British would accept a temporary association, if membership was ultimately definite. Whitaker's minute continued: 'Even the Dutch, who are well disposed to Britain, consider that exaggerated claims are being made about

---

[81] Van Elslande to Lynch on 6 June 1967, D/T, 98/6/861, S8131E, NAI.
[82] The French only answered the Irish request to make a formal visit to France in August 1967 (Maher, 1986).
[83] Dillon reported on a conversation with James Mellon, First Secretary, British mission to the EC, on Friday 23 June; Dillon's reports to Dublin, 26 June 1967, D/T, 98/6/859, S18081D, NAI.

the strength of the British economy. The British will have to make it absolutely clear that they do not expect the Community to accept any of the sterling reserve obligations'. Whitaker also noted that in general it had to be said that 'while the Dutch were extremely well disposed towards Ireland becoming a member at the same time as Britain, they could not be described as optimistic about the prospect of British membership within the next three years'.[84]

The Irish delegation, as a result of the round of informal discussions at The Hague, left the Dutch capital convinced that nothing dramatic was likely to happen in the near future. The Irish delegation travelled to Bonn for discussions from 26 to 28 June. Whitaker, in a minute dated 28 June, recorded and summarised the outcome of the talks on 27 June with Chancellor Henry Kiesinger and Ministers Franz Josef Strauss and Willy Brandt thus:

> The German Government welcome and will support Ireland's application for membership. ... The German Government is interested both for political and economic reasons to see Britain, Ireland and others in the Community (Statsecretar Schutz). The rate of progress towards enlarging the Community may not be as rapid as the German Government would hope (Strauss). The French attitude towards British membership was still rigid and it is not known whether it will continue to be so.

On the procedural front, Whitaker also recorded that 'the German authorities saw the necessity of giving the British application some priority but would be in favour of the greatest possible exchange of information and parallelism of negotiation and, particularly, of simultaneous membership of Britain and the other applicant countries, including Ireland'.[85]

Strauss enquired whether Ireland could join before or without Britain. Haughey, while saying that 'everything was possible', explained the grave economic difficulties that stood in the way of such a development. He finished by reminding Strauss that an even more serious situation would arise if Britain joined without Ireland. Brandt told the Minister for Finance, in private conversation, that Couve de Murville was not so negative about eventual British membership of the EEC. Germany advised the Irish to speak privately with the French. Whitaker further noted that the Chancellor and the two ministers were 'particularly preoccupied' in the present

---

[84] Whitaker's minute of meeting in The Hague, 23 June 1967, D/T, 98/6/859, S18081D, NAI.

[85] Whitaker's minute of meeting in Bonn, 28 June 1967, D/T, 98/6/859, S18081D, NAI.

circumstances as Europe was 'without any decisive or authoritative voice even in matters, such as the Middle East crisis, which affect Europe directly'.[86] The immediate aftermath of the Six Day War was not the time for Ireland to have pressed for stronger support for immediate enlargement of the EEC.

But whatever the international difficulties, the Six remained confident about deepening the process of integration. The Merger Treaty came into force on 1 July 1967, merging the three existing Communities – EEC, ECSC and Euratom – into one institutional entity. Lynch cordially acknowledged and congratulated the Commission on the merger in early July.[87]

The merger brought significant personnel changes in the Commission. Jean Rey resigned as Commissioner for External Affairs and took over from Walter Hallstein as President of the new (single) Commission of the European Community. This new structure had a number of effects on the workings of the Community itself (Urwin, 1991). The new structure, after the Luxembourg compromise, institutionalised the superiority of the Council of Ministers and the national state by giving it the power of veto.[88] Although the Commission could still place proposals before the Council, increasingly policy suggestions emanated from national governments. The power of veto meant that the Commission would not take decisive moves until COREPER had prepared the groundwork with individual national governments. The permanent representatives took on increased responsi-bilities and the representatives adopted ambassadorial status.

Rey's promotion to President of the Commission left a vacancy in External Affairs, a portfolio that had responsibility for the all-important question of enlargement. Rey had been enthusiastic about enlargement and his successor also proved to be supportive of the project. The Italian government, in July 1967, nominated Edoardo Martino to take over the portfolio of Commissioner of External Affairs. Martino arrived in his new posting at the height of discussions on enlargement. He proved to have been personally enthusiastic about achieving an enlarged EEC since 1959.[89] There is evidence of Martino's receptivity to bringing in new members in his personal papers.[90]

---

[86] Whitaker's minute of meeting in Bonn, 28 June 1967, D/T, 98/6/859, S18081D, NAI.

[87] Lynch to the Commission, Community Archives, Florence, EM 96.

[88] This arrangement remained unchallenged for sixteen years. Since the Council met infrequently this signified an increase in the influence of COREPER (Committee of Permanent Representatives).

[89] 'Démarrage dynamique de l'Europe des Six', *Panorama du Marché Commun* (September 1959, Paris).

[90] During a debate in the Commission on 3 October 1967, Martino committed his directorate general to investigating the political implications of delays to enlargement. Community Archives, Florence, p. 68, EM 159.

As Martino and the other commissioners took up their duties in Brussels, the Irish delegation continued its tour of the capitals of the Six in late July 1967. Accompanied by Haughey, Whitaker and McCann, Lynch visited Rome on 21 July for talks with Prime Minister Aldo Moro and Foreign Minister Amintore Fanfani.[91] In his opening remarks, the Italian Prime Minister commented that it was the first official visit of an Irish Prime Minister to Italy.[92] Moro indicated that his government supported Ireland's application for entry into the EEC and continued, 'Ireland is neutral while Italy is a member of NATO. The two countries have, however, acted together in the United Nations and the Irish initiatives in the United Nations have met with some success'. In that connection, Moro mentioned especially Irish efforts in the disarmament field to prevent the spread of nuclear weapons. Moro suggested that the Taoiseach might wish to exchange views on the present crisis in the United Nations.

Lynch replied that when Ireland applied for membership of the EEC, his predecessor had made it clear that Ireland accepted fully the political implications of the Treaty of Rome. Dublin sought a wider Europe not only for the economic benefits it would confer, but because a wider Europe could be more effective politically. Lynch also referred to the promises of support he had received in The Hague and in Bonn. Fanfani, referring to the attitude of the French, counselled patience. In reply, the Taoiseach wondered whether there was a danger that Britain would become less enthusiastic about membership of the EEC if a favourable response to its application was unduly prolonged. Fanfani discounted this danger saying that Britain was well aware of the need to remain steadfast. He said that Britain expected serious negotiations to be on the way at the earliest by mid-1968 and at the latest by December 1968, but that he regarded membership by 1970 as a little on the optimistic side.

The Taoiseach then enquired from Moro whether Ireland could count on Italian support for simultaneous entry with Britain to the EEC. Moro confirmed that the idea of different entry dates was not supported in the Six and in his opinion would be irrational. There might be different timing on decisions but the entry date should be simultaneous, he said, assuring the Irish delegation that Dublin could count on Italian support. Moro concluded the discussion by reaffirming that Italy favoured enlargement of the EEC, that Italy would not facilitate those engaging in obstructionist tactics, that the Italian government would help to prepare the way on the

---

[91] McCann's minute on Rome meeting, 21 July 1967, D/T, 98/6/862, S18981F, NAI.
[92] Lemass had made an official visit to the Vatican in 1965. Lemass had also met Moro on that occasion. However, Lynch's visit in 1967 was the first official visit of an Irish Taoiseach to Italy (Fitzgerald, 2000).

political side and that a new EEC excluding France was not a solution.[93] Returning home to Dublin, the Irish delegation was buoyed by the positive reception towards Irish membership in the Italian capital.

Having vigorously defended the Irish decision for membership in Dáil Éireann on 25 July,[94] Lynch set out with McCann the following day for Belgium. Haughey joined the party a day later.[95] The tactic to publicise and re-emphasise Ireland's position on future EEC political and defence union was very much in line with the central policy first adopted by Lemass in 1962 (see also Keogh, 2000).

The Irish delegation (consisting of Lynch, Haughey, Whitaker and McCann) was received on 27 July by Belgian Prime Minister Vanden Boeyants, the Minister for Foreign Affairs M. Harmel, the Minister for European Affairs M. Van Elslande and a number of senior officials. The Irish Ambassador to Belgium, Gerard Woods, and the Irish Permanent Representative to the EEC, Seán Morrisey, were also present at the exchanges.[96] Boeyants stated that his government supported the Irish application for membership of the EEC, as had also been the case in 1962. He was pleased with the recent declarations made by the Taoiseach about accepting the full political and economic implications of membership. Boeyants also noted that the agricultural side presented no real problem for Belgium but that, on the industrial side, a transitional period would be required. He also referred to the fact that Ireland had indicated in 1962 that it was prepared to accept the political implications of the Treaty of Rome, but he commented that Ireland was not a member of NATO and said that the Six wished to see members of the EEC also as members of NATO.[97]

In his reply, Lynch explained that the then Irish government had not joined NATO because of the partition of Ireland and of the fact that it was considered that an article in the NATO Treaty would require Dublin to

[93] McCann minute on Rome meeting, 21 July 1967, D/T, 98/6/862, S18981F, NAI.

[94] Lynch addressed the Dáil on 25 July 1967. The Irish government sent the full text of this speech to the acting Commissioner for External Affairs, Edoardo Martino. Community Archives, Florence, EM 96.

[95] Haughey delayed his departure to speak in the Dáil on the EEC. Cardon de Lichtbuer requested additional information on Ireland from Martino in the External Affairs Directorate General of the EEC on 6 May 1968 prior to his visit to Dublin on 28 May 1968. Haughey's speech to the Dáil on 26 July 1967 is contained in his reply to de Lichtbuer. Community Archives, Florence, EM170.

[96] Woods was Irish Ambassador to Belgium from 1966 to 1971. Morrisey was Ireland's Permanent Representative to the EEC from 1966 to 1970. Report on visit by Taoiseach to Belgian government, 28 July 1967, D/T, 98/6/863, S18081G, NAI.

[97] This is an interesting comment particularly in light of the fact that a year earlier France had decided to withdraw from NATO and had secured the removal of all NATO bases from French territory including SHAPE (Supreme Headquarters Allied Powers Europe). SHAPE moved to Belgium (Maher, 1986).

recognise the existing territorial limits of the country. According to the text of the Irish minute, he continued: 'Ireland desires unity and could not therefore bind itself to recognise the division of the country. It was only because of this that the Government of the day remained outside of NATO'. Lynch added that Ireland was not neutral and it was prepared to play a full political part in Europe in whatever way political unity might evolve, and it recognised that that could involve defence. Boeyants replied that he was very happy to hear that declaration as the point might come up many times in the discussions about the expansion of the EEC.[98]

Lynch led an official visit of the Irish delegation to the Community on 26 and 27 July. Extensive discussions took place between 27 and 29 July with Commissioner for External Affairs Martino, Vice-President Sicco Mansholt, Vice-President Raymond Barre and President Rey. Lynch repeated what he had said in the Dáil on 27 July 1967,[99] emphasising that Ireland 'shared the ideals which inspired the parties to the Treaty and accepted the aims of the Community as set out in the Treaty, as well as the action proposed to achieve those aims'. Lynch expressed Irish disappointment at the breakdown of the application process in 1962. He outlined what the Irish government had done to prepare for eventual membership. Lynch underlined how important adhesion was to the Irish government, because industrial and agricultural policies were drafted in the context of eventual membership. He argued that the Irish government had begun to make improvements economically. He emphasised Ireland's two unilateral tariff reductions of 10 per cent each in 1963 and 1964 and highlighted the Anglo-Irish Free Trade Agreement (AIFTA) in 1965. He argued that the AIFTA would help make Ireland's economy more efficient and more suitable for EEC membership. Lynch predicted the eradication of all tariffs between the two countries in the future.

Lynch asked whether Ireland's adhesion to the Community would be considered in tandem with Britain's, particularly considering their close economic ties. Director General of External Affairs Axel Herbst emphasised the difference between concurrent negotiations and adhesion itself. He said that he could not predict what form negotiations would take and therefore could not guarantee that the British and Irish applications would be considered together.

---

[98] Report on visit by Taoiseach to Belgian government, 28 July 1967, D/T, 98/6/863, S18081G, NAI.

[99] The Taoiseach also submitted a copy of the speech to all members of the Commission. Emile Noël forwarded Lynch's speech of 27 July 1967 to C. Calmes, Secretary General of the EEC Council, on 9 August 1967. A copy of the speech was forwarded to Commissioner Martino on 31 July 1967. Community Archives, Florence, EM 96.

Lynch said that the Irish government was preparing a report regarding the political, industrial and agricultural aspects of Ireland's application for EEC membership. Martino explained that the Commission was currently examining the applications for membership. The final version of its text would be available by 30 September 1967. This would form the basis for discussion in the Council in the first week of October. Martino questioned the economic consequences that Ireland's EEC membership posed for the Community as a whole and secondly, bilaterally, for the individual member states. Martino had already addressed the Commission regarding how important EEC political integration was internationally. Martino envisaged some difficulties in that area for Ireland's application. Therefore, he proposed that the present meeting should consist of an exchange of views on the Irish application.

Lynch said that Irish people were European-minded and, referring to the renewed application of 10 May, he repeated the points outlined in his briefing notes and addressed the issue of neutrality directly, stating that Ireland had no reservations on the political aspects of the Treaty of Rome. Haughey also pointed out Ireland's strong political commitment to the EEC. Herbst intervened at this point to stress the importance of gaining confirmation of that view.[100]

Martino continued that there was naturally a priority for negotiations with the United Kingdom, where the difficulties were greatest. The Commission knew about Ireland's wish for simultaneous entry into the Community and he emphasised that a series of entries was out of the question. He saw two questions arising (i) the free trade agreement with the UK and (ii) the fact that Ireland was not in EFTA, with the consequence that its tariff reductions were not as far ahead as those of Norway and Denmark. Lynch was heartened by the Commission's opinion on the need for simultaneous entry into the Community. He did not see Irish absence from EFTA as in any way a problem in view of the obligations Ireland had undertaken in the AIFTA, and that, even before the negotiation of that agreement, Ireland had undertaken two unilateral tariff cuts of 10 per cent as a preparation for free trade. When the AIFTA was fully in operation in 1975, he foresaw little difficulty in exposing Irish industry to further competition from the members of the Community.

Later that day the Irish delegation met the President of the Commission. Rey opened the proceedings by saying that the Irish visit was a very important one, in light of the Irish government's decision to reactivate its application for membership of the European Communities, and in view of

---

[100] Note prepared by the Department of External Affairs on meeting between Lynch and Martino, 27 July 1967, D/T, 98/6/863, S18081G, NAI.

the report that the Commission had been asked to prepare on the membership applications. Rey stressed that the Commission hoped that negotiations would take place and that they would be successful. Lynch replied by congratulating Rey on his appointment. He referred to Rey's predecessor, Walter Hallstein, and to the role he had played in the development of European unity. He then explained that his current visit to Brussels was one of a series that he was making to the European capitals. During discussions with Rey, Lynch assured him that the Irish application for EEC membership was '*toujours vif*' and re-emphasised some of the points he had made to Martino earlier that day.[101]

Having allowed Lynch to outline the Irish position, Rey replied that the Taoiseach's summary was clear and concise. He said that the Irish government had chosen wisely when they decided on the date of 1970 for possible entry into the Community. Lynch referred to the meeting which Lemass had had with the Council during the earlier negotiations, and said that matters were proceeding along different lines on this occasion. He emphasised that the Commission would meet the deadline of 30 September for handing in its report, and said that the numerous other tasks involved in the merger of the executives would not interrupt this work.

Lynch replied by saying that he saw no reason why the Irish should not commence negotiations in advance of the British, if it suited the Commission. He again referred to the need for simultaneous accession. As regards monetary problems, he said sterling would be strengthened if the UK joined the EEC. He again repeated that Ireland had no reservations on the political aspects of the Treaty of Rome. Haughey intervened to refer to the debate in Dáil Éireann and said that when replying he had spelled out fully Irish acceptance of the political and eventual defence policy involved and that no objections had been expressed. Rey said that was very important because the basic cause of the last rupture with Britain had been the political difficulties, defence, nuclear questions etc. He thought the situation was better in 1967.

Lynch commented that, as the Belgians had told him the previous day, growing pains were inevitable in the development of the Community and

---

[101] He also mentioned Ireland's 10 per cent unilateral 1963 and 1964 tariff reductions and the AIFTA that began in July 1966. Rey was particularly concerned about the pound sterling's unstable position in the world economy. Lynch pointed out that if Britain succeeded in entering the EEC it would have greater access to European markets and would be in a better position to resolve its financial difficulties. Lynch was also keen to point out that Irish adhesion would have to take place simultaneously with British adhesion. The Irish government also wanted to safeguard its relatively underdeveloped indigenous industry with transitional periods. EEC external affairs report (31 July 1967) of meeting held between Rey and Lynch on 27 July 1967. Community Archives, Florence, EM 96.

he thought it best that they should all go through this period together.[102] Lynch identified two problems. On the one hand, he thought it clear that the Community should be extended. On the other hand, it was important for Ireland that the negotiations should parallel those of the United Kingdom and that the two countries should accede to the Community at the same time.

Vice-President Barre referred to the close links between the British and Irish economies and asked for information on what the Irish situation was in monetary terms. The Minister for Finance replied that Ireland was a member of the sterling area, a creditor nation with official reserves amounting to £250 million sterling and that it had no basic monetary or balance of payments problems. Whitaker intervened to say that the reserves amounted to eight months' imports, a figure which was generally accepted as good in international finance. After a more extensive discussion on Irish agriculture, the meeting came to an end.[103]

In conclusion, Rey predicted that the Commission would not make a decision until October 1967 and emphasised that an enlarged Community needed a strong institutional structure. He felt that the monetary question would be a most serious obstacle to achieving stability. The meeting ended on a satisfactory but, as was to be expected, an inconclusive note.

The Irish delegation completed its tour of the capitals by paying a visit on 28 July 1967 to Luxembourg for talks with Prime Minister Pierre Werner, Minister for Economic Affairs Antoine Wehenkel and Minister for Agriculture Jean-Pierre Büchler. The talks followed the same pattern as previous discussions in Brussels with Luxembourg's Benelux partner.[104]

A second disappointment

Returning to Ireland, Lynch awaited news from Paris of a meeting with de Gaulle, Pompidou and senior officials. Instead of beginning his tour of the capitals in France, as had been considered most desirable, the Taoiseach was obliged to wait until 24 August 1967 when he received news that he would have to wait until November. Lynch was given the dates of 3 and 4 November for his meeting with de Gaulle and Pompidou. By that time, the

---

[102] Department of External Affairs note on meeting with Rey, 27 July 1967, D/T, 98/6/863, S18081G, NAI.

[103] Department of External Affairs note on meeting with Barre, 27 July 1967, D/T, 98/6/863, S18081G, NAI.

[104] Department of External Affairs note on meeting with the Prime Minister of Luxembourg and his Foreign and Agricultural Ministers, 27 July 1967, D/T, 98/6/863, S18081G, NAI.

outcome of discussions in Brussels would be clear. Commission President Rey organised a meeting on enlargement with the Council of Ministers on 23 October 1967. Rey also submitted guidelines which the Council could debate. French Foreign Minister Couve de Murville was concerned about Britain's ability to join the EEC due to its serious economic difficulties. According to Couve de Murville, discussions would mainly consider *'le tarif douanier avec tout ce que signifie le Commonwealth et l'agriculture'*. Couve de Murville stated that it was unrealistic to imagine that the Six would reach a common standpoint on these issues. Furthermore, he defined the negotiations in terms of discovering whether or not applicant countries effectively met the conditions required to adhere. Couve de Murville mentioned that in order to prepare for enlargement the Council had to do *'énorme travail'*.[105] It was evident that the French government still had reservations about British entry and the project for enlargement.

Lynch and the Irish delegation, made up of Haughey, Whitaker and McCann, left for the talks in Paris which were scheduled for early November.[106] They were to meet de Gaulle, Pompidou and Couve de Murville. In addition, Haughey was scheduled to meet the Secretary of State for Finance and Economic Affairs, Roland Nungesser.

On 3 November 1967, Lynch and de Gaulle had a private meeting.[107] The Taoiseach outlined, in the usual manner, the willingness of Ireland to join the EEC. De Gaulle, in reply, said that France had no objection whatever in principle to Ireland becoming a member. Indeed, he 'looked forward to the day when this would be possible'. He said that there were few problems as far as Ireland specifically was concerned but the UK candidature posed very grave problems indeed. Because those problems were complex and far reaching, de Gaulle indicated he had suggested to the British as far back as 1963 a form of association 'but this had not been well received'. He was still of the opinion that it offered 'a reasonable interim solution for the difficulties posed by the monetary and economic policies of the UK'. He had repeated the offer of association last May and it was still open for consideration.

De Gaulle then asked Lynch, because of the 'closeness of our economic ties with Britain', if Ireland had ever thought of association as a step

---

[105] Minutes of the Commission, 23 October 1967. Community Archives, Florence, EM 159.

[106] Report sent by A. de Baerdemaeker to Rey, Martino, Deniau, Hijezen and Toulemon on 14 November 1967 of meeting between Lynch and de Gaulle on 14 November 1967. Community Archives, Florence, EM 96.

[107] Whitaker drafted a minute of the meeting based on what he had been told afterwards by Lynch. The subject matter of the exchanges dealt exclusively with EEC matters. Whitaker's minute of Paris talks, 7 November 1967, D/T, 98/6/866, S18081I, NAI.

towards full EEC membership. Lynch replied very much along the lines of the briefing notes: Ireland had not 'seriously considered' associate membership, nevertheless if it appeared that British membership would be delayed for an unduly long time, Ireland would wish to explore the possibility of an interim arrangement with the Community envisaging ultimate membership at the same time as Britain. The conclusion of a satisfactory interim arrangement would, however, depend very much on the goodwill and support of France and the other members of the Community.

De Gaulle assured Lynch that such goodwill, as far as France was concerned, would be forthcoming. Later, de Gaulle had private conversations with both Whitaker and McCann and then hosted a luncheon in honour of the Irish delegation. Afterwards, de Gaulle received each member of the delegation individually. Whitaker took the opportunity to point out how Irish economic planning was being frustrated by not having any immediate possibility of entering the EEC while traditional markets in Europe were cut off by the use of a levy system.

In the afternoon, the entire delegation was received by Prime Minister Pompidou. He confirmed that France had no objection in principle to Ireland's membership and looked forward to the day when it would be possible for Ireland to join. Haughey failed to draw him on whether he saw Irish membership independently of Britain's accession. He made a reference to the possible breach of the AIFTA that such a development could cause. Pompidou said, according to Whitaker, 'that France was being blamed for enough without being guilty of disrupting trading arrangements of very long standing'.

On 4 November, a Saturday, the delegation met Couve de Murville and de Gaulle. The earlier part of the discussions revolved around the invitation by de Gaulle to consider associate membership. Lynch explained why that was not desirable for Ireland without Britain. Both de Gaulle and Couve de Murville were of one mind. De Gaulle treated at length the reasons why France was opposed to British entry at that time, placing emphasis on monetary, agricultural and Commonwealth problems, and 'the watering-down effect of the admission of so many new members on the character of the community coming later in the sequence'. He said that the French had offered the British 'an association arrangement to afford time for a solution but the reaction had been to treat this offer as an insult'. The British government did not appear to be disposed 'to face up to realities'. The French minister 'confirmed that the kind of interim arrangement or association which the French had in mind would be one whose end-product was full membership'. If the British entered into an interim arrangement with the Six, it would be easier for Ireland to do so. Couve de Murville said, however, that as far as France was concerned, 'the question of Ireland becoming a member independently of Britain was only a technical and not a political problem'.[108]

Before leaving Paris, Lynch signed a bilateral cultural agreement. But what had the visit actually achieved regarding Ireland's entry into the European Community? The Irish were fully aware of French opposition to anything other than associate membership for the British. The inevitable came to pass in December 1967. The French blocked enlargement. Thus ended the second attempt in which Lynch had been involved to bring Ireland into the EEC. There was no sense in Dublin of abandoning the objective to join the EEC. Instead, there was a return to the policy of 'dignified calm' advocated by Whitaker in 1962 and again in early 1967.[109]

In January 1968 Lynch was informed that the British were investigating the possibility of excluding France and arranging a meeting of the remaining five member states in early 1968. However, both the Commission and the Germans were opposed to such a development.[110] Meanwhile, Lynch set out to explore the French idea of an Irish interim arrangement with the EEC.[111] The British government, on hearing of the exploratory initiative by the Irish, communicated its opposition to Dublin. But the Irish Ambassador to France during the 1966 to 1970 period, Thomas V. Commins, pursued the matter in Paris. On 10 January he told the department that Alphand was receptive to the idea of McCann coming to Paris to discuss the matter.[112]

---

[108] Whitaker minute, 7 November 1967, D/T, 98/6/866, S18081I, NAI; there is a longer note on file covering the talks. This was probably prepared by the Department of External Affairs.

[109] Whitaker to Cremin, 1 March 1962, D/T, S17246D, NAI.

[110] On 11 January 1968 Ambassador Kennedy in Bonn contacted Dublin to report that the British proposal for a meeting of the Five plus the Four (applicant countries) had foundered on the rocks of German opposition. D/T, 98/6/868, S18081K, NAI.

[111] Ambassador Thomas Commins in Paris reported on 3 January that he had raised with Herve Alphand, Secretary General of the French Foreign Office, de Gaulle's idea for an interim arrangement between the EEC and Ireland. Alphand replied that he could not see how anything could be worked out on a practical plane for Ireland until such time as the British had made up their minds to take a step in the same direction. He emphasised that the French had never attempted to draw up a scheme for an interim arrangement because the British were so vehemently opposed to it. His honest view was that an interim arrangement would not be a practical proposition for Ireland in the absence of British participation. It would be necessary to wait until the British 'get their feathers unruffled'. O'Sullivan, Deputy Secretary General of the Department of Foreign Affairs, reported on a phone call he received from the Ambassador of Ireland to France. Commins reported on his conversation with Alphand. D/T, 98/6/868, S18081K, NAI.

[112] Alphand was leaving for India on 12 January and expected to be back in his office around 23 January, see O'Sullivan note, 10 January 1968, D/T, 98/6/868, S18081K, NAI.

Lynch authorised McCann's meeting with Alphand, which took place on 26 January 1968.[113] McCann came away with the firm impression that:

- The French did not regard as feasible, nor did they want, an interim EEC arrangement with Ireland independently of Britain. They did not show any great disposition to having an independent arrangement with, for example, Denmark or Norway
- If Britain should come around to exploring a possible interim arrangement, the French would examine it but would not commit themselves in advance as to the outcome and would certainly not agree in advance to a definite date for membership
- Nevertheless, there appeared to be French goodwill towards Ireland and it might be possible in those circumstances to secure some minor improvements in bilateral trade.[114]

However, the Danish, Irish, Norwegian and British applications were still on the table, as the Council of Ministers had in principal agreed to enlargement. Therefore, the EEC felt obliged to try. Three sets of proposals were put forward, aimed at providing for interim arrangements between the Six and the Four. On 20 January 1968 the Benelux countries put forward proposals to the Six and the Four proposing consultations and cooperation in the economic sphere (Urwin, 1991; Maher, 1986). On 15 and 16 February 1968 a combined German–French declaration set out a blueprint for an interim solution.[115] It envisaged a progressive reduction of trade obstacles. British Prime Minister Harold Wilson did not show interest in the project and reportedly felt that 'to pursue it would be to enter a blind alley which would lead nowhere slowly' (quoted in Maher, 1986, p. 236).[116] However, despite failure, at least it showed that France and Germany were prepared to contemplate interim arrangements with applicant countries (Maher, 1986).

---

[113] This contrasted with the period following the January 1963 veto when the Irish government only discussed interim arrangements for agricultural exports with the Community in March 1964. During this interval the Community had already settled its regulations governing trade, internal and external, in beef and dairy products. The Irish government secured a meeting to discuss interim arrangements with the EEC in March 1964. These regulations came into operation on 1 November 1964 (Maher, 1986).

[114] McCann added at the end of his minute, dated 26 January 1967: 'Ambassador Commins agrees with the content of this report and shares fully the conclusions expressed in this interpretative comment'. D/T, 98/6/868, S18081K, NAI.

[115] For text of German–French Declaration of 15 and 16 February 1968, see Community Archives, Florence, EM 169.

[116] During Anglo-Irish discussions on 14 February 1968 concerning interim proposals, Wilson reportedly revealed his views on the developing German–French declaration.

Meanwhile, Lynch met Wilson on 14 February 1968 for an exchange of views concerning the Council meeting of 18 and 19 December 1967 (Fitzgerald, 2000). Wilson told Lynch openly that the British government would prefer if Ireland did not accept any interim arrangement. The two leaders discussed the Benelux plan and the German–French declaration. It was agreed that the two countries should concentrate on the Benelux proposals which showed 'the best prospect for progress in the existing circumstances' (Maher, 1986, p. 236).

On 9 March 1968 the EEC Council discussed the various proposals for interim arrangements between the Six and the Four. Deadlock loomed as all arrangements were rejected. The Council, however, did agree to put forward proposals for an agreement that would prepare the way towards membership. There would be a preparatory phase of limited duration providing a procedure for consultation, trade cooperation and scientific and technological development. Following the preparatory phase, the Commission would indicate whether the conditions for membership were satisfied. In the meantime the Council should also strengthen its structure to be prepared for enlargement.

The Commission's proposals were accepted by the Council on 5 April 1968 and enlargement was discussed at successive monthly Council meetings. It was scheduled to come before the Council in May or June 1968.[117] In order to keep the matter alive, the Council recommended that it should continue to be discussed in Brussels among the permanent representatives of the individual states.

However, the Irish government viewed progress as being very slow. EEC enlargement was the subject of a Department of Finance report covering the period January to March 1968 and a second report was prepared to review developments during May.[118] On 23 May Whitaker wrote to McCann, enclosing a copy of the second report: 'The interpretative comment is deliberately pessimistic in tone, but not, I think, excessively so'. He added that the document had been prepared before 'the recent developments in France, which could have quite unpredictable consequences for the Community'.[119] In fact, the student riots and street unrest in Paris contributed indirectly to the resignation of de Gaulle in April 1969 (Lacouture, 1991a and 1991b), but in mid-1968 few could see such a development.

---

[117] Conclusion to Commission report on Ireland, Britain and Denmark's application to join the EEC, Community Archives, Florence, EM 169.

[118] Department of Finance, 'Digest of Developments in the European Community and in Trading Groups – Quarter ended 31 March 1968', D/T, 99/1/494, S18081N, NAI.

[119] Whitaker to McCann, 23 May 1968, enclosing Department of Finance memorandum, signed E. J. Brennan, 24 May 1968, D/T, 99/1/494, S18081N, NAI.

The way clear

The situation moved forward very swiftly. De Gaulle was replaced by Pompidou. The road to enlargement opened up. Patrick Hillery, who became Minister for External Affairs in 1969, took the lead in Ireland's negotiations. At the same time, violence in Northern Ireland became a matter of international concern. The principles on which Ireland negotiated entry into the EEC and the other two Communities were deeply influenced by the experiences of the Irish government earlier in the decade. Dublin wished to become a full member of the Communities. The idea of associate membership had been roundly rejected. The Irish government accepted the ultimate political objectives of the EC. Dublin made it clear in negotiations that, if Ireland was to be admitted, it would not become the slowest ship in the convoy en route to full integration. Quite the contrary in fact. Dublin adopted a very strong Community spirit and made its position clear to Brussels. There were assurances that Irish neutrality would not stand in the way of Ireland fully embracing membership of the Communities. By the time the referendum on entry was held in May 1972, the Irish government had grown much more confident in its handling of EEC policies. A decade of false starts had provided time for Ireland to work through its apprenticeship.

In the intervening years, Ireland's role in what is now called the EU has continued to be rooted in support for the fulfilment of the aspirations of the Treaty of Rome. Ireland, reluctant to join in the 1950s, changed its position in 1961. Securing membership in 1972, the next thirty-five years would witness dramatic changes in Ireland's position in an international context. As a member of the EU, Ireland at once developed a much greater economic independence from Britain. At the same time, membership has obliged both London and Dublin to work more closely together, particularly on trying to bring about a solution to the crisis in Northern Ireland. Ireland also works at a much more extensive and self-confident level within other multilateral organisations. Ireland has found its place among the nations of the world. Gone is the diffidence of de Valera for membership of multilateral organisations, as expressed at the Council of Europe in the latter part of the 1940s.

3

Ireland's New Economic Strategy and the Beginnings of European Integration

T. K. Whitaker[1]

Introduction

The movement towards greater economic cooperation in Europe was an important backdrop to the discussion of public policy in Ireland in the 1950s and 1960s, and in particular set the context for the debate about Ireland's strategy for economic development.

By the 1950s it was clear that continental Europe was preparing to abandon the tradition of trade protectionism, which had been so prevalent before World War II. This was for many in Ireland an ominous development, and in many ways a challenge to Ireland's traditional approach to economic policy.

The provisions of the 1957 Treaty of Rome establishing the European Economic Community included the dismantling of tariff barriers between member countries, and the coordination of trade policies vis-à-vis non-members. Equally, the European Free Trade Association founded in 1960 involved the dismantling of barriers to trade. There had also during the 1950s been discussions about establishing a wider free trade area across Western Europe. These developments were closely monitored in Ireland to assess their implications and consider appropriate courses of action.

The new approach adopted in the 1950s to domestic economic planning, the dismantling of tariffs on external trade, and ultimately accession to the European Economic Community, were all key ingredients within an overall strategy of promoting economic growth and development.

---

[1] Synthesis of an interview with Mark Callanan on 27 March 2007.

Early European cooperation

Ireland was a participant in some of the early economic and political organisations developing in Western Europe in the immediate post-war period. These included the Council of Europe, but more important from an economic perspective was the OEEC (Organisation for European Economic Cooperation), which was linked to the receipt of Marshall Aid under the European Recovery Programme. Ireland also participated in international as well as European organisations during this period, including, from 1957, both the World Bank and the International Monetary Fund.

Membership of organisations like the OEEC and the Council of Europe helped Ireland to move away from its rather isolated position in Europe. While Ireland was a member of European bodies such as these, in practice of course it was very much on the fringe of things, even if its general approach was to try to be as positive and cooperative as possible in the work of such organisations.

The OEEC helped reduce quantitative import restrictions, facilitate trade and intra-European payments, and assisted in the receipt of European Recovery Programme funds.

One of our key priorities in the Department of Finance at this time was to get whatever help or advice we could from different quarters in developing new and more effective economic policies. In this respect, the OEEC was very useful in terms of building up contacts and sources of information on economic developments in various countries. In particular, J. Flint Cahan, the Canadian Deputy Secretary of the OEEC, was a very useful contact as a respected economist well versed in economic recovery conditions in major European countries. He was sent a draft of the first chapter of *Economic Development* (1958), and contacts in the OEEC were generally eager to help with progressive suggestions and advice.

Those of us involved in seeking to promote economic development in Ireland were also aware of the French approach to economic recovery and planning under Jean Monnet and his successor as head of the French *Commissariat Général du Plan*, Pierre Massé. For example, we invited representatives from the *Commissariat Général du Plan* to come to Dublin in early 1962 to talk to us about the French modernisation plan in the context of the preparation of the Second Programme for Economic Expansion for Ireland. Ireland also used contacts to gather information on forward-looking approaches to economic recovery in a variety of locations, from the Vanoni Plan in Italy to the Tennessee Valley Authority in the United States.

The Irish approach to economic planning therefore certainly drew inspiration from abroad, albeit with slightly different terms being used – in particular phrases such as 'economic planning' and 'plans' were avoided, reflecting a concern at the time not to invite parallels with the Soviet-style planned economy.

European cooperation and domestic debate

After discussion in the mid-1950s on a large West European free trade area involving most OEEC countries came to nothing, two different and more ambitious alternatives emerged: the European Economic Community (EEC) and the European Free Trade Association (EFTA).

The six founding EEC member states – Belgium, France, Italy, Luxembourg, the Netherlands and West Germany – of course went on to sign the Treaty of Rome in 1957. Had Ireland been in a different economic situation at the time, and not been so dependent on Britain, the EEC would have held a number of attractions at the outset. This was particularly so because of agricultural price support. However, it would have been impossible to desert the privileges Ireland had in the British market and its trade association with that market. A decision to join the EEC without Britain, never a realistic prospect at the time, would have effectively meant replacing trade preferences with the UK with tariffs.

Some of the British negotiators involved in the initial discussions leading to the Treaty of Rome saw the idea of a 'common market' as wishful thinking. Some in Ireland shared that view too, particularly those who favoured retaining a protectionist trade policy.

While there was no immediate reaction in 1957 within government circles in Ireland to the signing of the Treaty of Rome, Seán Lemass as Taoiseach saw its significance. There were of course politicians who distrusted the idea of giving away an element of sovereignty.

EFTA also came onto the horizon – involving the UK, Austria, Denmark, Norway, Portugal, Sweden and Switzerland, who signed the Stockholm Convention in 1960. Lemass posed the question whether Ireland should be interested in this idea, and requested a review of the impact of free trade on protected industries. This spurred a debate over the merits or otherwise of retaining protectionism or embracing free trade, and prompted a review of the effect of removing tariffs. Some of the arguments surrounding this debate have been highlighted in a recent publication (Whitaker, 2006). I was almost alone in arguing that Ireland should consider joining, not because of any direct benefit or that EFTA held any great appeal in itself, but because it might set Ireland on the path of the gradual reduction of tariffs and in that way make us more efficient and prepared for entry into a more worthwhile free trade relationship.

While it was considered, it was probably never likely that Ireland would join EFTA, largely because it provided no real advantage in terms of agricultural support. Ireland already had preferential trade status with Britain, which made up almost 60 per cent of the population of EFTA at the time, and only modest trade ties with the other EFTA members.

Certainly when the light appeared at the end of the EEC tunnel, Ireland decided that this was the best strategy. Policy-makers in Ireland were conscious of the rapid growth rates in continental Europe at that time – faster than those in Britain. Irish exports to the continental European market were also increasing significantly.

These developments in European cooperation, in particular the establishment of the EEC (the Six) and of EFTA (the Seven), were closely monitored in Ireland. They also coincided with one of the bleakest periods in the Irish economy in the mid-1950s, with stagnation, high unemployment and high levels of emigration.

From a Department of Finance perspective, the developments in European cooperation offered external support for a complete reversal of Ireland's domestic policy of protectionism. It was very helpful that these external developments had taken place, because if Ireland had been confronted with a Europe that had returned to protectionism after World War II it would not have seen any of the changes that ultimately took place.

Our argument in terms of the domestic debate was that the decision of thirteen countries (the EEC and EFTA states) to dismantle tariffs and increase mutual trade made it more difficult, but also more urgent, for Ireland to become more competitive. Remaining entirely isolated from such developments over the long term, which seemed to be subtly mooted by some, was a recipe for continuing high levels of unemployment and emigration. It was also government policy by this time to encourage foreign investment, and remaining isolated from European trade groupings would make Ireland less attractive to foreign industrialists.

In a 1959 Department of Finance memorandum entitled 'Reasons for Reducing Protection', it was argued that

> ... it is only through enlarging its sales on export markets that Irish industry can in future provide jobs in increasing numbers for those seeking a livelihood in Ireland ... We cannot hope to share in the economic advance of Europe if we merely try to safeguard our industrial status quo ... The urgency of action to bring down the cost and improve the quality of our manufactures is made all the greater by the emergence of the Six and the Seven (quoted in Whitaker, 2006, pp. 51–52).

Applications to the EEC in the 1960s and further preparation

Effectively Ireland was in the position of shadowing Britain's approach to joining the EEC. Through diplomatic channels and contacts in the British administration, the Irish government could read the signs about Britain's intentions to seek EEC membership. It was clear by 1961 that Britain planned to put forward an application. In due course, Ireland submitted its application for EEC membership.

Of course, many of the attractions of the EEC were much more material than idealistic, and the arguments surrounding the debate over membership were largely put in economic terms. While there was an element of idealism, too, in terms of uniting Europe and preventing future wars, one would have to say that this was probably something of which only a minority of Irish people were conscious.

As a small economy with a small domestic population, open markets had to be to Ireland's benefit. *Economic Development* had signalled the change of direction towards an open, export-oriented economy, but of course this strategy was predicated on the ability of Irish exporters to sell to other markets. The external context was therefore uppermost in policy-makers' consideration during this period. The opening passages of *Economic Development* (1958, p. 2) also reflected on the challenges posed by events in Europe:

> The possibility of freer trade in Europe carries disquieting implications for some Irish industries and raises special problems of adaptation and adjustment ... It seems clear that, sooner or later, protection will have to go and the challenge of free trade be accepted. There really is no other choice for a country wishing to keep pace materially with the rest of Europe.

Indeed the policy changes heralded in *Economic Development* constituted the essential groundwork for joining a 'common market'. An application to join the EEC in 1961 would not have been credible if Ireland was to insist on maintaining high protective tariffs. In the end of course, Ireland did not join the EEC until a decade later, given General de Gaulle's opposition to British membership (see Chapter 2).

In fact, we were conscious in Ireland of the possibility of a veto of British accession by de Gaulle. Both Con Cremin in the Department of Foreign Affairs and I had read de Gaulle's *Mémoires de Guerre*, in which he had indicated clearly what his policy for European integration would be after World War II, and more specifically his intentions as to which countries would be involved in European integration: '*réunir les pays qui touchent au Rhin, aux Alpes et aux Pyrénées*'. That rather specific geographic delineation clearly did not envisage including Britain as part of the process.

In retrospect, de Gaulle's veto of EEC enlargement to include Britain, which in turn meant that Ireland would not join the EEC in the early 1960s, was possibly a blessing in disguise, at least from an Irish perspective. The delay in joining the EEC gave Ireland breathing space to conduct analysis to assess the implications for Ireland of the dismantling of protectionism with a view to preparing ourselves for participation in economic integration, and to adjust to the obligations of membership. For example, the Committee on Industrial Organisation surveyed different industries to assess what was needed to make them competitive in the early 1960s. A Second Programme for Economic Expansion was prepared with a view to Ireland becoming a member of the EEC.

A decision was also taken to lower tariffs unilaterally on imported goods in 1963 – on the basis of the inherent benefits of a change in policy. I argued at the time that this would help maintain the psychological impetus in adjusting to EEC conditions. It also acted as a pressure valve for industry, because if tariffs had not been reduced at least to some extent before membership Ireland would ultimately have had to make more drastic reductions upon membership. The decision to introduce a unilateral reduction of tariffs also acted as an indication of Ireland's determination to join the EEC.

Another significant development was the Anglo-Irish Free Trade Agreement (AIFTA) of 1965, which set in motion an inevitable dismantling of tariffs and a mental preparedness on the part of industry for EEC membership. The AIFTA was an important and clear signal to industry of the direction Ireland was going, that change was coming and that it was necessary to prepare for that change. It also opened the way to an expansion of exports.

The waiting time was very useful to us, so in retrospect perhaps Ireland owes de Gaulle a vote of thanks for delaying enlargement. It certainly was to our benefit to delay, because we saw the writing on the wall and did something about it. It also meant that when Ireland ultimately joined, in 1973, its economy was better prepared than it would otherwise have been.

4

The Single Market: 'Constantly Evolving and Adapting'

Michael Mulreany, Anthony Foley and Margaret Mary Malone

Introduction

On the twenty-fifth anniversary of the Treaty of Rome, which marked the foundation of today's European Union, *The Economist* featured a tombstone on its cover. The message was clear: the European Community (as it then was) was moribund. Twenty-five years later, for the fiftieth anniversary, *The Economist*'s cover featured the statue of a lady of uncertain age looking in a hand-mirror under the headline 'Europe's mid-life crisis'. Within this cycle of birth, demise and recovery the single market plays a key role. Indeed the European single market concept can be found in the Spaak Report a year prior to the Treaty of Rome. Of course a single market is part of a venerable economic succession:

- First, a free trade area with no tariffs or quotas
- Second, a customs union which places around the free trade area a common external tariff against the rest of the world
- Third, the single market adds free movement of goods, services, capital and labour – the so-called four freedoms
- Finally, an economic and monetary union unifies economic policies and has a single currency.

A well-functioning single market is commonly seen therefore as an important staging-post in the journey to economic union but, of course, has in its own right highly significant economic consequences such as scale economies, increased competition and improved competitiveness in the world economy.

Much progress was made in the early days of the EEC due to favourable economic circumstances. Indeed, tariffs and quantitative restrictions (quotas) were removed ahead of schedule by 1968. Yet by the early 1980s the single market aspiration was becalmed for an array of reasons. Member

57

states, partly in reaction to the severe recessions caused by increased oil prices in the 1970s, acted out of self-interest and hid from competition behind non-tariff barriers which often masqueraded as regulations to protect the health and safety of consumers. The decision-making process was hamstrung by the requirement for unanimity among member states on single market issues. The Community seemed lost in a process of harmonisation in which it sought standardisation on matters such as health regulations and food standards – to the delight of tabloid journalists who pondered the demise of traditional measures such as the pint of beer and, as Neal (2007) reminds us, the prospect of the single European condom size. The foregoing obstacles to progress seemed all the more worrying because of concerns prevalent in the 1980s that Community performance on economic growth, price stability and employment was lagging behind the United States and Japan, with the US in particular taking the lead in scaling back regulation and 'big government'.

Such was the unpromising background against which a new Commission under Jacques Delors took office in 1984. Two years later however, based on the White Paper drawn up by Lord Cockfield, Vice-President of the Commission, the Community enacted a landmark reform of the treaties in the Single European Act, the legal framework for the single market programme.

The Single European Act was important primarily in providing impetus to the single market, but it also had other significant features (see Chapter 12 for further details on the Single European Act). It was the first major package of treaty reform in the EC since the original treaties were signed. The use of a white paper was new to the Community, as was the use of a tight and legally binding deadline – 31 December 1992 – for the achievement of the ambitious objectives it set out. The Act empowered the Council of Ministers to adopt up to two-thirds of the proposals related to the single market programme by means of qualified majority voting (QMV), thereby enabling quicker decisions. The exceptions related to the social rights of workers, the free movement of persons and fiscal provisions. The expansion of the use of QMV brought to an effective end the national veto, the threat of which had inhibited any bold legislative initiatives from the Commission since the Luxembourg Compromise of 1966.

The Act also broadened the EC policy sphere to include environmental policy and science and technology policy, and paved the way for economic and monetary union. Finally, the increased competitive pressures created by removing internal economic frontiers led to a range of compensatory social solidarity policies aimed at economic and social cohesion, specifically the reform and doubling of the structural funds (see Chapter 5).

Integrating the markets of the EC member states was an ambitious 'supply side' exercise: the reduction of wasteful costs and the promotion of competition would reduce prices and thus stimulate demand; as production responded, economies of scale could generate fresh reductions in costs. The increased competition would stimulate innovation and enhance EU competitiveness in the world economy. Clearly the single market was linked to enhancing economic growth and increasing employment. At the same time, Delors, as a committed European integrationist, sought to harness the stimulation of economic growth to serve a political agenda to relaunch and galvanise the process of European integration itself.

The White Paper was ambitious: it set out some 282 proposals (this figure eventually increasing to 302) mostly in the form of EC directives to remove the remaining barriers to the free movement of goods, services, capital and people. These proposals aimed to remove three types of barrier to free trade: physical, technical and fiscal.

Physical barriers existed in the form of customs controls, which imposed administrative costs and also costs due to delays in processing the cumbersome documentation necessitated by transport regulations. These barriers were addressed in several ways: a 'single administrative document' simplified the controls, transport quotas into and out of each member state were abolished, and 'cabotage' rights (i.e. the freedom for a carrier from one member state to transport goods from an origin to a destination within another member state) were granted.

Technical barriers existed in the form of specialised product standards and regulations for health and safety, nationalistic public procurement regimes, controls on movement of capital and restrictions on the movement of services and labour. The removal of technical barriers caused by differing standards and regulations was facilitated by a landmark European Court of Justice judgment in 1979 in the Cassis de Dijon case. This judgment established the principle of mutual recognition, which in essence meant that if a product was fit for sale in one member state then it was fit for sale in any other member state. This meant that in future there would need to be a mixture of harmonisation of rules and the mutual recognition of rules. The single market process also involved the opening up of public procurement, the releasing of controls on capital movements and the freeing of services such as financial services.

Fiscal barriers existed in the different rates of VAT and excise duties and in the different tax rules among member states. These differences distorted trade away from higher-taxed member states. The single market process tackled these distortions by increasing the level of standardisation of VAT rates and by other measures including the abolition of duty-free sales within the EC.

Benefits of the single market

The single market promised considerable economic gains. The removal of trade barriers opened up the prospect of member states specialising in the production and trade of goods and services in which they were efficient relative to others, i.e. in which they enjoyed absolute or comparative advantage. The large, barrier-free market also gave scope for the economic benefits deriving from competition and from the achievement of economies of scale.

The physical, technical and fiscal barriers imposed costs. These costs – the so-called 'costs of non-Europe' – were analysed and estimated in the Cecchini Report (Commission of the European Communities, 1988). The reduction of these costs would generate not only the direct benefits of the single market, but also indirect benefits, such as those deriving from innovation, accruing over a period of time. The Cecchini Report estimated that GDP in the EC would increase by between 2.5 and 6 per cent due to cost reductions deriving both from the removal of trade barriers and the achievement of economies of scale. Indeed, if member states were to pursue appropriate macroeconomic policies, then GDP could grow by as much as 7 per cent.

Ex-ante estimates on such a large scale are fraught with difficulties. The first major ex-post study, the Monti review (1996), was more downbeat: it estimated that the single market had raised GDP by approximately one per cent by 1994. Coming so quickly after the advent of the single market, this review could not hope to capture more medium-term benefits. These were picked up to some extent in a second ex-post analysis (European Commission, 2003) published for the tenth anniversary of the single market programme, which estimated that GDP had grown by 1.8 per cent due to the single market. This is considerably short of the expectations generated by the Cecchini Report.

There are, of course, difficulties in arriving at an agreed estimate. It is, for example, hard to attribute growth effects to specific single market measures and there are difficulties in accounting for dynamic effects which only become apparent over time, such as the cumulative interaction of growth, investment and further growth. Even so, it seems that the direct economic benefits of the single market have to be regarded as significant rather than outstanding.

The European Commission (2003) estimated that 2.5 million new jobs were created in the EC from 1993 to 2003 and that the increase in wealth attributable to the single market during the same period was some €877 million. EU exports to third countries increased from 6.9 per cent of EU GDP in 1992 to 11.2 per cent in 2001. The single market had helped to more than double new inflows of foreign direct investment into the EU as a percentage of GDP.

Benefits for the citizen

In certain respects the optimism of the Cecchini Report's estimations are unfortunate in that they distract from the single market's significant achievements. The European Commission (2007a) articulated the achievements of the single market for citizens as follows:

- An increase of 2.2 per cent in GDP over the period from 1992 to 2006, equivalent to an increase of €480 per person in 2006
- The right to work and live abroad – a right which has been exercised by over fifteen million EU citizens. EU nationals enjoy important, if limited, political rights in the country in which they reside. For example, they may stand for election and vote in municipal and European (but not national) elections. EU migrant workers have the right to equality of treatment concerning employment, pay, conditions of work and so forth. The European Health Insurance Card facilitates reimbursement of healthcare costs incurred during a temporary stay in another member state. There are programmes to facilitate the mobility of researchers and for the automatic recognition of qualifications in a range of professions including architects, dentists, doctors, midwives, nurses, pharmacists and veterinary surgeons
- Greater ease in travelling to other member states, particularly those who are party to the Schengen Convention which abolished passport controls between certain member states
- Greater ease of studying abroad, with over one million students having completed part of their studies in another member state
- A wider choice of high-quality goods and services – Eurobarometer figures show that three-quarters of citizens believe that the single market has helped improve the range and quality of goods and services
- Lower prices for telecommunications, transportation, banking and insurance and so forth, due to the opening up of national markets and the increase in competition
- Consumer protection, with consumers enjoying full consumer rights when buying in another member state
- Savings in government expenditure due to more transparent and competitive public procurement rules.

Benefits for business

The benefits for businesses include:

- A single market of approximately 500 million people which creates new export opportunities for business and enables the achievement of economies of scale

- Greater ease of cross-border trade as 'border bureaucracy' such as customs clearance documentation has declined. Mutual recognition has meant that businesses that trade within the EU need authorisation only in their home member state
- Greater ease of starting or buying a business. For example, EU competition law creates standards for mergers and competition. EU regional policy supports small and medium-sized enterprises (SMEs) in terms of finance, management and marketing
- Greater coverage by EU standards: this facilitates goods which are in compliance with the required standards to move freely between member states, simplifies procedures, enables technical interoperability and ensures high safety standards
- Greater opportunities, through the opening up of public procurement, to bid for public sector contracts in other member states
- Cheaper finance for business, particularly when the Action Plan for Financial Services reaches completion
- Lower telecommunications and electricity costs where markets have been opened to competition.

Perceptions of the single market

What do ordinary European consumers believe have been the effects of the single market? A Eurobarometer survey carried out in early 2006 among the then EU-25 member states found that the majority of those polled perceived the effects of the single market as broadly positive in terms of competition (67 per cent), the range of products (73 per cent) and their quality (58 per cent).

Most people in all states surveyed, with the exception of one, believed that increasing worker mobility could help combat unemployment. The exception was Germany, possibly because German economic recovery has proven to be long and arduous.

The majority of respondents also believed that the single market had facilitated travel between member states (72 per cent), while more than one-third had considered the possibility of living in another member state (36 per cent). Such results may indicate an incipient positive change in popular attitudes towards labour mobility in Europe, which has traditionally been poor. This is in stark contrast to the US where labour mobility has long been an accepted part of life and a major factor in achieving lower unemployment.

How complete is the single market?

The single market is more complete in some areas than in others. There have been delays and a lack of uniformity in implementation.

The directives underlying the single market had to be transposed into national law and then implemented. It took over three years for the process of transposing the original '1992' directives to be largely completed. Indeed, in 1997, the Commission introduced an Action Plan for the Single Market to finalise the original single market programme and reboot the process. New single market directives have been introduced on a regular basis and the concern over implementation gaps led the Commission to introduce a single market scoreboard to monitor transposition. Performance varies between member states with, for example, some Scandinavian members having a good record and some of the original founders, such as Germany, France and Italy, lagging behind. However, somewhat amusingly, there seems to be a good correlation between the acceleration of the rate of transposition of directives by a member state and the imminence of that member state assuming the presidency of the Council of the EU.

In January 2007 the *Internal Market Scoreboard* showed 1.2 per cent of single market directives were not implemented in time. Six months later this had slipped to 1.6 per cent. The average deficit therefore remains above a new one per cent interim target agreed by the heads of state and government in March 2007. This new target is expected to be reached by the end of 2009 at the latest.

The scoreboard is a useful method of focusing attention, but in itself is insufficient. There is a need to think 'beyond the scoreboard'. Not only should a directive be transposed in time but it should be properly thought through and implemented. The emphasis on proper transposition and implementation, and the need for political will to drive the process can be expected to increase in future, as major EU directives are likely to contain more vagueness due to the compromises necessary to get agreement among all member states.

Compliance with existing legislation is also an issue. For example, figures to date show that only 16 per cent of all EU procurement is publicly advertised and open to cross-border bidding (European Commission, 2004b). Potential savings are significant. Public authorities that apply the EU's procurement legislation have paid 34 per cent less than authorities that did not. The Irish government estimates that it could save €1 billion over the next five years from e-procurement. The Italian government has already saved €3.7 billion out of a total of €23 billion of purchases in 2003. Greater efficiency in public procurement goes some way to helping member states satisfy the fiscal deficit limits required by the Stability and Growth Pact. Notwithstanding the potential savings, some national governments continue to find it difficult to resist the temptation to reserve the more lucrative contracts for home companies, while pursuing opportunities in neighbouring states.

In a similar vein, the market for services remains fragmented, though the recent adoption of the Services Directive (see below) is an important development in liberalising this sector of the European economy. Such liberalisation is expected to create new opportunities for economic growth, investment and employment and to broaden consumer choice as well as to enhance productivity.

The Services Directive

The majority of the legislative proposals for the single market were transposed by member states broadly on schedule so that the single market largely became a reality during 1993, albeit with some exceptions which took several more years to address. One notable exception was the area of services, which was to become a much more important part of the European economy than it had been in the early 1990s when the emphasis was primarily on the free movement of goods.

Nowadays the services sector is estimated to account for approximately 70 per cent of economic activity but only 20 per cent of intra-EU trade. More trade in services therefore promises further economic growth, though for Ireland the 'exportable proportion' of services is less than that of manufacturing (see Table 4.1). Integrating services markets could result in an increase in bilateral trade and foreign direct investment in commercial services by between 15 and 35 per cent (McCreevy, 2005). However, exports of services are constrained both by regulatory barriers and the nature of the services sector itself.

Table 4.1: *Export propensity of services and manufacturing, Ireland 2004 (% of output in manufacturing and turnover in service)*

Manufacturing	82.5
Indigenous	33.4
Foreign	96.4
Services	7.1
Computer and related activities	42.0
Wholesale trade	0.4
Retail trade	1.4
R&D	7.9

Source: CSO Annual Services Inquiry 2004

Services have always been an element of international trade including, for example, tourism, transport, postal services and insurance. The Irish policy framework identifies a separate specific category of internationally traded services such as software, consulting services, R&D, healthcare, education and training, digital media and financial services. In this category of internationally traded services, which is unique to Ireland, the export element is more important. This is naturally the case as the generally non-traded services, such as retail, are excluded.

The current international services export situation is quite similar to the manufacturing situation at the beginning of the single market in 1992. Exports are dominated by multinationals, indigenous firms export a relatively small proportion of sales, and overall the exports are highly concentrated in financial services and software (see Table 4.2). Software accounts for 72 per cent of foreign firms' international services exports, while the equivalent figure for indigenous firms is 57 per cent.

Table 4.2: *Exports and export proportions: International services, Ireland 2005*

	Sales (€ billion)	Exports (€ billion)	% exported
Indigenous	5.7	2.1	36.8
Foreign	25.2	23.9	94.8
Total	30.9	26.0	84.1

Source: Forfás, Annual Business Survey of Economic Impact

The Commission proposed the Services Directive in 2004 in order to liberalise the provision of services in the EU and promote competitiveness and economic growth. The Bolkestein Directive as it was originally called (after European Commissioner Fritz Bolkestein, who first proposed it) was one of the most hotly contested pieces of EU legislation ever to be piloted through the EU's legislative system and was in essence the final plank in the effort to complete the single market. The Services Directive was subject to the codecision procedure, which meant it had to be adopted by both the Council and the European Parliament, thus providing the latter with considerable power to influence the final outcome. Following protracted negotiations between the two institutions, the heavily amended directive was finally adopted jointly by the Council and the Parliament in December 2006.

The directive creates a legal framework to enable freedom of establishment and free movement of services between member states. It addresses the reality that barriers continue to exist to the free movement of services, for example due to the administrative burdens or legal uncertainties associated with trading services. This is of major concern at a macroeconomic level given that 70 per cent of GDP and employment in member states is generated by services, and also at a sectoral level due to the high incidence of SMEs in the provision of services.

The directive has reasonably broad coverage, but, due to derogations or to the prior existence of EU legislation for certain services, it does not apply to financial, transport, electronic communication, audiovisual and gambling services. Neither does the directive apply to social services such as social housing or healthcare or to non-economic services. There are also derogations in the postal, electricity and gas sectors as well as water distribution and waste treatment. These derogations are noteworthy. In the case of Ireland, for example, financial services, which are of course covered by other EU directives, are a major part of the country's service exports.

A key aim of the directive is administrative simplification. Member states are required to examine procedures and formalities for access to a service activity and, where necessary, simplify them, establish points of single contact, ensure that relevant information is accessible, and that procedures and formalities can be completed at a distance or by electronic means.

In order to promote freedom of establishment, member states are required to apply certain criteria to schemes which authorise services – such authorisation schemes should be non-discriminatory; justified by an overriding concern for the public interest; proportionate to the public interest; clear, objective and accessible; and made public in advance.

Member states are not permitted to apply requirements which, for example, discriminate on the ground of nationality. They are required to evaluate whether there are discriminatory requirements such as obligations on businesses to take a specific legal form, bans on businesses having more than one establishment in a member state or specifications on the minimum number of employees. Overall, member states must be guided by the aforementioned principles of:

- Non-discrimination (according to nationality or location of the registered office)
- Necessity (i.e. requirements must be justified by an overriding concern for the public interest)
- Proportionality (i.e. requirements must not go beyond what is necessary to attain an objective).

To promote the free movement of services, member states are required to respect the right of providers to provide services in a member state other than that in which they are established. Once again, any requirements which are imposed must respect the principles of non-discrimination, necessity and proportionality.

The directive also deals with the quality of services and the rights of recipients of services, including information and non-discrimination.

Importantly, it also requires administrative cooperation in the form of mutual assistance among member states to ensure that providers, and the services they provide, are effectively supervised.

The directive is clear in its intent. Even allowing for the numerous exceptions and derogations, it applies to a significant part of the dominant sector in modern economies. It is clear that businesses and particularly SMEs feel the burden of administrative requirements in services. In Ireland, business representatives have frequently adverted to administrative burdens, and official reports have also acknowledged it. Any action, not least at EU level, is welcome and works with the grain of Irish policy-making.

However, achieving progress with a single market for services is difficult. Compared to physical goods, services tend to be more complicated. The vested interests among service-providers are powerful. And services, though referred to by the same name, can differ significantly from member state to member state. Indeed the nature of services continually evolves, for example due to technological change. Products, such as software, once classified as manufactures may just as well be seen as services. To compound matters the data on services in Ireland emerge slowly. In mid-2007, for example, we were still using data on services from 2004 and 2005.

It is not surprising therefore that the Services Directive, when first proposed, was strongly contested and that the directive which eventually emerged showed signs of compromise. The directive is clear however in expressing an aspiration of achieving a genuine single market for services by 2010. In pursuing this objective the member states have certainly set themselves an ambitious target.

As the focus of the single market shifts to services, it is interesting to note that Ireland's services trade performance is much weaker than its merchandise trade performance. In both cases, however, the data are significantly influenced by the accounting policies of the multinational companies located in Ireland.

The merchandise account is heavily in surplus, though this surplus has been declining each year since 2002. In 2006, exports of €83.4 billion exceeded imports of €58 billion, yielding a surplus of €25.4 billion. On the services account in 2006, exports of €55.1 billion fell short of imports of €62.5 billion, yielding a substantial deficit of €7.4 billion. Indeed services imports exceeded merchandise imports. The detailed services performance and the summary balance of payments account for merchandise and services are shown in Table 4.3.

The biggest single element in both services exports and surpluses is computer services, which largely comprise the electronic distribution of

Table 4.3: *Services trade, Ireland 2006 (€ billion)*

Sector	Exports	Imports	Balance
Merchandise	83.4	58.0	+25.4
Services	55.1	62.5	−7.4
Transport	2.3	2.0	+0.3
Tourism and travel	4.3	5.4	−1.1
Communications	0.4	0.8	−0.4
Insurance	8.8	7.2	+1.6
Financial services	6.2	3.8	+2.4
Computer services	16.7	0.5	+16.2
Royalties/fees	0.8	16.6	−15.8
Business services	14.9	26.0	−11.1
Other	0.6	0.2	+0.4

Source: CSO, Balance of Payments 2006

software. Other major surplus sectors are insurance and financial services and there is a slight surplus in transport. The biggest deficit occurs in royalties and licences but deficits also occur in tourism and travel, communications and business services.

Ireland clearly has some way to go to become a strong services exporter. By contrast, when the single market gathered pace in the 1990s, Ireland performed strongly in merchandise trade and was well placed to capitalise on the opening up of the market. The situation with services in 2007 is simply not the same, though we must re-emphasise that some of the performance reflects accounting practices rather than real market-priced trade.

A look at the geographic pattern of services trade in Table 4.4 shows that Ireland has a surplus with the EU-25 (as it was when the data was collected), as well as with Asia and Africa. The overall deficit is largely due to services trade with North America.

Table 4.4: *Geographic pattern of services trade, Ireland 2005 (€ billion)*

	Exports	Imports	Balance
EU-25	30.9	27.4	+3.5
North America	4.2	19.1	−14.9
Asia	3.5	1.3	+2.2
Africa	0.7	0.3	+0.4
Total (including other regions)	46.1	56.2	−10.1

Source: CSO, Services Exports and Imports 2007

The detailed sectoral aspects of services trade with the EU-25 are set out in Table 4.5.

Table 4.5: *Services trade with the EU-25, Ireland 2006 (€ billion)*

Sector	Exports	Imports	Balance
Transport	1.9	0.9	+1.0
Tourism and travel	2.6	3.1	–0.5
Communications	0.3	0.5	–0.2
Insurance	5.1	3.7	+1.4
Financial services	2.7	1.1	+1.6
Computer services	12.0	0.2	+11.8
Royalties/fees	0.1	4.7	–4.6
Business services	6.2	13.2	–7.0
Total	30.9	27.4	+3.5

Source: CSO, Services Exports and Imports 2007

It is interesting to consider some of what might be deemed non-traditional services within the category of business services. For example, in legal, accounting and professional services, exports to the EU-25 amounted to €157 million compared to imports of €413 million. R&D exports were €211 million compared to imports of €545 million. In essence, the scale is small but the performance is in deficit.

As with the single market in 1992, a key opportunity for Ireland is the better facilitation of exports through the removal of barriers; though, of course, there can be welfare gains in the form of lower-priced and better-quality imports as overall EU production avails of absolute and comparative advantage. In addition, the Services Directive, in facilitating the right of establishment, increases competition in domestic markets thereby benefiting consumers.

Analysis of Irish exports benefits from a recognition of the dualism between indigenous and foreign direct investment firms. In 1992 the expectation was that the foreign sector would thrive and that more modest gains would be expected from indigenous exports. This was because, despite the easing of both the costs and the difficulties of exporting, basic commercial weaknesses such as small scale, weak product portfolio, low technological capacity and weak management and finance would persist in the indigenous sector. This has largely turned out to be the case.

While indigenous employment, exports and sectoral mix have improved, often above the EU average performance, the indigenous export performance is dwarfed by the performance of multinationals and still displays many of the weaknesses that existed prior to 1992. In effect, fifteen years of the single market have not fundamentally transformed indigenous export performance. It has certainly helped in the process but it has not changed the basic position.

Table 4.6 compares 1991 and 2004 data for manufactured exports. Overall export growth was enormous. The 2004 level is five times that of

Table 4.6: *Manufactured exports, Ireland 1991–2004*

	Total		Foreign		Indigenous	
	1991	*2004*	*1991*	*2004*	*1991*	*2004*
Exports (€ billion)	16.5	80.8	12.2	74.6	4.3	6.2
Sales (€ billion)	26.5	97.9	14.2	79.4	12.3	18.6
% Exports/sales	62.3	82.5	85.9	94.0	35.0	33.3
% Share of exports	100	100	73.9	92.3	26.1	7.7
% Increase exports 1991/2004		390		511		44

Source: CSO, Census of Industrial Production 1991, 2004

1991 but this was driven by multinational firms. In 2004 exports by multinationals were six times the 1991 level.

Indigenous exports grew over the period but only by 44 per cent. Their share of exports declined from 26.1 per cent to 7.7 per cent. The proportion of indigenous sales which was exported remained virtually static at 35 per cent in 1991 compared to 33.3 per cent in 2004. O'Malley (2004) notes that several indigenous sectors had a good export performance relative to EU standards between 1991 and 2001. Although the relative performance was good, it was inadequate to transform the overall indigenous export performance as was required given the low base from which it began in the early 1990s.

The recent indigenous services export performance is better than that for manufacturing, but manufactured exports still exceed services exports by a ratio of 3.6 to 1. Between 2000 and 2005, as illustrated in Table 4.7, indigenous manufactured exports were static, while services exports (on the Forfás international services definition) grew by around 8 per cent per year. Total exports grew by 5.5 per cent, while services exports grew by 50 per cent. Software exports grew by 10.7 per cent, while other services exports grew by 87.9 per cent.

Table 4.7: *Total indigenous exports (manufacturing and international services), Ireland 2000 and 2005*

	2000 *(€ billion)*	2005 *(€ billion)*	*% change*
Total	9.1	9.6	5.5
Manufactured	7.6	7.6	~
International services	1.4	2.1	50.0
Software	0.75	0.83	10.7
Others	0.66	1.24	87.9
Services share (%)	17.8	22.8	28.1

Source: Forfás, Annual Business Survey of Economic Impact 2005

Services exports, both traditional (such as tourism) and international (such as consulting and healthcare), are identified as having strong potential for Ireland (Forfás, 2004). This is particularly important because Ireland's competitive position in basic manufacturing will progressively weaken. However this chapter has shown that Ireland's services trade performance currently leaves much to be desired. Ireland has a serious deficit. It depends on multinationals for 92 per cent of service exports. There is a strong dependence on finance which is outside the Services Directive remit. On the positive side, the growth rate of indigenous international service exports is performing much better than indigenous manufacturing exports, albeit from a lower base.

Ireland was one of the first economies to promote the development of non-traditional exports. An international services programme was established as part of the industrial policy framework in the early 1980s. The performance discussed above, therefore, reflects two decades of active support and illustrates the difficulty of the task.

Of course, not all the implications of the Services Directive are for trade. The directive and other relevant directives, such as the Professional Qualifications Directive, have important implications for national administrations. For example, the need to exchange information so that the providers of a service from one member state can establish in another (one thinks of the Polish plumber) requires the linking of competent authorities with appropriate structures and technical solutions.

Within member states there will be a need for one-stop shops to deal with business registration, VAT registration and the assessment of qualifications in a streamlined fashion. This in turn requires an assessment of the appropriate structures and of staffing and resources.

Reinvigorating the single market

As the fiftieth anniversary of the Treaty of Rome approached, the EU looked to further development in a number of areas prominent among which was the single market. In *A Citizens' Agenda: Delivering Results for Europe*, the European Commission (2006a) emphasised the importance of a 'fully functioning' single market alongside other key issues on the policy agenda such as security and justice, enlargement, the EU in the world, and EU solidarity policies to promote quality of life, social cohesion and increased opportunity.

The Commission specifically identified gaps in the single market in areas such as energy, financial markets and obstacles to the free movement of labour, with consequent effects on energy prices, bank charges and so forth (European Commission, 2006a). The Commission pointedly asked why it was so difficult for a citizen in one member state to get insurance in another. It also referred to potential improvements in roaming charges for mobile phone users and the prospect of a Community patent. Looking externally, the Commission saw a competitive single market as a major feature of the EU's response to globalisation.

As a consequence of these reflections, the Commission proposed a fundamental review of the single market. In October 2006, following a public consultation, the Commission reported the views of stakeholders on the future of the single market (European Commission, 2006d). These stakeholders included citizens, member states, trade unions, consumer organisations, NGOs, academia, chambers of commerce and businesses running the gamut from manufacturing and construction to professional and technical, and finance and insurance.

The respondents, while favouring the single market, identified gaps in areas such as financial services, insurance, transport, energy, taxation, intellectual property and the free movement of labour. The respondents also agreed on the next steps needed to complete the market including improved implementation and enforcement, better regulation, fostering innovation, investment in information and communication and taking account of the global context. Deriving from these, the respondents made practical suggestions. For instance implementation and enforcement might be improved by means of guidance in the form of transposition workshops or by sanction in the form of more efficient infringement procedures. Innovation might benefit from closer synergy between competition policy and the single market, more robust evaluation of the effects of policy proposals on business, and reductions in red tape.

The Commission published an interim report in February 2007 in which it outlined a vision for the single market in the twenty-first century. The following gives a flavour of the vision:

> 21st century Europe is indivisible from the world economy. Its prosperity has and will continue to flow from dismantling barriers and creating open markets. This openness has been made possible and facilitated by a strong regulatory framework. The single market principles remain sound. The challenge of the 21st century is to adapt the application of these principles: to secure the right regulatory framework, to ensure that markets function properly, to promote competitiveness and to respond to the dynamism and change that flows directly from Europe's engagement with the world economy. The goal of the 21st century single market is to make markets work better for the benefit of European citizens, consumers and businesses, and to promote a more competitive and sustainable Europe (European Commission, 2007a, p. 4).

As a consequence the single market should focus efforts in six areas: consumers, integration of the economy, the knowledge society, good regulation, sustainability and globalisation.

For consumers, the single market should be more active, for example in assuring quality of goods and services – for imports as well as those produced internally. The single market could help assure and protect consumers in areas such as health services and in cross-border or e-commerce transactions.

The single market could in future help further integrate the EU economy, whether in facilitating business to operate or labour to move across borders, and in the creation of trans-European networks and pan-European financial markets.

In promoting the knowledge society, the single market could help address fragmentation in markets, such as telecommunications, which are central to such a society. The single market could also, for example, bring clarity to intellectual property rights.

Recognising that thriving markets pose environmental threats, the Commission articulates the need for appropriate accompanying policies – regional, social, employment, educational and environmental.

Within the global economy, the Commission argues that the single market can help influence global standards and norms through the leadership it has shown in developing rules and standards in areas ranging from product safety to the environment to corporate governance.

Within the EU, the Commission recognises the need to improve the implementation and enforcement of laws, reduce the administrative burdens of compliance and evaluate which laws work and which do not.

To realise its vision the Commission advocates 'new aproaches' – though some are hardly new – such as ensuring the better functioning of markets, the simplification and modernisation of rules and the active enforcement of EU law and competition rules. In order to respond to global markets the Commission refers to possible initiatives such as systematic monitoring of prices to establish whether the benefits of global markets are being passed on to consumers. It also sees possibilities in greater convergence of regulations with those in the global economy and more regulatory cooperation between the EU and its main trading partners. There is also, in the Commission's view, scope for greater decentralisation, for instance in the form of a stronger role for national regulators and by improving the networking between member states of administrative and judicial and regulatory authorities. And, of course, there is the ever-present need for improvements in access and communications, for example in the form of rationalised information sources, better publicity, access to one-stop shops for SMEs and so forth.

The reports outlined above heralded a final report on the theme of a single market for citizens in the twenty-first century, to be published before the end of 2007. This report will be supplemented by reports from each member state – Ireland's report is being prepared by Forfás. Although the report is not available at the time of writing, we can safely expect that the themes identified in the February 2007 report will re-emerge. Action to assist the consumer is necessary in facilitating access to financial services, healthcare services and safe food and medicines. To promote an integrated EU there is a need to facilitate the mobility of labour. The knowledge economy requires action on e-communications, patent protection and the mobility of students and researchers. A well-regulated Europe requires action on e-government and the simplification of laws and rules. We can also expect that there will be greater emphasis on the importance of SMEs. A sustainable Europe requires action on the social aspects of the single market, including the social agenda. A single market open to the world requires action in monitoring world prices (to assess whether the benefits of open trade are passing through to consumers), benchmarking EU rules and standards against the rest of the world and encouraging the convergence of regulation in world markets.

To improve the governance of the single market we can expect action plans to facilitate access and the flow of information, to enhance cooperation between single market authorities at member state and EU levels, a more focused infringement policy and enhanced reporting of the transposition of EU legislation and progress of the single market (such as in the single market scoreboard).

It is evident that the single market is, to use the Commission's phrase, 'constantly evolving and adapting to new realities' and that it will never be 'finalised' or 'complete' (European Commission, 2007a, p. 3). The Commission has clearly identified gaps in the single market and recognises that as markets evolve they throw up new types of barrier. It is disappointing, though not surprising to those who observe the development of the single market, that such major gaps persist even after fifty years.

Conclusion

At the start of the 1990s Ireland, as a small, open economy, looked forward to the completion of the single market and the more competitive environment it heralded. In a study at that time, we concluded that Ireland was in a relatively good position to compete in the single market (Foley and Mulreany, 1990).

The Irish economy in 2007 has transformed fundamentally from that of 1990. High unemployment has been transformed into virtual full employment, the numbers at work have approximately doubled, income levels have increased to make Ireland one of the the richest EU member states and net emigration has been replaced by net immigration. Despite this very impressive performance we must however acknowledge that in 2007, as in 1990, the export performance of the economy is heavily dependent on foreign direct investment rather than indigenous innovation and commercial capability.

There are many determinants of Ireland's overall strong performance, including foreign direct investment, partnership, macroeconomic stability, low taxes, education, labour supply and economic competitiveness. The direct and indirect effects of the single market on Irish economic performance take their place alongside these other significant causes of Ireland's transformation.

Like the other main achievement of the EU, namely the preservation of peace between member states on the European continent for an unprecedented six decades, the virtual completion of the single European market in manufactures is largely taken for granted by European citizens almost fifteen years on. Such an abstract economic objective was never calculated to capture the popular imagination. As Jacques Delors, President of the European Commission for ten years and chief architect of the project, put it: 'You can't fall in love with the single European market'.

For Delors, an ardent European federalist in the tradition of Jean Monnet and Robert Schuman, completing the single market was not an end in itself; it was decidedly a means to an end, that is, the deepening of European integration. In short, removing the remaining borders to the free movement of goods, services, capital and people was a step closer to some form of political union as yet undefined or clearly stated.

Though people may not fall in love with the single market, they are happy with its practical benefits, whether they take the form of the right to live and work abroad or, simply, cheaper air travel and mobile communications. The success of the single market contributes to a better standard of living and the development of the single market is an important feature in the EU's vision of the future, including the Lisbon Strategy for increasing economic growth and creating more and better jobs.

The new wave of single market implementation has a services, and indeed a governance, focus. As a small, open economy Ireland should welcome moves to facilitate easier and more cost-effective trade. Services are particularly important for an economy which is losing its competitiveness in basic manufacturing, hence a double welcome for services liberalisation. However, the liberalisation gives no guaranteed solution for the problems of services exports such as the overall deficit, dependence on software and financial services and high dependence on multinationals.

The 'new' single market approach provides a better environment for services trade, but is only one of the determinants of success. Domestic innovation, enterprise capability, size of company, management, skills and competitiveness will matter to a great degree.

Current expectations surprisingly mirror those we anticipated for 1992. Service-based foreign direct investment will improve in the sectors where high skills matter, but not in low-cost sectors. Indigenous service exports will be boosted, but the main determinants of success will be found elsewhere. Once again, much as we argued in 1990 for manufactures, domestic policy needs to be directed at the areas which promote commercial competence and competitiveness so as to maximise the services export potential of the new single market.

5

Cohesion in the European Union: The Negotiations that Shaped Modern Ireland

Peter Brennan[1]

We do not anticipate that it will be necessary to seek any special financial assistance from the Community ...
Statement by Seán Lemass to ministers of the governments of the member states of the European Economic Community, Brussels, 18 January 1962

Introduction

Economic and social cohesion is one of the most important objectives of the European Community and lies at the very heart of European integration (Christophersen, 1994). Therefore it should come as no surprise that the issue of cohesion has been at the epicentre of hard political bargaining at EU level for decades.

Ireland's perspective about cohesion, as follows, is a good summary of this key EU policy:

> Cohesion policy has been at the heart of what the European Union is all about. It encompasses the principle and philosophy of solidarity at its best. Member States commit themselves to measures aimed at strengthening the competitiveness of less developed regions and countries with a view to reducing disparities in prosperity levels across the EU. This commitment to bringing about a shared prosperity underpins the ambition of bringing about greater European integration. The objectives of cohesion policy support the overall political ambitions of the Union. Cohesion policy shows EU citizens, particularly those in the poorer regions and countries that European integration comprehends more than just providing a single market (Parlon, 2004, pp. 4–5).

---

[1] This chapter is based on material from a forthcoming book *The EU Negotiations that Shaped Modern Ireland* to be published by Blackhall Publishing.

The structural and cohesion funds are the main instruments of cohesion policy.[2] The main structural funds are the European Agricultural Guarantee and Guidance Fund, Guidance Section (EAGGF),[3] the European Social Fund (ESF) and the European Regional Development Fund (ERDF).

This chapter narrates Ireland's contribution to the debate on EU cohesion policy, a debate which has its roots in the pre-accession period. Ireland has had an enormous influence in shaping EU policies aimed at securing policy, political and financial commitments to assist Europe's less-developed regions (LDRs). Without this dogged and consistent determination, Ireland would have got much less than the €18 billion in EU co-financing received to date from structural interventions since 1973. It is also arguable that Ireland's negotiators in the first two decades of membership laid the foundations for a period of economic convergence which has resulted in Ireland having a gross domestic product (GDP) per capita of 141.4 per cent of the EU-27 average.[4]

The emergence of cohesion policy

The Spaak Report, which was produced by a committee set up by the 1955 Messina Conference, set out the initial views of the Six on Community financing. The pivotal theme in the report was the weak performance of the European economy, characterised by lower productivity and less efficiency than the US economy. The report also anticipated the setting up of an investment bank to support economic development and adjustment, and a social fund designed to improve the quality of the European labour force. These proposals were predicated on the view that the creation of the common market would lead to considerable economic change in the location of industry, labour mobility and methods of production. The provisions of the Treaty of Rome, which were modelled closely on the Spaak Report, set down the basic principles for what subsequently became known as cohesion policy. Due to the fact that the six founding member states were relatively homogenous in terms of economic development, the issue of disparities between the regions was not considered in any detail in

---

[2] Evans (1999) provides a comprehensive account of the EU structural funds.

[3] Under recent reforms of the Common Agricultural Policy (CAP), the EAGGF has, since 2007, been reorganised into two new funds: the European Agricultural Guarantee Fund (EAGF) and the European Agricultural Fund for Rural Development (EAFRD).

[4] This figure is taken from EUROSTAT data published in February 2007. GDP per capita is expressed in terms of purchasing power standards and covers 268 NUTS-2 regions in the twenty-seven member states on the basis of latest available statistics i.e. 2004 data. The convergence rate for Ireland's Border, Midland and Western (BMW) region at 100.1 per cent per capita is well short of that for Ireland's Southern and Eastern (S&E) region at 156.5 per cent.

the Rome Treaty. Thus while the treaty spoke about the need for harmonious development, it did not provide for a legal mechanism to deliver such an objective. The predominant laissez-faire ethos of the Rome Treaty precluded a strong role for the Community at the outset.

Ireland's accession negotiations opened in Luxembourg on 30 June 1970 (Maher, 1986).[5] The four applicant countries were put on notice that the Six were working on a plan for the achievement of economic and monetary union (EMU). The report on EMU by Pierre Werner, the Prime Minister of Luxembourg, was subjected to close scrutiny in Ireland's Department of Finance and Central Bank, as both were concerned with the implications which EMU could have on Ireland, situated as it was on the periphery of an enlarged Community and with a markedly lower level of economic development when compared with the existing member states. The assessment led to the conclusion that there was a need for the adoption of a Community regional policy to deal with the problem of regional disparities which would otherwise be exacerbated. The view was that any assurances that might be obtainable from the Community would best be incorporated in a special protocol for Ireland similar to that accorded to Italy in 1957 when the Treaty of Rome was negotiated. In December 1970 Ireland presented to the Community negotiators an analysis of the Irish economy, with particular reference to its regional and structural deficiencies and the policies applied by the Irish government to make good the situation. On 15 February 1971 the Irish government outlined its objectives in relation to economic development in the context of the EMU project.

On 22 March 1971, on foot of the completion of the Werner Group's Report in October 1970, the Council adopted a resolution and three decisions on EMU, which recorded the political will of the member states to achieve EMU in stages by 1980. One of the principal features of the Union was to be a 'Community policy with the appropriate means to resolve the most important problems in the regional and structural fields'. It also asked the Commission to bring forward measures to 'initiate solutions to the priority problems in the regional and structural fields'. As part of this ambition, a new impetus was given to the development of a coherent and comprehensive regional policy at Community level. The resolution expressed approval in principle to the use of the EAGGF for regional development purposes. It was also agreed to create a regional development fund. The Irish government indicated its readiness to cooperate fully with the Council's resolutions and decisions on EMU.

---

[5] Maher's account of Ireland's accession negotiations by one of its principal negotiators provides a unique insight as regards the dynamics of the politics and policies of the period.

In the immediate period ahead, the negotiations moved on to other priorities. However, on 12 July 1971, Ireland's Foreign Minister Patrick Hillery presented to the Community a memorandum defining in greater detail the nature and extent of Ireland's regional development problems and the measures needed to solve them. The minister sought a commitment that the Community would employ all the means at its disposal to supplement Irish government programmes aimed at removing existing imbalances, and that in further development of a comprehensive Community regional policy full account would be taken of the special problems of Ireland in this field. It was agreed by the Community side that the matter would be the subject of further study.

In subsequent informal contacts with the Commission team, the Irish delegation indicated the government's preference for a protocol which would recognise Ireland's special needs in the matter of regional and structural disparities. The protocol proposal was under consideration by the Irish side for quite some time but quite deliberately was not mentioned until the negotiations were well established. In October 1971 final agreement was reached on the protocol on the economic and industrial development of Ireland, which was eventually added as an annex to the Act of Accession (Protocol 30). This agreement was facilitated by a concurrent deal on the retention of Irish industrial incentives.[6]

The pre-accession summit held in Paris on 19 and 20 October 1972 approved a communiqué which set out the principles on which the development and further strengthening of the EC should be based after enlargement. This was an important meeting for Ireland as it secured commitment about the development of a Community regional policy and agreement that a high priority should be given to the aim of correcting the structural and regional balances which might affect the realisation of EMU. Specifically, member states agreed to coordinate their regional policies. The Commission was tasked to prepare a report analysing the regional problems which would arise in the enlarged Community. The summit believed that the creation of the ERDF, along with a coordination of regional aids, should permit, progressively with the realisation of EMU, the correction of the main regional imbalances in an enlarged Community. Thus, prior to Ireland's accession, there was not only evidence but also political will to assist the less-developed regions to meet the challenges of

---

[6] The declarations made by the Community side (Aldo Moro, Minister for Foreign Affairs of the Italian Republic) and Dr Hillery at the sixth ministerial meeting between the Community and Ireland, held on 19 October 1971, drew on the treaty commitment to the harmonious development of the economies of the member states by reducing the differences existing between the various regions and the backwardness of the less-favoured regions.

EMU. While the term had not been coined at that stage, cohesion policy was seen as an inclusive part of the EMU process.

The results of Ireland's accession negotiations were presented by way of a White Paper (Government of Ireland, 1972).[7] On EMU, it was noted that a greater measure of discipline was required in economic-policy-making to ensure that member states did not pursue conflicting or divergent policies. It was government policy that EMU would help achieve Ireland's economic and social objectives. The protocol, which was described as an 'outstanding achievement in the negotiations', was seen (correctly) as a major step in the direction of putting in place a Community regional policy to counterbalance the effects of EMU. The White Paper said that, as a result of the protocol, Ireland could proceed with development plans secure in the knowledge that 'we will be able to operate an adequate system of development aids and supports and that Community resources will be available to assist us' (p. 18).

Accession and the ERDF

The accession of the UK and Ireland in 1973, followed by the Mediterranean enlargements of the 1980s, altered the political and economic framework within which the issue of economic divergence and peripherality would be debated. Both countries attached particular importance to the need to develop regional policy at Community level, not least because their membership increased the economic disparities between member states.[8] The UK's interest in regional policy, however, was quite different to Ireland's as the problem regions in the UK were characterised by industrial decline rather than rural or agricultural problems; hence the UK could not benefit as much from the CAP. The ERDF, in part, would redress this funding shortfall. The doctrine of the *juste retour* – a strict balance sheet approach to payments/receipts from the Community budget – took its roots in this period.

Very soon after membership, the Commission sent the Council the (George) Thompson Report on the regional problems in the enlarged

---

[7] The text of the Accession Treaty was published in a special (unnumbered) version of the EEC *Official Journal* on 27 March 1972. On 10 May 1972, 83.1 per cent of the Irish electorate (some 1,041,890 voters) approved the proposal to amend Article 29 of the Constitution of Ireland in order to allow the state to become a member of the European Communities. The European Communities Act 1972 became law on 6 December 1972. Ireland deposited its instrument of ratification on 16 December and along with the UK and Denmark (Norway having voted against membership) joined the EEC on 1 January 1973.

[8] Another driver was the UK's experience of developing its own regional policy (see Milward, 1992).

Community (Commission of the European Communities, 1973). Garret FitzGerald, Ireland's Foreign Minister, (attending one of his first EU meetings) made it quite clear that Ireland supported the report when it was discussed by Foreign Ministers at their meeting on 14 and 15 May 1973. He also made the point that other Community policies should be assessed as regards their impact on regional development; this aspiration was later adopted in treaty language. Given the support received at Council, the Commission wasted no time in bringing forward its proposals to set up an ERDF.

Ireland undertook a tour of capitals over the autumn to make the case that the proposed level of resources bore no relationship to the country's needs in comparison to other regions of the Community. Quiet diplomacy was put aside however at the Foreign Affairs Council held on 15 October 1973, when Ireland's Foreign Minister made it clear that the Commission's proposals failed to take account of the key findings of the Thompson Report; failed to give adequate expression to the treaty's objective to achieve harmonious development; failed to make provision for any variations in the level of permissible aid payable having regard to the degree of intensity of regional problems; failed to take account of the ability of member states to co-finance their own regional aid programmes; and failed, most notably, to take any account of Protocol 30.[9] Days later, Commissioner Thompson told the European Parliament that the unique character of the Irish problem which was given expression in Protocol 30 was recognised from the beginning by the Commission in the sense that Ireland is the only country where the entire country has been accepted as falling within the criteria in the ERDF Regulation (Article 5), and that the Commission would have flexibility to vary the rate of Community contribution according to the degree of need.

The adoption of the ERDF in 1975 was a notable milestone, and was not unrelated to the pressure applied by Ireland and the UK to have such an instrument adopted.[10] Certainly, the high-level inter-state bargaining at the Paris Summits in 1972 and 1974 facilitated the adoption of the ERDF

---

[9] Throughout the debate and negotiations on the ERDF and Community regional policy, FitzGerald underlined that his concerns applied equally to Northern Ireland on the basis that the problems of development of the entire island must be considered together in the context of Community regional policy.

[10] Regulation (EEC) No. 724/75, OJ L 73 of 1975. In 1975 the ERDF's budget was just €150 million. The adoption of the ERDF regulation was one of Ireland's successes during its first presidency of the Council of Ministers. Padraig O hUiginn, the Director of the Secretariat of the Council of Ministers at the time with responsibility for the ERDF proposal, subsequently became Secretary (General) of the Department of the Taoiseach and was closely involved in the first rounds of structural funds negotiations.

during Ireland's first presidency of the Council.[11] It was agreed that each member state could apply for grants up to a given percentage i.e. its quota, which in Ireland's case was 6 per cent of the total budget of 1.3 billion units of account (UAs), with a modest 250 million UAs for its first year of operation.[12] This generated by far the highest per capita return compared to other member states; Ireland got some €10.77 per capita which was more generous than the next less prosperous member state (Italy at €3.67 per capita). This initial high allocation, as well as Ireland's growing share of the ESF (which was the responsibility of Patrick Hillery as a member of the Commission) was an excellent outcome for Ireland's negotiators. These above-average allocations ensured that subsequently, and as the size of the structural funds budget increased, Ireland continued to secure relatively high per capita transfers. One other important decision taken at the time which had long-term implications was that eligible regions would be chosen with reference to a percentage of GDP of the Community average.

Richie Ryan, Ireland's Minister for Finance, did not waste any time and on 24 July presented the Commission with the Irish government's first global allocation for the full €19.4 million allocated to Ireland for 1975. Ireland was the first member state to present its applications. The Irish administration's dexterity in getting projects to Brussels became one of the hallmarks of Ireland's EU membership.

In 1979 the ERDF's rules were changed quite substantially. The fund's budget was increased to €1.1 billion per annum (from 1980). The aid rates were increased and a non-quota section was set up. The Commission was given power to determine regional development priorities on the basis of regional development programmes (RDPs) submitted by member states. Ireland's first ever RDP was submitted by the Department of Finance to the Commission in December 1977. It consisted essentially of the recently published White Paper on national development (1977–1980), together with background material of an analytical and descriptive nature.

---

[11] The heads of state and government also decided at the Paris Summit in December 1974 to meet three times a year and whenever necessary as the Council of the European Communities and also in the context of European Political Cooperation. The first meeting of the 'new formula' Council took place in Dublin Castle, with the then Taoiseach Liam Cosgrave in the chair, on 10 and 11 March 1975. The author was a member of the Irish delegation to the Council. For an account of the Council and its modus operandi refer to de Schoutheete and Wallace (2002).

[12] For convenience, the euro (€) is used where monetary values are mentioned. Prior to the euro, the Community budget was expressed in UAs, which were based on a basket of nine European currencies on the basis of fixed rates. For example, at the time the ERDF was adopted in 1975, £1 was the equivalent to 2.4 UAs. On 1 January 1978 the UA was replaced by the European Unit of Account which reflected the market value of the different national currencies. The Community budget was expressed in ECUs (European Currency Units) before the introduction of the euro on 1 January 1999.

Subsequent RDPs, updating the 1977–1980 RDP, were submitted to the Commission in 1979 and 1980. In April 1981 the Department of Finance presented what was described as its 'second generation' RDP, prepared in line with Commission recommendations and guidance. Thus a decade before anyone ever heard of such a thing as a national development plan, the Irish administration was becoming familiar with the technique of identifying priority projects for EU co-financing.

The link between EMU and cohesion

In a memorandum presented by the Irish government to the European Council meeting in Rome on 1 and 2 December 1975, Taoiseach Liam Cosgrave made the case for improvements in the Community's institutional processes having regard to Ireland's experience since accession. In a comment which may seem odd over thirty years later, Ireland stated that until and unless there was a radical change in the way key economic decisions were taken, little progress could be made towards the approximation of economic conditions in the member states and so towards economic integration. Ireland pressed for a realistic programme to achieve EMU and stated that there should be a quantification of the scale of Community action and resources that would be necessary to counteract the centripetal effects of EMU and to ensure a smooth transition during which the disparities in the economic and social spheres between member states would be narrowed sufficiently to make the achievement of EMU practicable. The memorandum concluded: 'Unless we accept the logic of this progression, EMU will remain forever on the far side of the horizon'. This visionary policy statement was made a decade before the Commission brought forward its proposals on economic and social cohesion. Thus from the earliest days of membership Ireland articulated a policy which saw EMU and cohesion on both sides of the same coin.

During the 1970s the Commission began the slow process of developing a role for the Community in matters of regional policy and a stronger role in social policy. The literature on regional economics at the time endorsed the view that the benefits of market integration would be felt unevenly. The Commission drew support for its views from analyses of fiscal federalism, in particular the 1977 MacDougall Report on the role of public finance in integration. However, there were signs that the Community's commitment to economic convergence policies was not shared by all. The Commission published a report on 'European Union' in June 1975 which set out not only the various approaches to 'European

Union' but also the forms the Union might take.[13] A key aim for the Union was to achieve social progress and economic development for the peoples of Europe and the diminution of regional and social disparities. Briefing the Dáil (after his attendance at the Hague Summit held on 29 and 30 November 1976 which discussed the report), the Taoiseach accepted that the report was a 'major signpost on the way to European integration', but very much regretted that there had been no meaningful debate about the scale of Community action needed to counteract the centripetal effects of EMU while narrowing the economic disparities between member states.

Addressing the Dáil after attending the Rome Summit of March 1977, the Taoiseach pointed out that in the early 1970s Ireland's GDP per capita was almost 54 per cent of the Community average. By 1975 the figure had fallen to 48 per cent. Building his argument he said that the objective of ending regional disparities required a new approach, not only to budgetary flows but also to the interpretation of industrial and competition policy. He went on to make the unusual statement that: 'We cannot contemplate a situation where regional funds and policies are allowed to languish while these other regulatory policies of the Community are applied with vigour and enthusiasm'. While not arguing against the unity of the markets, the Taoiseach firmly believed that the application of policies favouring unduly the central areas of the Community contradicted one of the fundamental purposes of the Community. He concluded by adding that this situation strikes against any hope of reducing regional imbalances and, therefore, any hope of attaining EMU.

The subsequent Jack Lynch government (from July 1977) maintained the Irish position which had developed since accession on the link between EMU and cohesion. During a visit of Commission President Roy Jenkins to Dublin in February 1978, the Taoiseach made it clear that Community policies, in the absence of a regional policy, should take account of the differences between central and peripheral regions; the 'peripheral' card was played for the first time.

The Oireachtas took a keen interest in European developments throughout this period. For example, in considering the 1978 EMU Action Programme submitted by the Commission on 20 February 1978, the Joint Oireachtas Committee on Secondary Legislation concluded that EMU could lead to a widening of regional imbalances and to further unemployment unless the Community committed itself to a regional policy

---

[13] This was based on a report prepared by Leo Tindemans, the Belgian Prime Minister, who was given a mandate by the Paris Summit of December 1974 to prepare wide-ranging recommendations on how to achieve a 'European Union'.

which would ensure a significant redistribution of resources from the richer to the poorer regions.[14]

Helmut Schmidt, Chancellor of the Federal Republic of Germany, chaired the Bremen Summit on 6 and 7 July 1978 which instructed Finance Ministers (ECOFIN) to 'formulate the necessary guidelines for the competent Community bodies to elaborate the provisions necessary for the functioning of a durable and effective scheme of closer monetary cooperation [the European Monetary System (EMS)]'. Such a common approach should, according to the Council's conclusions, 'reduce regional disparities'. The Council also noted 'that action needed to be taken to strengthen the economies of the less prosperous member states in the context of EMS'. Finally the link was made between EMU and cohesion policy. Over the following months ECOFIN discussed the technical aspects of EMS but did not make any commitments regarding Ireland's case for resource transfers. In November both the Taoiseach Jack Lynch and Tánaiste George Colley lobbied other member states, including the French President, the German Federal Chancellor and the British Prime Minister. This lobby effort bore an instant dividend.

The European Council held in Brussels on 4 and 5 December agreed to set up an EMS (on a voluntary basis) from 1 January 1979. As part of the agreement the Council decided that measures would be taken to strengthen the economies of the LDRs. It was proposed that Ireland and Italy would be the main beneficiaries of subsidised loans from a new Community financial instrument.[15] At the end of the meeting Ireland indicated (as did Italy) that it was not in a position to take a decision on participation in the EMS, but would do so as soon as possible. The Irish government published a White Paper on the EMS later in the month. It summarised the case made by Ireland for resource transfers and concluded that there were no inherent

---

[14] A Joint Committee of the Houses of the Oireachtas on the Secondary Legislation of the European Communities was established on 26 July 1973 (see Chapter 11). The committee had power to examine and to report to both Houses on draft Commission proposals, acts of the EC institutions, regulations made under the European Communities Act 1972 and other instruments made under statute and necessitated by the obligations of membership of the Communities. At its first meeting, held on 3 August 1973, Charles J. Haughey TD was elected chairman. There is no doubt Deputy Haughey's experience with the committee and its response to EU proposals had an influence on his government's approach to the later Delors I package negotiations.

[15] The new community financial instrument (the NIC) was adopted by the Council in October 1978. The first loans for Irish infrastructure and energy projects were signed on 17 September 1979. The first loans attracting EMS interest subsidies were for infrastructure projects and were approved in late 1979. The loans covered water supply and waste water (sewerage) projects, electricity generation and distribution, peat bog development and peat processing, road improvements and arterial and land drainage.

drawbacks in the EMS that would preclude Ireland's membership. In a statement to the Dáil on 15 December the Taoiseach said the government had decided to participate in the EMS from the outset. He added that Ireland had received assurances from two (unnamed) member states that Ireland would get substantial resources in excess of the amount agreed at the European Council. By today's standards the amounts involved were modest, but in 1979 what was on offer was more than the combined receipts from both the ERDF and the ESF.

Slow but steady progress

At the European Council in April 1978, the Taoiseach pressed again for a correcting mechanism to be brought forward where the regional impact of Community policies was harmful. Specifically he stated there was a danger that policies to overcome unemployment might be tailored largely or exclusively to meet the more recent problems of the central regions of the Community. Ireland requested a special meeting of the Council to discuss regional policy. The Council's conclusions stated that 'the pursuit of greater internal cohesion, implying also a reduction in regional imbalances, constitutes one of the key objectives of the Community enterprise'. The Commission set up a comprehensive system of analysis and policy formulation on foot of the conclusions of the meeting of the Council. The Commission also decided to undertake a systematic assessment of the regional impact of Community policies.

Perhaps the most significant initiative prior to the Single European Act was the publication of *The Regions of Europe, First Periodic Report on the Social and Economic Situation of the Regions of the Community* (Commission of the European Communities, 1981). This document, for the first time, set out the facts and the figures about the socioeconomic situation in the regions. The concept of cohesion was first articulated in detail in this first periodic report. The Commission undertook to prepare proposals regarding priorities and guidelines for Community regional policy. The starting point was the statement in the 1979 Council resolution that 'regional policy is an integral part of the economic policies of the Community and the member states'. The emphasis was therefore on assessing the capability of regions to adapt their economies to changing circumstances and to develop their indigenous resources to the fullest possible extent. The momentum was maintained with the publication of the second periodic report in 1984 (Commission of the European Communities, 1984). This report gave Ireland and the other less-developed regions, including Greece from 1981 and Spain and Portugal from 1986, all the hard evidence they needed to make the case not only that economic and social cohesion should become one of the principal tasks of the Union, but also that a substantial increase in the Community budget was needed to fulfil this political ambition.

In the decade after membership, Ireland, almost single-handedly but with much sympathy from the Commission, fought the good fight for a fair deal to reflect the country's poor standard of living when compared with other member states. The policies agreed during this period – most importantly the link between EMU and the need to address the requirements of the LDRs, the idea of concentration of resources, and the preparation of RDPs – were the building blocks upon which a more developed policy on cohesion was based in the context of the reforms brought forward by the Commission President Jacques Delors.

Cohesion policy since the Single European Act

The Commission's work programme for 1985 cautioned that regional disparities 'could become a permanent source of political confrontation' and urged that the south of Europe should be given a fairer share of the benefits of economic development.[16] This message was taken up by Delors in addressing the European Parliament in March 1985, when he warned that enlargement negotiations with Greece, Spain and Portugal had 'revealed a tension in Europe which is a tension between north and south. It stems not only from financial problems but from a lack of understanding, from a clash of culture, which seems to be promoting certain countries to turn their backs on the solidarity pact that should be one of the cornerstones of the Community'.[17] Thus, during the intergovernmental conference (IGC) on the Single European Act (SEA), the Commission advocated a substantial redistribution of resources to the LDRs.[18] In the Commission's view, the reduction of disparities and the strengthening of economic and social cohesion should go hand in hand with the implementation of the single market.

---

[16] *Bulletin of the European Communities*, EC S/1-1985, p. 15.

[17] *Bulletin of the European Communities*, EC S/4-1985, p. 5.

[18] The SEA was the outcome of the conference of representatives of the governments of the EC member states, which the heads of state and government decided to convene at the Milan European Council in June 1985. The IGC completed its work in January 1986. The treaty was signed by member states at The Hague the following month. The Irish government approved the SEA in January 1986. The Irish Supreme Court ruled, in the case Raymond Crotty v. An Taoiseach and others, in April 1987 that a constitutional referendum was necessary in order for Ireland to ratify the SEA. The SEA entered into force on 1 July 1987. An explanatory guide to the SEA was published in 1986 (Government of Ireland, 1986).

In reporting to the Dáil on the outcome of the Brussels European Council held on 29 and 30 March 1985, Taoiseach Garret FitzGerald, in a wide-ranging speech, addressed the issue of economic convergence and said this required a scale of funding 'far beyond anything currently available'. He referenced the MacDougall Group on the Role of Public Finance in European Integration (1977), which concluded that substantial increases in spending would be needed to help reduce inequalities in living standards if all member states were to have a single currency and an integrated economy. While the MacDougall Group had recommended a Community budget of 2 to 2.5 per cent of GNP, an earlier report had suggested that 5 per cent of Community GNP was required.[19] Thus, well in advance of the SEA and the Delors I package, Ireland knew quite well the scale of resources required to turn the theory of cohesion into practice.

Thus, the goal of economic and social cohesion became an important part of the debate during the 1980s on economic convergence and political integration of the EU. The SEA – combined with the accession to the Community of Greece, Spain and Portugal – brought about fundamental changes in the structure of the Community and the obligations of the member states. The SEA improved significantly the institutional system and set new objectives for the Community, notably the completion of the single market by 1992 and the strengthening of economic and social cohesion. In the Commission's view, the SEA represented a new frontier for European integration.

In anticipation of the entry into force of the SEA, the European Commission did not lose time in setting in motion a process to translate the treaty's ambitions on cohesion into reality. Named after the Commission's President, the Delors I package on the future financing of the Union involved a decision-making process that was, perhaps, one of the most difficult, most technical and certainly the most protracted ever in the Union's history (other than IGC negotiations on treaty change). Agreement on the Delors I package took one year from the time the Commission made its formal proposals in February 1987 to the decisions taken at the special Brussels European Council in February 1988. This package was arguably ambitious and the conclusions agreed in February 1988 were both far-reaching and strategically important. The successful outcome laid the foundations for the adoption of multi-annual financial perspectives, including the Delors II package (1993–1999) and Agenda 2000 (2000–2006). With hindsight, however, it is hard to imagine that the

---

[19] This was the Marjolin Group Report on EMU published in 1975. Professor Marjolin was a former Vice-President of the Commission. His group of fifteen experts was asked to fine-tune the EMU strategy agreed in 1969.

Union's leaders spent so much time squabbling over a mere 0.15 per cent of Community GDP.

When the Council decided in February 1988 to double the structural funds' budget by 1993, Delors called this 'a second Marshall Plan' (cited in Dinan, 2005a, p. 376). Negotiations involved highly complex issues, including the reform of the CAP, new regulations for the structural funds, and the comparability and uniformity of national GNP statistics, to mention but a few. The Commission established a critical policy and political link between the implementation of the single market programme and a stable budgetary framework for the EU's finances. Delors was convinced that the SEA needed financial underpinning in a number of important respects and he sought to take advantage of a 'window of opportunity' to stabilise and regularise budgetary politics in the Union.

Behind the technical discussions on the Commission's proposals lay careful assessments of what the package might mean for national contributions to, and receipts from, the Union's budget. Tortuous negotiations on what were on the face of it minor technical points underlined the seriousness with which all the member states approached the negotiations on the Delors package. These proposals would transform many beneficiaries from the budget into net contributors for the first time.[20] The difficulty in reaching agreement can be explained partly by the comprehensive nature of the dossiers under consideration, but was mostly due to the high stakes involved. The member states were being asked to agree to a major change in the rules which would leave many of them financially worse off. The broad outline of the agreement reached at the Brussels Summit in February 1988 corresponded to what the Commission wanted to achieve.

The first reform of the structural funds took effect on 1 January 1989. It was agreed that the amounts allocated for the funds would be doubled in real terms between 1987 and 1993 and that there would be a particular concentration on the LDRs facing the greatest problems, i.e. regions with a per capita GDP below 75 per cent of the Community average, including Ireland, were designated as Objective 1 regions.

The Irish government's view prior to the IGC on the SEA was that, despite the very considerable benefits which Ireland and other member states had received from the Community's structural funds since 1973, serious economic and social disparities existed between the peripheral and less prosperous regions of the Community and the more advantaged central regions (Government of Ireland, 1986). In the Irish government's

---

[20] Laffan (1997) provides an overview of the development of the Union's budgetary arrangements and procedures.

assessment it was important that the SEA specifically provided for a balanced commitment to achieving greater economic and social cohesion. All the more so as Ireland took a lead at the IGC in pressing for the inclusion in the SEA of provisions on cohesion and submitted proposals which 'are extensively reflected in the cohesion provisions agreed' (Government of Ireland, 1986, p. 23). In the Irish government's view, the SEA provisions on cohesion represented a renewed and strengthened commitment to reducing regional disparities within the Community. Particular importance was given to the creation of a legal basis in the treaty for the ERDF. Furthermore, the task of reducing regional disparities was also for the first time recognised in the body of the treaty as central to a harmonious economic and social development of the Community. The stipulation that the cohesion objective was to be taken into account in the implementation of all common policies of the Community and the single market was, according to the Irish government, of particular importance for the LDRs such as Ireland. Finally, the government said the Commission's review of the structural funds would afford an important and early opportunity to give practical effect to the SEA's commitment to strengthened and more effective action to reduce regional disparities. The SEA strengthened the provisions as Ireland sought, not only in relation to setting out firmly the objective of economic and social cohesion, but also by specifying many of the instruments to be used to achieve it.

It was made clear to the general public that Ireland's net budgetary transfers from the Community would be jeopardised if the electorate did not vote to ratify the SEA. At the time (1985), net transfers amounted to some 13.6 per cent of current government revenue. This argument suggests that the principle of the *juste retour* was not far from the Irish government's deliberations. In submitting the proposal to ratify the SEA to the government, the Department of Foreign Affairs remarked (quite correctly as it emerged) that vigilance would be necessary to ensure that Ireland's interests in regard to the effectiveness of and receipts from the structural funds are fully protected in the overhaul of the funds envisaged in the SEA.

The link between constitution-building in the Union and a budgetary settlement was once again evident after the signing of the Maastricht Treaty on European Union (TEU) in 1992.[21] The TEU gave a further boost to economic and social cohesion as not only were the provisions on

---

[21] The TEU was adopted by the European Council after a marathon negotiation session which ended in the early hours of 11 December 1991. The twelve heads of state and government concluded work which had been taking place in two parallel IGCs on EMU and on political union. For an account of the Maastricht IGC, see Keatinge (1992).

cohesion amended in a significant manner, but a specific protocol on cohesion was also added to the treaty. The Delors Commission published its second budgetary proposals just five days after the signing of the TEU in February 1992. The Commission adopted a formula similar to the Delors I package by proposing a multi-annual budgetary strategy, organised around six categories of expenditure. Budgetary increases were earmarked for structural expenditure, further strengthening the redistributive aspects of EU finances. The negotiations on the Delors II package took place in the aftermath of the Danish 'no' vote on the TEU and the September 1992 exchange rate mechanism (ERM) crisis. Unlike the euphoria of 1987/88, the political atmosphere in 1992 was one of turbulence and a loss of confidence in the European project. For example, the final phase of negotiations on the Delors II package was in the hands of the UK presidency, which was reeling from the forced departure of sterling from the ERM and the protracted TEU ratification crisis in Westminster (Laffan, 1997).

The Delors II package deliberately built upon the agreement reached on the first five-year medium-term strategy, including a further commitment to structural funds spending, a new cohesion fund, a containment of agricultural spending, and a seven-year financial perspective (1993–1999). Negotiations on Delors II proved no less tortuous and difficult than the original agreement. In many ways, the environment was much less conducive to a successful outcome this time around. The stakes were truly high. So much so that at a critical stage Delors sent a letter to all delegations, reinforcing his arguments about the *raison d'être* of the Commission's proposal and the unacceptability of a UK presidency compromise tabled at the later stages in the negotiations, just prior to the Edinburgh European Council of December 1992. He ended his letter as follows:

> I can but repeat my conviction that the ambitions of Maastricht cannot be achieved piecemeal. Closer cohesion, greater competitiveness, stronger Community policies and wider external responsibilities all go together. What is at stake is the impetus of the European venture and its transition into economic and social terms and into foreign policy terms (quoted in Laffan, 1997, p. 68).

The December 1992 Edinburgh Council agreed the EU's financial perspective for the period from 1993 to 1999. As part of this package, the budget for the structural interventions was increased from €18.6 billion in 1992 to €30 billion in 1999 (in 1992 prices). Of this amount, some €15 billion was approved for the cohesion fund, which was adopted in 1993.

From the beginning of the negotiations for the Maastricht Treaty, Ireland attached a high priority to achieving a further strengthening of the provisions on economic and social cohesion. A greater emphasis on this aspect of Community policy was seen as essential to the wellbeing and durability of any Union which was likely to emerge from the negotiations. Furthermore, there was a wish to see a framework established which would provide the basis for the cohesion mechanisms of the Community to keep pace with future integration. Finally, with regard to EMU in particular, there was a concern that, in the absence of mechanisms to assist in the redistribution of the undoubted benefits which EMU would bestow on the Community as a whole, the more central and prosperous regions would gain disproportionately. Thus, the Irish government had a clear negotiating strategy to ensure that the Maastricht Treaty contained the fullest possible recognition of cohesion as a basic objective of the treaty and that this recognition was accompanied by firm commitments to measures, including financial measures, to achieve this objective. While the treaty amendments themselves were very satisfactory, Ireland made it clear in the negotiations that there should be additional commitments of a practical nature relating to cohesion. As these commitments are contained in a protocol on cohesion included as part of the treaty they have the highest legal status short of being in the treaty itself.

All of these developments were greatly in Ireland's interest, in particular the provision that EU co-financing would not place an excessive burden on national matching funds. Ireland was committed to pursuing a convergence programme aimed at ensuring full participation in the final stage of EMU. The package of texts on cohesion was considered very satisfactory from the point of view of Ireland. The Irish government was determined to ensure that the treaty provisions were implemented in an effective way. Between the treaty provisions and the protocol provisions, Ireland expected substantial increases under more flexible conditions in the transfer of resources to support economic and social cohesion in the years ahead. This was a fundamental aspect of the government's strategy during the Delors II negotiations and it was deployed with a high sense of urgency and at the highest political level. The securing of Ireland's alleged €8 billion at the December 1992 European Council was a highlight.[22]

---

[22] Ireland got an assurance at the summit from the Commission (but not from member states) as regards a formula for Ireland's likely share of the funding expressed as a percentage of available funds for the Objective 1 regions, which was interpreted to be worth €8 billion. The harsh reality is that the Commission did not deliver on its promise. In any event, there was an element of double-counting as 1992 was included in the calculation, whereas the financial perspective covered the period from 1993 to 1999.

Much of the remainder of the 1990s was spent bedding down the implementation of the investment programmes required to draw down EU co-financing. In 1998 the Commission made considerable progress in making a direct link between the intensity of permissible state aid with the designation of regions for the purposes of the structural funds. Strict rules on regional aid were contained in regional aid guidelines as part of the Agenda 2000 budget package through to 2006.

The Commission's Agenda 2000 budgetary proposals were adopted, largely unchanged, by the Berlin Summit in December 1999. Fundamental reform could not be avoided with the enlargement of the EU in May 2004. The negotiations on the financial perspective for the 2007 to 2013 period were the most complex, vexatious and difficult of the four budgetary negotiations since Delors I. Many of the reforms agreed in 1988 were reversed in 2005, with the views of the net contributors prevailing.

Some reflections

The structural funds and the preparation of four national development plans (NDPs) have had an important impact on Ireland's economic and social development. Leaving aside the volume of monies received, the structural funds resulted in the introduction of a system of national planning, the use of programme evaluation techniques, the introduction of multi-annual budgeting, a recognition of the need for value for money for public (and EU) spending and the opportunity to make a genuine impact on regional development. Ireland was divided into two regions as a consequence of the structural funds rules. The social partners and regional representatives were given an opportunity to contribute to regional development issues because the Commission insisted that partnership was part of the deal. On the other hand, as Ireland's economic convergence improved, the level of EU funding fell; tougher regional state aid rules were imposed; and since January 2007 the NDP does not include an element of EU co-financing.

One could argue that EU cohesion policy has never reached its full potential as it continues to be based on the cohesion and structural funds with little evidence to date of a common approach at national level to the cohesion imperative. EU co-financing is often seen as offsetting national expenditure, and the priority of such expenditure more often than not reflects domestic and not EU priorities. The Commission has admitted that, after almost twenty years, the precise impact at EU and at national level of some €480 billion in cohesion spending is hard to quantify.

Over a sustained period since 1957, when the Rome Treaty was adopted, cohesion policy has developed in an incremental manner but with a clear and consistent strategic focus. The Commission, the principal contributor and driver of this policy, makes the case that regional disparities must be reduced across the EU. Ireland too played a proactive and influential role in shaping EU cohesion policy. Successive Irish governments never gave up on the mantra that the extent of Ireland's regional disparities required significant transfers of EU resources. The messaging became easier once Greece, Spain and Portugal joined in the 1980s. But it was not until the Delors II negotiations that the power and influence of these four countries (the cohesion four) bore fruit. In the new financial perspective (2007–2013), the cohesion and structural funds represent around 36 per cent (€308 billion) of total EU spending. Nobody can dispute that the efforts of the cohesion four, and Ireland in particular, have had a dramatic impact in terms of putting Europe's cohesion to the forefront of the political agenda.

Ireland has had a soft landing. The decisions taken by the European Council in October 2002 about the financing of the CAP until the 2013 budget secured a key policy objective for Ireland. As the European Council decided to cap the Community budget at around one per cent of EU gross national income, Ireland's contributions will not be as great as had been forecast when the arithmetic was done on the original Commission's proposals for the period post-2006. Ireland will become a net contributor, but only it appears towards the end of the period of the 2007–2013 financial perspective. The BMW and S&E regions will get EU co-financing of €750 million over seven years to 2013. To put this in context, the expenditure programmed in the NDP for the same period is €184 billion (Department of Finance, 2007). Unlike the situation during the Delors packages, the amount that Ireland received was not the subject of intensive haggling with the Commission, but a mathematical consequence of a methodology which applied to all member states. Although no longer an EU requirement, the Irish government published a seven-year NDP on the grounds that medium-term planning of this nature is one of the positive side-effects of Ireland's experience with the structural funds.

The negotiations on the financial perspectives have been characterised as involving 'side-payments' to some member states as a quid pro quo for their acceptance of unpalatable elements of the overall compromise deal. The only side-payments agreed during the negotiations on the current financial perspective were rebates to the net contributors. In fact, one might conclude that the EU has confirmed its reputation as a regulatory giant and a budgetary dwarf.

In successfully securing some €18 billion in EU co-financing from the cohesion and structural funds since 1973, senior Irish civil servants, particularly from the Departments of Finance and of Foreign Affairs, have played a key role in the negotiations at EU level as indeed have almost all Taoisigh and their senior government ministers. One might conclude 'that they have done the state some service'.

6

Europe and the Revolution in Irish Agriculture

Tom Arnold

Introduction

The story of the revolution in Irish agriculture over the past fifty years is a story about big political choices at European level, about Ireland adapting to the challenges and opportunities of EU membership, and about the deep economic, social and cultural changes in Irish society. It is also about the key agents of change, from Taoisigh, ministers, civil servants and social partners to mothers on farms, who made the decisions, took the risks and shaped the future.

The past fifty years must be situated within a longer historical narrative covering the major decisions that shaped Irish and European agriculture. The narrative must also take account of the profound changes in the Irish economy and in Irish society over the past half-century.

This chapter has two parts. The first part deals with the main political and policy changes which occurred during the following four periods:

- The decades, and indeed centuries, pre-1958, when decisions taken outside Ireland, particularly in Great Britain, had a dominant influence on Ireland's political and economic life
- The period from 1958 – when the publication of *Economic Development* foreshadowed a major change in Irish economic policy – to 1973, the years during which Ireland prepared for and negotiated entry to the EEC
- The period from 1973 – when Ireland started the process of aligning to the EEC's Common Agricultural Policy (CAP) and higher prices – to 1992 – when Commissioner Ray MacSharry pushed through fundamental policy reform. The key part of this reform was the move from supporting farm product prices to supporting farm incomes through direct payments
- The period from 1993 to 2007, during which the CAP was further reformed, with additional cuts in price support coupled with an

increasing move to direct income support, and greater emphasis on rural development, environmentally friendly farming, food safety and animal welfare. This period also saw increasing external pressure on the CAP, with demands for lower protection and support levels for European farmers and greater access to European markets for third-country suppliers.

The second part examines the economic and social changes over the period, particularly since Ireland's accession to the EEC in 1973. The changing role of agriculture in the Irish economy and the changing structure of the agricultural and food sector are examined. And some of the key political, administrative and institutional actors, within Ireland and Europe, who were instrumental in bringing about this change are identified.

The period before 1958

Pre-1958 – Shaping forces in Britain and Europe
In 1958 agriculture was the dominant sector in the Irish economy, accounting for 25 per cent of GNP and employing 400,000 people, which represented nearly 40 per cent of total employment (Kennedy *et al.*, 1988). But the sector had many structural weaknesses, which are discussed further below. There were a number of critical shaping forces, both within Ireland and as a result of the decisions and policies of Great Britain and Europe, which provided the backdrop to that situation (Crotty, 1966).

The big political forces may be briefly identified. The two World Wars of the previous decades, the second of which had ended just thirteen years earlier, had brought terrible cost and destruction to Europe and the wider world. The Great Depression of the 1930s had led to mass unemployment in many countries. Ireland's political and economic life had been intertwined with that of Britain over centuries and now, less than forty years after achieving independence, its government and people were striving to give practical effect to that independence.

British policy towards its agriculture from the mid-nineteenth century had had a decisive influence on the market possibilities and the economic interests of Irish farmers. The Industrial Revolution in Britain of the late eighteenth and early nineteenth centuries created a mass workforce which needed cheap food. The 1832 Reform Act reduced the influence of the landowning aristocracy. These and other factors led to the political decision in 1846 to abolish the Corn Laws, which had provided tariff protection for British farmers, and to usher in Britain's cheap food policy, which was to operate unchanged until the 1930s and, in a modified form, until Britain joined the EEC in 1973.

The political geography of Europe had been reshaped during the nineteenth century, with many of the modern European countries establishing their boundaries and statehood. Although some countries had their own version of an Industrial Revolution, all of them maintained a strong agricultural sector with a greater level of political influence than applied in Britain. This was reflected in the later decades of the nineteenth century when most European countries introduced tariffs to protect their agricultural sectors in response to low food prices caused by cheap cereal imports from the US and Russia and meat imports from Australia made possible by developments in shipping and refrigeration (Tracy, 1982).

A second wave of agricultural protectionism occurred in response to the Great Depression of the early 1930s. Food prices fell sharply due to the drop in worldwide demand. As part of the widespread resort to tariff protection, tariffs for agricultural products were sharply increased in most European countries. The most spectacular development was Britain's conversion to protectionism for its agriculture in the autumn of 1931, albeit at a substantially lower level than its European neighbours.

The increase in tariffs was not the only instrument that governments across Europe used to support their farming sectors. State intervention in agricultural markets increased in a number of ways, including the establishment of commodity boards, guaranteed prices, subsidies to growers and import quotas. The principle of government intervention to support farmers and to protect them from free trade in agricultural products was now broadly accepted and would, two decades later, underpin the creation of the CAP.

The early post-war years had seen additional decisions with important implications for Irish agriculture. The 1947 Agriculture Act in Britain introduced a modern-day version of a cheap food policy while supporting British farmers by instituting a system of deficiency payments to make up the difference between the price they could get on the British market and a guaranteed price.

At European level, the Schuman Plan and the moves to establish the European Coal and Steel Community in the early 1950s represented steps towards economic integration and recovery. Two separate initiatives on freeing trade for agricultural products were discussed during the 1950s.

In 1953 France took the lead in supporting the concept of a 'Green Plan' for Europe, whereby the countries of Europe would organise their agricultural markets in common. In 1954 the Organisation for European Economic Co-operation (OEEC) – set up in 1948 to administer the Marshall Plan which brought substantial US aid for the reconstruction of

Europe – initiated negotiations aimed at a progressive freeing of trade in agricultural produce for its fifteen member countries. These negotiations finally broke down in 1958 (Kennedy and Skelly, 2000).

By this time, however, the six founding members of the EEC had signed the Treaty of Rome in March 1957 and the EEC had come into being in January 1958. The Rome Treaty provided for a Common Agricultural Policy (CAP) to replace the national agricultural policies of the Six. This represented a political compromise at two levels: first, it was a recognition that free movement in industrial goods could not be achieved if there were substantial differences in food prices, and hence in labour costs, between the member states; second, France, the Netherlands and Italy were, in effect, agreeing to open their markets to industrial goods while Germany was opening its market to agricultural exports from the others (Tracy, 1982).

Article 39 of the treaty set out the objectives of the CAP, which are in summary:

- To increase agricultural productivity
- To ensure a fair standard of living for the agricultural community
- To stabilise markets
- To ensure the availability of supplies
- To ensure supplies reach consumers at reasonable prices.

Under the CAP, market organisations for the main products were established from the early 1960s, based on three principles:

- A single unified market for agricultural products
- Community preference – a system of protection at the EEC's external border against low-priced imports
- Financial solidarity – spending on the CAP to be borne by the central Community budget.

As discussed below, these principles would prove very attractive to the Irish government and farmers when the option of joining the EEC arose a decade later.

Pre-1958 – Shaping forces for Irish agriculture
The Famine or Great Hunger of the 1840s was the defining event of the nineteenth century for the island of Ireland. It caused the death of over one million people, the emigration of a further one million people and the beginning of a period of population decline which was not reversed until the 1960s.

One of the legacies of the Famine was a hunger for land among Irish tenant farmers. The Land League, founded in 1879 by Michael Davitt, gave expression to the demand for land reform. The mobilisation of mass support for this demand and the political skill of Charles Stewart Parnell and his Irish Parliamentary Party in the British House of Commons paved the way for a series of major Land Acts from the 1880s onwards.

The Land Acts, the last of which was in 1923 under the new Free State government, led to massive changes in land ownership and farm structure. In 1870, before agitation for land reform began, 3,800 landowners with over 1,000 acres, most of whom were landlords, owned 80 per cent of the land of the (32 county) Ireland. There were almost 500,000 tenant farmers with holdings of more than one acre (Moody, 1981). By 1930 the Land Acts had turned tenants into owners: there were then 338,000 farm holdings of more than one acre in the (26 county) Free State, only 29,000 of which were over 100 acres (Dooley, 2004).

At the creation of the Free State in 1922 the population was 3.25 million and the workforce was 1.25 million. Over half the workforce worked on the land, with many farmers, and their 'relatives assisting', operating at a miserable subsistence level (Whitaker, 1983).

The Department of Agriculture and Technical Instruction, established in 1900, had worked to improve standards of production in the early decades of the twentieth century. Notwithstanding that, and the priority given to agricultural development by Irish governments from the 1920s onwards, Irish agriculture in the 1950s was still very underdeveloped. Its development had been hindered by its structural and technical deficiencies and by the lack of markets for Irish agricultural exports.

In 1949 a report on Irish grassland prepared by an external expert stated that he had seen 'hundreds of Irish fields which are growing just as little as it is physically possible for the land to grow under an Irish sky'. With the poor fertility of Irish land and the desperate shortage of fertiliser, 'it is a miracle that some of the land is able to grow grass at all' (Daly, 2002, p. 279).

Animal health standards were a major problem. A pilot study in 1951 found that 30 per cent of the cattle and 44 per cent of the cows tested positive for tuberculosis with a further 9 per cent of the cattle and 14 per cent of the cows giving inconclusive results. The bovine TB eradication programme, a voluntary nationwide programme of TB testing, was launched in 1954. A key part of the impetus for this programme came from the commitment of the British government to eradicate TB by 1961. This meant that Irish cattle would be excluded from Britain after that date unless they were certified as free from TB.

The market situation for Irish agricultural exports was also a major constraint. During the 1950s the market was effectively confined to Britain, with few exports to Europe or the wider world. An indicator of the limited market opportunities for Ireland was that, as part of the 1948 Anglo-Irish trade agreement, Britain had insisted that it should receive 90 per cent of Irish cattle exports. With reservations, the Irish government agreed to this. The reservations were because the government wished to open outlets for Irish cattle and meat on the continent. But the Irish beef processing industry was very underdeveloped in the 1950s. Even by 1958 the only beef processing occurring was the slaughter of cows which had tested positive for TB (reactor cows); all prime cattle were exported live to Britain (Sheehy, 1997).

The Irish government had participated earlier in the decade in the discussions – the Green Plan and the OEEC talks – about European free trade in agricultural products. The Departments of Finance and of Agriculture saw little benefit in these discussions and were seriously worried that, should the discussions lead to an agreement, Ireland's preferential treatment in the British market could be severely diminished with little gain on the European markets. A report drawn up by senior civil servants in 1957 noted that 'the prospects of expansion of agricultural exports would continue to lie mainly in the British rather than in continental markets' (Daly, 2002, p. 333)

But the moves towards freeing of trade and greater economic integration within Europe contributed to a reassessment of economic policy. In 1956 the government set up an interdepartmental committee, chaired by T. K. Whitaker, Secretary of the Department of Finance, to examine the probable effects on Ireland's interests of an association of member countries of the OEEC in a free trade area. The work of this committee had a key role in preparing the shift in political and official opinion which was to underpin the move from the policy of protectionism introduced in the 1930s under the first Fianna Fáil government to one where interdependence with other European economies was assumed (Murphy, 2005; Bradley, 2006).

From ending protectionism to EEC membership, 1958 to 1973

Economic Development, written by T. K. Whitaker in 1958, is seen as the seminal policy document which heralded a new departure in Ireland's economic policy. It provided the basis for the First Programme for Economic Expansion, which stated that economic growth offered the only means of reducing emigration and unemployment and warned that the imminent free trade area in Europe represented a significant challenge (Lee, 1989).

In *Economic Development* (1958), agriculture was seen as the most dynamic sector for achieving economic growth. Eight chapters dealt exclusively with agriculture and three of the remaining seven discussed agriculture at some length. Expansion of livestock was set as a key objective – additional livestock and livestock products could be produced and exported without state protection or subsidy, which was not the case for dairy or crop products. Improved grassland could carry bigger numbers of cattle and sheep without a commensurate increase in cost.

In July 1960 Taoiseach Seán Lemass outlined Ireland's future policy on Europe. He noted that the first objective would be to protect Ireland's trade relationship with Britain, which he described as 'the keystone of our external trade structure' (Daly, 2002, p. 364). A second objective would be to secure markets in Europe.

Protecting the access of Irish agricultural exports to the British market was central to this vision. On the day Lemass outlined the government's policy on Europe, the National Farmers' Association (NFA) urged the government to seek to join the EEC without waiting for Britain. But this view was dismissed as unrealistic, given that Britain took 75 per cent of Irish exports.

British policy towards Europe at the time was, however, under review. In 1961 Britain decided to apply for EEC membership, and Ireland also submitted its application at this time (see Chapter 2). Negotiations on the terms of membership commenced between the European Commission and the British government in 1962. Formal negotiations on Irish membership were not opened, although a number of discussions were held between Irish ministers and the Commission.

As negotiations between the Commission and Britain on possible membership terms proceeded during 1962, it became clear that there were major disagreements on agriculture. Britain was seeking favourable import arrangements for beef, lamb, butter and sugar from its Commonwealth partners into an enlarged EEC. While Ireland was not a party to these negotiations, it had a clear interest in ensuring that import quotas for Commonwealth produce should be as low as possible (Tracy, 1982).

In any event, President de Gaulle's veto of British membership in January 1963 brought the issue to a temporary halt. Ireland's application for membership remained on the table but it was generally acknowledged that Ireland would not join unless Britain became a member.

While the French veto on progress towards enlargement of the EEC was regarded as a political setback, it meant that Ireland had additional time to prepare for eventual EEC membership (see also Chapter 3). Irish political and business leaders were acutely conscious that much of Irish industry was uncompetitive and would need time to adjust to freer trading arrangements. The negotiations for revised trading arrangements with Britain, which began in 1964, provided an opportunity both to improve markets for Irish agricultural produce in Britain and to prepare for a world with lower tariffs for industrial goods.

The Anglo-Irish Free Trade Agreement, signed in December 1965, provided that Britain would remove all protective duties on Irish manufactured goods imported to the UK from July 1966. In return Ireland would remove all duties on British manufactured goods over the next nine years. A key part of the agreement on agriculture was that the waiting period before Irish cattle qualified for British deficiency payments was reduced to two months (the reduced waiting period for payment of the subsidy would increase the price of cattle on the Irish market). And the Irish government undertook to endeavour to prevent the number of store cattle – which accounted for 40 per cent of agricultural exports to the UK – exported to Britain falling below 638,000 annually (Daly, 2002).

The improvement in access to the British market did not, however, lead to any significant improvement in farm incomes. The early 1960s had seen the economy grow by 4 per cent annually, double the rate forecast in the First Programme for Economic Expansion. But it was the industrial sector rather than the agricultural sector which had provided most of the growth.

The growing income gap between the farm and non-farm sector thus became a significant political issue. Aggregate farm income remained flat over the period from 1964 to 1966, notwithstanding an increase in the price of milk and additional government support for the agricultural sector. In 1966 discussions on farm incomes between the government and the farm organisations became increasingly fractious, with the NFA leading a farmers' march to Dublin, a sit-down outside the Department of Agriculture, the jailing of farm leaders following road blockages and refusals to pay fines and, in early 1967, some short-lived commodity strikes.

But the government operated under significant constraints in improving the lot of farmers. In 1966 Minister for Agriculture Charles Haughey pointed out that with over 30 per cent of the population making their living on the land and a high proportion of agricultural produce exported, there were limits to the possibility of exchequer support to bolster farm income. This point was evident in subsequent years as higher levels of price support, particularly for milk, allied to production increases led to significant increases in state spending on agriculture.

Ireland's application for EEC membership was reactivated in May 1967. The EEC member states agreed in principle on enlargement at the Paris

Summit in December 1969 and negotiations opened in June 1970 with four potential new members, namely Britain, Denmark, Norway and Ireland (Maher, 1986).

In April 1970 the Department of Agriculture published a report entitled *Irish Agriculture and Fisheries in the EEC* and the government issued a White Paper on the implications of EEC membership (Government of Ireland, 1972). The Department of Agriculture's main concerns related to transitional arrangements for Irish agriculture, Anglo-Irish trade during the transition period and measures to protect animal and plant health.

As membership of the EEC became an increasing prospect, the potential benefits came into sharper focus for both the government and farmers. The government looked forward to significant budgetary savings. In the years immediately preceding EEC accession, the Irish exchequer was spending 3.4 per cent of GDP on price support to farmers and this cost would now be paid for by the common EEC budget (Sheehy, 1997).

For farmers, participation in a CAP based on a single European market for food products, Community preference and common funding had huge attractions. When the referendum on membership was held in May 1972, the farm organisations were enthusiastic supporters of a 'yes' vote, which was duly delivered with 83 per cent of the electorate in favour of membership.

From EEC entry to CAP reform, 1973 to 1992

Ireland's early years in the CAP system
The period from 1973 to 1992 includes Ireland's five-year transition to full membership of the CAP, the economic shocks caused by the two oil crises during the 1970s and the growing surpluses produced under the CAP. These surpluses cost the Community budget a considerable amount to dispose of, depressed international commodity markets and damaged the interests of traditional agricultural exporters. This led to a decision to include agriculture in international trade negotiations which started in 1986. This combination of internal and external pressure led to radical reform of the CAP in 1992. The key milestones towards that reform are traced below.

The CAP began to apply in Ireland from 1 February 1973, one month after Ireland's accession. Irish agricultural prices had risen sharply from 1968 to 1972 in anticipation of EEC membership but in 1973 prices were still substantially below the Community average. The transitional arrangements were designed to bring Irish farm prices in line with Community prices by the end of 1977.

The CAP represented a major change in the way in which support was provided to the Irish agricultural sector. About 95 per cent of the CAP budget – which accounted for some two-thirds of the total EEC budget – was spent on price and market support with the remaining 5 per cent spent on measures to improve the structure of the European farm and food sector. The CAP budget was administered through the European Agricultural Guidance and Guarantee Fund (EAGGF), better known through its French acronym FEOGA. The Guidance Fund financed the structural measures; the Guarantee Fund addressed the price and market support.

The price and market support arrangements were designed to keep European prices at guaranteed levels which were, for the most part, considerably above world price levels. This price gap was maintained through a combination of import tariffs and quotas, intervention purchases and other measures to support internal prices, and export refunds to make up the difference between European and world prices (see, for example, Nugent, 1999, Chapter 15, for an introduction to the workings of the initial CAP system).

Support under the FEOGA Guidance Fund consisted of funding for a series of farm structural regulations on farm modernisation, early retirement and socioeconomic measures. The farm modernisation scheme was the most important of these and, when it came into operation in February 1974, it subsumed all existing departmental schemes for land drainage, farm buildings and capital equipment.

The Guidance Fund also covered grants for the modernisation of the food processing sector and, from 1975, for a scheme for designated disadvantaged areas, which provided cattle headage payments for farmers. The range of payments in these areas was expanded in subsequent years and the area of the country classified as disadvantaged was extended through a series of reviews which lasted until the 1990s (Daly, 2002).

These arrangements were implemented by a new Fine Gael/Labour coalition government, headed by Liam Cosgrave, which was elected in February 1973. Mark Clinton was appointed Minister for Agriculture. He oversaw the early years of EEC membership for Irish farmers which brought, for the most part, positive developments in terms of price increases, additional support measures and significant investment by farmers.

Towards the end of 1973 the first oil crisis, in the wake of a war in the Middle East, led to economic recession and inflation. In 1974 there was a collapse in cattle prices arising from a rapid increase in livestock numbers, a shortage of fodder and a shortfall in factory capacity. Large-scale intervention purchasing of beef was instituted to support prices. This pattern of substantial intervention, allied to the other price support measures available under the CAP, was thus instituted early on in Ireland's EEC membership and was to remain a prominent feature of support arrangements until CAP reform in 1992.

Following the 1974 cattle crisis, incomes recovered due to a number of factors. The volume of farm output increased and farm prices received an annual boost as the transition to EEC prices occurred. The combination of output and price increases resulted in real farm incomes doubling between 1970 and 1978. Over the period farmers made significant investments in their farms and in improving housing standards, and they substantially increased their borrowings (Sheehy, 1997).

But in the following two years, 1979 and 1980, interest rates doubled from 9 per cent to 18 per cent, largely as a result of the second oil crisis, and farm prices fell by 23 per cent in real terms, due to rising surpluses in the Community. Irish farmers were caught in a vicious price/cost squeeze, average incomes were halved, falling back to pre-EEC levels and a significant number of farmers were plunged into a severe credit crisis.

The 1980s – Quotas and cutbacks

The early 1980s saw a steady recovery in farm incomes. But depressed world food markets and growing European food surpluses held in intervention stocks and then exported with large subsidies were adding to the pressure for reform of the CAP.

There was also a high-level political dimension in that Britain was pressing for a reduction in its budgetary contribution to the Community, a formula for which had been fixed at the time of enlargement. The cost of the CAP was a key factor in the size of the British budget contribution. British Prime Minister Margaret Thatcher famously 'wanted her money back' and a compromise was reached at a European Council meeting in 1984 which provided for a budget rebate for Britain.

The most significant decision taken at this time to control the cost of the CAP was the introduction of milk quotas in 1984. Although the Irish government and the farm organisations were initially opposed to the introduction of milk quotas, the only realistic alternative, if cost control of the CAP was to be achieved, was substantial price cuts for milk. This could be shown to be more damaging to farm income and to the entire economy.

The Irish government's strategy shifted to getting the best possible deal under a new milk quota regime. Strong negotiations by Taoiseach Garret FitzGerald and Minister for Agriculture Austin Deasy resulted in Ireland being granted a special deal due to its stage of relative underdevelopment and the fact that agriculture, and specifically dairying, represented a larger share of the economy in Ireland than in other member states.

The 1984 quotas provided for a reduction of 7 per cent on the 1983 Community milk output, and most member states received a national quota equal to their 1981 output. Ireland's 1984 quota was based on a 4.63 per cent increase on its 1983 output (Daly, 2002).

The introduction of milk quotas signalled only a temporary respite from the pressure to reform the CAP. European exports of subsidised surpluses were contributing to depressed world commodity markets during the first half of the 1980s. This was damaging the interests of other major agricultural exporting countries such as the US, Australia, New Zealand and Canada.

The depressed world commodity markets and the rising costs of national agricultural budgets lay behind the decision that agriculture would be part of the new round of international trade talks, launched in 1986 in Punta del Este (the Uruguay Round). None of the previous rounds of post-war trade agreements negotiated under the General Agreement on Tariffs and Trade (GATT) had included agriculture in its disciplines.

The Uruguay Round negotiations were to drag on for seven years, with agreement finally being reached in December 1993. They became directly linked with decisions on radical reform of the CAP, which was agreed in May 1992. Two Irishmen, Ray MacSharry, European Commissioner for Agriculture and Rural Development, and Peter Sutherland, Director General of the GATT, were to play key roles in bringing these separate negotiations to a conclusion.

The MacSharry CAP reforms, 1992
The proposed CAP reform, presented in a Commission discussion paper *Reflections on the Common Agricultural Policy* in February 1991, had three main objectives:

- To keep intact the common price system, including Community preference as regards imports, and free movement of products within the Community
- To preserve financial solidarity, i.e. full Community financing of market measures
- To introduce measures that would guarantee price competitiveness and a reduction in surpluses, and would provide farmers with realistic alternatives to increasing food production.

After very difficult negotiations a final agreement on a reform package was reached in May 1992. Most elements of the reform proposed by the Commission had been accepted, albeit in modified form. There were substantial reductions in guaranteed prices with cereals reducing by 29 per cent compared to the 35 per cent proposed, and beef prices reducing by 15 per cent as proposed (MacSharry, 1999).

The key policy change in the reform was the switch from price support to a 'mixed system' of continuing but lower price support plus 'coupled' direct payments. These direct payments were linked to a certain level of production, for example the number of suckler cows, male cattle, ewes etc. and hectares of cereals, oilseeds and protein crops.

Another important part of the reform package was the introduction of a set of 'accompanying measures'. These consisted of three schemes: one to promote afforestation; a second to promote early retirement of farmers; and a third as payments for the 'public good' of improving the rural environment in the form of the Rural Environment Protection Scheme (REPS). The accompanying measures were a continuation of a growing emphasis at European level on rural development. In 1988 the Commission had published a report, *The Future of Rural Society*, which indicated the need for an integrated rural policy that would create alternative sources of income in rural areas (European Commission, 1988). Funding for rural development had received a major boost in 1988 with the decision to double the budget for structural funds: the FEOGA Guidance Fund, the European Social Fund and the European Regional Development Fund (see Chapter 5).

When Ray MacSharry took up his post as Commissioner in January 1989, rural development was added to the title of the portfolio for the first time, in recognition that the mandate was not limited to supporting agricultural markets, but needed to be broader in terms of developing rural areas, as had been reflected by the decision to double the structural funds (MacSharry, 1999).

The decisions on CAP reform introduced a new era for Irish farmers and a set of administrative challenges both for farmers and for the Department of Agriculture. Instead of supporting farm prices through price support, which involved operating intervention stores and dealing with a relatively small number of food processors and exporters, the department was now faced with distributing direct payments to over 150,000 farmers. These payments would represent an increasing part of net farm income which put considerable pressure on ministers and the department to deliver payments on time. Farmers faced the challenge of meeting the administrative and form-filling requirements for these direct payments. A new era had begun.

The GATT (Uruguay Round) negotiations

The outcome of the CAP reform was crucial to securing an agreement in the GATT negotiations. Following their launch in 1986, there had been slow progress in the negotiations until 1990 when progress accelerated. At a GATT ministerial meeting in Brussels in December 1990, the EC found itself isolated. MacSharry (1999, p. 301) concluded:

> The situation required a strategy that would enable the Community to establish a more realistic position such as would tempt our trading partners into seeking a basis for agreement, rather than pursuing a strategy of isolating Europe. The position had to be based on what the reform of the CAP could guarantee. Otherwise, the Community would find itself being pushed towards concessions without any assurances that commitments agreed at international level could be delivered 'on the ground'.

With the decisions on CAP reform agreed in May 1992, a critical next milestone in securing final agreement was the meeting held the following December between the US and EU negotiators in Blair House in Washington. The two sides agreed a package of measures they could accept as part of an overall settlement which would require the assent of all the GATT negotiating parties.

When final agreement was reached in December 1993, under GATT Director General Peter Sutherland, the Uruguay Round was the first global trade agreement to deal comprehensively with agricultural products. The agreement involved commitments, over six years, to reduce domestic support to agriculture, to convert import charges and other restrictions to tariffs and to reduce them, and to reduce the volume of subsidised exports and expenditure on refunds.

The agreement was to apply from January 1995 and provided for discussions on a further round of trade talks to begin in 1999. It was generally agreed that the concessions made in the Uruguay Round would not have any significant short-term effects on the protection and support levels provided to European farmers, given the changes already agreed as part of the 1992 CAP reform.

From CAP reform to … more CAP reform, 1993 to 2007

Even in advance of agreement on CAP reform and the Uruguay Round, it was recognised, at political and official levels, that policy change was on the way.

The Department of Agriculture and Food's *Agriculture and Food Policy Review*, published in 1990, was based on the assumptions that 'competition will intensify (GATT, EC anti-surplus action, Eastern Europe), that public emphasis on the environment, the growing importance of consumer concerns and progress in technology will continue' (p. vi). The review also acknowledged that 'the Irish food industry has been, to a considerable degree, support led rather than market led in its behaviour since its entry to the EC' (p. vi). One of its four recommended policy objectives was that 'the sector must shift gradually but decisively away from a production and support orientation to a concentration on what the market requires' (p. vi). The decisions on CAP reform and the outcome of the Uruguay Round validated the need for the policy directions recommended by the review.

The policy directions set by CAP reform and the Uruguay Round would intensify in the fifteen years from 1993 to 2007. This period brought two further significant reforms of the CAP – Agenda 2000 in 1999 and the Luxembourg Agreement of 2003. This latter agreement led to the 'decoupling' of direct payments to farmers from production.

In addition, European agricultural policy and rural development policy became increasingly integrated. Food safety issues loomed large, influenced by consumer concerns following outbreaks of BSE and Foot and Mouth Disease. EU enlargement also loomed large and eventually occurred in 2004 with the entry of ten new member states, with Romania and Bulgaria following in 2007 and bringing the number of members to twenty-seven.

The Agenda 2000 CAP reform decisions agreed in Berlin in 1999 continued the MacSharry reform process – further price support cuts for beef and cereals and a further switch to direct payments which were coupled to production.

In 2002 the Commission launched a mid-term review of the Agenda 2000 decisions. This culminated in the Luxembourg Agreement of 2003, which involved a fundamental change of policy – the switch from direct payments which were coupled to the farmer producing certain levels of production, whether livestock or crops, to payments which were decoupled (i.e. not linked to production). The support price for milk was also reduced and a dairy direct payment introduced.

Under the new decoupled system, direct income payments (in the form of a single farm payment (SFP) based on specified reference years) are linked to respect of certain standards in relation to protection of the environment, animal health and welfare and public health.

Member states were given some latitude in the timing and methodology of introducing decoupled direct payments. Ireland chose to opt for full decoupling from January 2005.

In addition to the changing arrangements for price and income support for European farmers, the trend towards the increased integration of agricultural and rural development policy, already noted as part of the

1992 CAP reform, has continued. That reform introduced three accompanying measures – on the agri-environment (REPS), forestry and early retirement for farmers. These three schemes, together with the Disadvantaged Areas Scheme (in place since 1975), became known as the CAP accompanying measures in the 1994–1999 EU budget. In the 2000–2006 budget, they were known as the CAP Rural Development Fund measures.

The EU budget for 2007 to 2013 has taken this process further. CAP now consists of Pillar 1, which funds the SFP and some remaining market supports; and Pillar 2, the CAP Rural Development Fund, which funds the previous CAP Rural Development Fund and the Agricultural Structural Fund.

As was the case in the early 1990s, decisions on CAP reform were intertwined with the negotiations on wider international reform of agricultural trade policy. This reform was to be negotiated within the framework of the World Trade Organization, the successor to the GATT created as part of the Uruguay Round agreement.

A new round of negotiations was launched in November 2001 at Doha, Qatar. The Trade Ministers declared that the interests of developing countries should receive priority in this round: in consequence, it has been named the Doha Development Round.

In August 2004 a 'framework agreement' on agriculture was reached, covering the following elements:

• A substantial improvement in market access for all products, i.e. substantial cuts in import tariffs
• Phasing out of export subsidies by an end date to be decided
• Conversion of most domestic farm support to a non-trade-distorting (decoupled) form
• Special favourable treatment for developing countries.

Some progress was made in the negotiations at a ministerial meeting in Hong Kong in December 2005, including a conditional agreement to eliminate export subsidies by 2013. However, the negotiations broke down in July 2006 and at the time of writing it is not clear whether they can be brought to a successful conclusion.

Looking back over the almost thirty-five years of Ireland's EU membership, the scale of the policy change at European level is clear. The direction of policy, particularly since the 1992 CAP reform is also clear – reduced domestic support, more competition from imports and greater focus on meeting the demands of the consumer and on respecting higher environmental standards.

And over the past twenty years, since the decision was taken in the context of the start of the Uruguay Round negotiations that agriculture should be subject to international rules and disciplines, European agriculture has become more integrated with the world trading system.

The revolution in Irish agriculture, and how it happened

Against the background of the major policy changes outlined above, the final part of this chapter examines the changing role of the Irish agricultural and food sector, and some of the structural changes that came about. The chapter concludes by identifying some of the key agents of change, both individuals and institutions, who contributed to the revolution in Irish agriculture over the past half-century. Naming individuals who have played a significant role in change is highly subjective and, in the available space, choices have to be made. The full story of how the revolution in Irish agriculture occurred merits fuller treatment in future research.

The changing role of agriculture in the Irish economy

In examining the changing role of the agricultural and food sector in the Irish economy, the obvious measures are in relation to GDP, employment and exports, as shown in Table 6.1. The rapid economic growth over the past fifteen years has meant that agriculture's relative importance in terms of share of GDP and employment is now on a par with many other developed countries, but agricultural and food exports – at almost 10 per cent of total exports in 2006 – remain of major significance.

Table 6.1: *Irish agriculture since 1973*

	1973	*1990*	*2006*
Primary agriculture's share of GDP (%)	18.3	8.5	2.3
Agriculture, forestry and fishing's share of total employment (%)	24	14.9	5.4
Agricultural exports as a % of total exports*	50	15	9.8

* Figures for 1973 and 1990 refer to 'agri-based exports'; figure for 2006 refers to agri-food, drinks and tobacco.
Sources: Department of Agriculture, Fisheries and Food, 2007; Forfás, 2000; CSO, 2004; and 'Compendium of Irish Agricultural Statistics' on the Department of Agriculture's website (www.agriculture.gov.ie)

EU membership played a key role in contributing to these changes. The financial consequences of the CAP were significant for farming and for the wider economy. Firstly, there were the budgetary transfers arising under the FEOGA Guarantee and Guidance Funds for price support and structural measures respectively. Secondly, there were transfers from European consumers as trade in agricultural produce took place at prices above world levels. Taking these two elements together, Matthews (1988) estimates that CAP transfers to Ireland between 1979 and 1986 represented some 7 per cent of GNP over the period. This was a time when there was heavy use of the price support mechanisms – intervention purchase, aids to private storage, export refunds – for the main agricultural products of milk and beef.

With CAP reform in 1992 and the shift from price to income support, the nature of support to the agricultural and food sector has changed significantly. In addition, the rapid growth of the non-farm economy from the early 1990s has reduced the relative importance of flows from the CAP. But they still remain significant. In an updating of his earlier work, Matthews (2001) estimates that agriculture's net economic contribution for the 1998 to 2000 period – taking the budget and trade effects into account and making some other adjustments – amounted to 1.9 per cent of GNP.

Major structural changes have occurred within both the farm sector and the food industry. In reviewing the changes in 1990 in farming since Irish entry to the Community in 1973, the *Agriculture and Food Policy Review* noted the growth in part-time farming which had occurred, as evidenced by the large drop in the number of principal occupation farmers below 12 hectares (30 acres). Furthermore, it highlighted the considerable structural change at individual enterprise level, with an increasing proportion of production coming from a smaller number of producers (Department of Agriculture and Food, 1990).

These trends have continued. The *Report of the Agri-Vision 2015 Committee* noted a clear pattern of ongoing consolidation of farm structures. The total number of farms declined by over 23 per cent between 1980 and 1991; between 1991 and 2002 this figure fell by a further 20 per cent. Assuming a continuation of this trend and the positive macroeconomic situation, and factoring in the changes in EU farm policy, the report forecast that, by 2015, the farm population would fall to 105,000. Of these, about one-third would be economically viable, another one-third non-viable but with off-farm employment and the last one-third classified as 'transitional' where the farm business is not economically viable and neither the farmer nor spouse have an off-farm job (Department of Agriculture and Food, 2004).

The structure of the food sector has also been transformed since Irish entry to the EU. The FEOGA Guidance Fund played a significant role in providing investment capital for restructuring the food processing industry from the 1970s. During the 1980s and 1990s a number of rationalisation programmes aimed at modernising specific sectors, including dairy and meat processing, were implemented.

A particularly important development occurred in the mid-1980s when changes in cooperative and company law enabled the larger dairy cooperatives to transform their business into public limited companies, become part of the stock exchange and thereby access capital markets. Although the mid-1980s were still characterised by heavy use of intervention purchasing for dairy and beef products, some of the more progressive leaders in the food industry, such as Denis Brosnan of the Kerry Group, were seeking to diversify and become less dependent on European market support arrangements. The combination of the improved access to capital markets and the more market-oriented strategy laid the foundation for the transformation of the likes of the Kerry Group and Glanbia – created through a merger of Avonmore and Waterford cooperative societies – from milk processing cooperatives to the diversified global food companies of today.

Agents of change – Political and administrative
Given the importance of Ireland's entry to and membership of the EU to the future development of Irish agriculture and the wider economy, how the political and administrative systems would adapt to avail of the new opportunities that arose and how they would manage the risks were issues of critical importance. This section discusses some of the people who have played key roles since 1973.

Mark Clinton was the Minister for Agriculture for the early years of Ireland's membership. Notwithstanding the cattle crisis of 1974 referred to above, he presided over a period of major change and general optimism for the Irish farm sector. Prices increased steadily as Irish farm prices aligned upwards to the CAP guaranteed prices. This was the era when the outcome of the negotiations in the Council of Agricultural Ministers was likely to be the lead item on the main television news – and the news from the Council during those early years of membership was normally good for Irish farmers.

The negotiating climate for Irish Ministers for Agriculture became more difficult in the late 1970s and into the 1980s. The negotiations on the milk quota in 1984 have already been referred to. The combined efforts of Taoiseach Garret FitzGerald and Minister for Agriculture Austin Deasy were required to achieve a result which was perceived to be a positive outcome for Ireland.

Ireland was also perceived to have achieved positive outcomes from the various major negotiations on CAP reform from 1992 onwards. Joe Walsh served as Minister for Agriculture for most of the period from 1992 to

2005 and built up a reputation as a solid and experienced negotiator at European level.

The common purpose of successive Ministers for Agriculture, from 1973 onwards, was the preservation of a CAP which would continue to deliver benefits to Irish farmers and, by extension, to the Irish economy. This led to the situation that, for much of the 1970s and 1980s, Irish farm production was more focused on European support arrangements than on the market – which may have delayed the development of a more diversified and market-oriented food industry. But the case may also be made that Irish negotiators, at political and official levels, played an important role in reforming the CAP while paying understandable attention to the political realities at home.

At European level, Ray MacSharry, as Commissioner for Agriculture and Rural Development from 1989 to 1993, oversaw fundamental reform of the CAP. Indeed, historians will likely judge that MacSharry ranks among the three most important Commissioners for Agriculture over the fifty-year period under discussion, alongside the 'father of the CAP', Sicco Mansholt, Commissioner from 1958 to 1972, and Franz Fischler, the Commissioner from 1995 to 2003 who oversaw much of the post-MacSharry reform.

Successive Irish Ministers for Agriculture were, it is widely accepted, well served by the officials in the Department of Agriculture. In her study of the Irish administration's approach to dealing with European affairs, Laffan (2001, p. 58) states:

Of all the domestic departments, Agriculture actively embraced Europeanisation from 1970 onwards ... The department built up considerable expertise in the complexities of the policy, established contacts throughout the Agriculture Directorate General in the Commission and placed national experts in key units of that Directorate ... the department seeks to influence the Commission at the drafting stage and will try to voice its preferences long before a set of proposals gets to the full Commission. It is essentially unique among Irish departments in having an inside track in the Commission.

It has been traditional that ministers are accompanied to key European negotiations by the secretary general of the department. Over the period of EU membership, successive secretaries general – Jimmy O'Mahony, Donal Creedon, Michael Dowling, John Malone and Tom Moran, along with officials at different levels, have been successful in building coalitions at European level that helped secure favourable political outcomes to negotiations.

Within the European institutions, Irish officials played a significant role in shaping and administering agricultural policy. In the Commission these included Tom O'Dwyer, John Scully, Marcus McInerney, Mary Minch who served in MacSharry's cabinet, and Maeve Doran and Gerry Kiely who served in Fischler's cabinet.

Agents of change – Economic and social

The policy changes arising from EU membership required massive adaptation on the part of Irish agriculture and rural society. This adaptation has been facilitated by the development of many new institutions dealing with education, science and technology and improved marketing of produce. The development of farm organisations and the growth of social capital in rural Ireland have also been of importance.

As indicated above, Irish agriculture in the 1950s operated at low levels of technical efficiency. The succeeding decades have brought massive advances, due to significant capital investments, the generation and dissemination of improved technology, improved communications and rising standards of education.

An Foras Talúntais (AFT) – the Agricultural Institute – was established in 1958, charged with promoting and coordinating agricultural research and communicating its findings. The idea of such an institute was suggested as early as 1949, as part of the Marshall Plan, but disputes lasting through the 1950s involving the Department of Agriculture and the universities about who should be responsible for different aspects of agricultural research delayed agreement on its establishment (Daly, 2002).

Dr Tom Walsh, an eminent soil scientist, was appointed as the first Director of AFT. Relationships between AFT and the Department of Agriculture were difficult for a number of years, with disputes over budgets and respective responsibilities frequently arising. But, under the energetic leadership of 'the Doc', a team of bright young scientists, many of whom held doctorates from US universities, produced a stream of technology during the 1960s and 1970s which contributed to significant productivity increases in Irish agriculture.

The mid-1960s saw the introduction of continental beef breeds and increased use of artificial insemination for both the beef and dairy sectors.

Translating new technology into changed production practices required cooperation between the department, AFT, the farm advisory services which were under the control of county committees of agriculture until the late 1970s, and the farm organisations. The gradually increasing level of education in rural Ireland and the improved flow of information to farmers about market conditions and methods of improved farming played an important role in helping farmers adapt to new circumstances.

The national broadcasting station, RTÉ, played an important role in the transformation. In the 1960s a particularly innovative programme, *Telefís Feirme*, demonstrated methods of improved farming. This was presented by Justin Keating, a veterinary surgeon by profession, who later became a minister in the Liam Cosgrave-led coalition government of 1973 to 1977. Discussion groups were formed by Macra na Feirme and other farming organisations, often in association with the local farm adviser, to view these programmes.

The station also facilitated the improved dissemination of information about farm prices in different parts of the country. The legendary Michael Dillon presented his weekly programme, *Mart and Market*, which was required viewing for cattle farmers around the country, at least for those who had access to a television. In the print media, *The Farmers' Journal*, under editor Paddy O'Keeffe and later Matt Dempsey, has been a vital source of market and technical information for farmers since its establishment in the 1950s.

We have seen above the major problems Ireland faced in finding markets for its agricultural and food exports before 1973. The combination of additional market opportunities, improving technology and increased investment led to a significant expansion of agricultural output in the first decade of membership – before the quotas and production restrictions under the CAP began to bite. In the early 1960s the government set up an advisory committee to conduct the first detailed review of agricultural markets since the 1920s. Decisions taken on foot of this review led to the establishment of the Irish Dairy Board (Bord Bainne) in 1962 to improve the marketing of dairy products. Its first Managing Director was Tony O'Reilly, later to become a successful international businessman. In 1964 the Pigs and Bacon Commission was strengthened and in 1969 CBF, the Meat and Livestock Board, was established for the promotion of meat products. Following entry to the Community, the statutes and roles of certain of these bodies had to be changed to conform to European competition law (Daly, 2002).

The farm organisations played an important role in advocating for Ireland's entry to the Community, in helping their members adjust to the opportunities it presented and in representing the interests of their members. Macra na Feirme had been established in 1944 as an organisation to improve the social and cultural life of young farmers and rural dwellers. Over the future decades it played a hugely important role in improving informal educational and social opportunities for its members – with the further beneficial effect that it acted as an unofficial marriage bureau for many young rural people.

The NFA was established in 1955 for the purpose of representing the economic interests of farmers. The NFA (now the Irish Farmers'

Association) drew heavily on farm leaders who had been members of Macra. The organisation soon established itself as the predominant voice on behalf of the agricultural sector and, as already noted, had advocated as early as 1960 that Ireland should seek membership of the Community, even if the UK did not join. Hederman (1983, p. 112) comments, 'The record of initiative, organisational ability and awareness of international developments shown by the farming community in Ireland between 1948 and 1960, in both long-established and new organisations, is impressive. Set against the economic and political background of the period it is outstanding'.

The other main farming organisations were the Irish Creamery Milk Suppliers Association (ICMSA), which had been established in 1950, and the Irish Agricultural Organisation Society (IAOS), later to become the Irish Co-operative Organisation Society (ICOS).

It would also be deeply unjust if a narrative on the development of Irish agriculture over the past fifty years was to omit mention of the important role played by farm women in that development. While national statistics provide little information about the role of women in farming, O'Hara (1998, p. 2) notes in her study dealing with women, farm and family in Ireland:

Despite their invisibility in the public role of agriculture, farm women are self-evidently at the heart of family farming which clearly involves more than the individual male farmer/operator working his land ... Many farm women contribute substantially to farm production for the market and for home consumption and, almost invariably, undertake almost all the domestic work in the farm household and (sometimes) elder care. When they work off the farm, their income is often essential to the family's well-being.

The growth in part-time farming and the diversification of farm household income over the past twenty or thirty years has been in no small measure due to the increasing role played by women in the workforce.

O'Hara identifies a further key role played by farm women which is highly relevant to the transformation of farming structures that has occurred and the movement of people out of farming. She argues that farm women have for many decades 'used their influence as mothers to secure for their children livelihood options outside of family farming. Their commitment to success in this is reflected in the remarkable levels of educational participation among farm children' (1998, p. 10). This situation applied particularly in the west of Ireland, where farms were too small to provide full-time employment for the next generation.

While very few women were involved in making the big political decisions about agricultural policy at European level over the past fifty years, women were making the decisions at household and farm level which translated these political decisions into the life-changing choices that altered future employment patterns and how the structure of farming would evolve.

Conclusion

In reviewing Irish agriculture over the past half-century, the most striking feature is the scale of the changes which have occurred. Ireland has undergone an agricultural and economic revolution over the period. Notwithstanding a number of continuing economic and social problems at the start of the twenty-first century, that revolution may be seen as what economists call a 'virtuous development circle' which has involved a deepening of economic, social and institutional capital. And Ireland's EU membership, its involvement in the CAP system set up under the Treaty of Rome, and the subsequent reforms of that system, have been of central importance to that revolution.

For Irish agriculture, the 1960s was a decade of preparation in the hope of entering the Community. The 1970s saw that hope realised and farmers responding to the new opportunities. The 1980s was the era of cutbacks and production restraints as pressure built for CAP reform, which was eventually delivered in 1992. The 1990s brought the growth associated with the Celtic Tiger economy, which itself became a major force for change in farm structures. Young farm and rural people were increasingly well educated. More opportunities were available in the wider economy, while the prospect of making a full-time living from most farms continued to decline.

The coming decades will inevitably see profound changes. Price prospects for agricultural and food products are reasonably optimistic in the medium term as a result of global economic growth, pressure on resources and the impact of global warming. The stalled WTO trade talks will at some point have to be brought to a resolution and the trend towards freer international trade for agricultural products, and more competition for Irish farmers, will re-assert itself. The resourcefulness and capacity to adapt, which has been so evident over the past fifty years, will continue to be needed.

7

The Adaptation of Irish Foreign Policy to Europe

Nicholas Rees

Introduction

The formation and conduct of foreign policy has traditionally been an area in which nation-states have sought to preserve their sovereignty and have been reluctant to cede powers. The history of European integration is littered with early attempts to form political, security and defence communities, which faltered and failed in the face of national opposition. The ceding of some economic sovereignty and the pooling of authority in the European Coal and Steel Community, and later in the European Economic Community, were not matched by early attempts at political and security integration. It is, therefore, intriguing to observe that the European Union has incrementally increased its role in international affairs, ranging from the Commission representing the member states in trade negotiations to the coordination by the EU presidency of member state positions at the United Nations to developing common EU foreign policy positions and actions on international issues such as the Middle East, Africa and UN reform.

The degree of EU involvement varies depending on the area under examination, which reflects its highly differentiated role and legal standing with regard to trade, aid, political affairs, security and defence cooperation. The extent to which the EU is an actor, or has a presence, in international affairs, has been the subject of much discussion in the academic literature (Allen and Smith, 1990; Hill, 1993; Bretherton and Vogler, 1999), but what is not in doubt is that the EU's role in international affairs has had an impact on and shaped the way in which member states formulate and conduct their foreign policies.

This chapter examines the impact of Europeanisation on Irish foreign policy by looking first at the historical context of Ireland's involvement in the EC/EU, the national-level institutions involved in policy formation and the aspects of Irish foreign policy that traditionally made Ireland distinctive as a small, 'neutral' state with a strong commitment to

121

multilateral international institutions such as the UN and its agencies. The chapter aims to consider what impact and in what ways the pre-existing domestic structures and policies have conditioned how Irish foreign-policy-makers act in Europe. It examines the impact of the EU's growing role in international affairs on the making and conduct of Irish foreign policy, focusing especially on the adaptational pressures to change, as well as the policy preferences and the role of domestic political elites and public opinion. It looks at the adaptation and change that occurred in institutional structures and policy over the period since membership up to the present day. Finally, the chapter assesses the sources and degree of policy learning and adaptation and what impact Europeanisation has had on Ireland's foreign policy outlook and role in international affairs. It is argued that Irish foreign policy remains distinctive, based on a set of underlying values and sense of purpose, but that it is embedded in a European context that shapes Irish foreign policy behaviour.

Irish foreign policy pre-1973 – Institutions and policy development

In order to assess the relative impact of Europeanisation, as well as other factors such as domestic change and international considerations, on Irish foreign policy, it is important to recognise that the formation of the state and the distinctiveness of Irish nationalism, reflected in the thinking and views of Irish political leaders and public opinion, have uniquely shaped the formation of Ireland's outlook and standing in international affairs. At an early stage and up to the present day, Irish political leaders had to balance a principled set of foreign policy positions with a pragmatic approach to securing economic and political benefits for the state as and where possible. Ireland, like many small states, has lacked the economic and military clout to influence the behaviour of other states, and has therefore in its foreign policy had to win advantage and acceptance for its views through skilful political negotiation and coalition-building.

State formation and policy development
Ireland's early foreign policy outlook was a product of the state formation process, arising out of a protracted campaign for independence from Britain, followed by a bitter internal civil war over the nature of that independence. The formation of the state was contested and the deep-rooted political divisions in the country between opponent and supporters of the Free State Treaty left a lasting mark on the political landscape. Ireland's relationship with Britain remained a defining characteristic of

early Irish foreign policy, reflected in the desire to bring about a united Ireland and the reluctance to break all links with Britain, on the grounds that they might provide a means of gaining control over Northern Ireland and recognising Ireland's continuing dependence on British markets.

Outside of this area, Irish foreign policy in the 1930s was largely focused on the League of Nations and participation in imperial conferences, reflecting the continuing association with the British Commonwealth until 1948. Ireland's ambiguous political and security relationship with Britain was maintained throughout the World War II period, and it was only in 1948 that the Republic of Ireland Act broke the final constitutional link with Britain (see O'Halpin, 1999).

In this context, Irish foreign policy was largely aimed at ensuring and supporting the development of the state and its assertion of independence and sovereignty on the international stage. Indeed, what emerges from most examinations of this period is the inevitable mix of principled and pragmatic thinking that influenced the direction of Irish foreign policy, which is a continuing feature of Irish foreign policy today. Irish statesmen, while not significant players on the international stage during this period, did at times hold important roles, notably Seán Lester, who was the last Secretary General to the League of Nations (1936). The state did form a fledgling diplomatic service with a limited number of overseas embassies and trade missions established in Geneva (1922), London (1923), Washington (1924), Paris (1929), Berlin (1929) and the Holy See (1929).

Moreover, as archival evidence from the Department of External Affairs (now Foreign Affairs) suggests, Irish politicians and diplomats were involved with, and at times were courted by, European political leaders in the run-up to and during World War II (Girvin and Roberts, 2000). The island of Ireland was geo-strategically significant, providing an important military transit base for allied operations in Northern Ireland, as well as providing a useful transit point in the South for those travelling by air via Foynes between the US and Europe. The German government also courted Irish diplomats, seeing Ireland as a potential ally and possible invasion point. In this environment the Irish state's declared policy of military neutrality served to provide a pragmatic means of ensuring that the country remained out of the war, while covertly it used its position to support the allies, albeit with caution given the potential threat of German aggression and Ireland's ambiguous relationship with Britain.

In the post-war era Ireland was on the periphery of European events, participating in the Organisation for European Economic Co-operation (OEEC, established as part of the European Recovery Programme) and the Council of Europe, but remaining largely outside discussions focused on the reconstruction of Europe and the restoration of state structures. In the

Cold War climate Ireland's policy of military neutrality was broadened and used to justify Ireland's position as a 'neutral state' in international affairs. The main focus of Irish foreign policy was on Britain and the partition of the island, although this began to change by the late 1950s as Irish statesmen espoused a broader set of foreign policy principles and increasingly began to look towards Europe. These principles were first stated by Liam Cosgrave, Minister for External Affairs, in the Dáil in 1956 as being: support of the UN charter; independence of blocs in the UN; and a commitment to preserve Christian civilisation in opposition to communism (Keatinge, 1973). Frank Aiken, Minister for External Affairs (1951–54, 1957–69) emphasised the principle of independence in Ireland's position as a state in the UN. Indeed, membership of the UN opened up new opportunities for Ireland at a time when the state was seeking to internationalise: Frederic Boland became President of the UN General Assembly in 1960; Ireland participated in the UN peacekeeping mission to the Congo in 1960; it served on the Security Council in 1962; and it played a leading role in the formation of the Treaty of Non-Proliferation of Nuclear Weapons. This provided the bedrock of Irish foreign policy, and is still relevant today in understanding Irish positions on international affairs and in European institutions.

As Ireland engaged on the international stage, albeit as a small player, the state's politicians, economic-policy-makers and diplomats increasingly focused on the development of the European Economic Community and the economic benefits of being in the common market. In particular, concerns about the state of the Irish economy, unemployment and emigration in the 1950s led to domestic discussions about ways in which Ireland might develop its economy. This generally reflected a view that domestic economic policy, which has focused on import substitution and domestic capital development, had failed. The publication in 1958 of the First Programme for Economic Expansion (1958–63), brought about under the stewardship of T. K. Whitaker, Secretary of the Department of Finance, marked a shift in thinking and focus aimed at attracting multinational corporations to Ireland and developing international trade relations.

The fundamental reorientation of Irish economic policy inevitably had knock-on consequences for Irish foreign policy. At the height of Ireland's involvement in the UN, the state's politicians and diplomats were increasingly beginning to pursue a European course, although there was criticism that Frank Aiken, as Minister for External Affairs, showed limited interest in Europe (Keatinge, 1973). The likelihood that Britain might join the EEC inevitably raised questions as to whether Ireland should also do so, given that as of 1960 two-thirds of Ireland's trade was with Britain and

Ireland could not afford to remain outside the Community if Britain joined. This would have risked economic isolation and exclusion, which the state could not afford, and there was a strong domestic lobby in favour of membership (Hederman, 1983). As it transpired, British membership was blocked by the French veto in 1963 thereby effectively postponing Ireland's application, although only until 1967 when Ireland renewed its application. In the interim, Ireland signed an Anglo-Irish Free Trade Agreement with Britain in 1965, reflecting economic concerns and aimed at creating a more open economy and developing trade. Ireland eventually signed the Treaty of Accession in January 1972 and joined the EEC in 1973. In a referendum held in 1972 the Irish people voted by 83 per cent in favour of membership, with 17 per cent opposed, with a turnout of over 70 per cent.

The issues debated in the lead-up to the referendum (which were largely concerned with the economic impact of membership on the state, the implications of joining the EEC for Irish sovereignty and independence, and whether Irish neutrality would be threatened) reflected the mix of pragmatism and idealism evident in the practice of Irish foreign policy (Coakley *et al.*, 1997). In the end economic considerations dominated over political and foreign policy concerns, reflecting the view that Europe offered the only real alternative for a small state like Ireland. The formative experiences of this era fundamentally shaped Ireland's foreign policy outlook and orientation, thereby strongly influencing Ireland's positions and policies within the EC/EU up to the present. The evolution of Irish foreign policy and the impact of Europeanisation on institutions and policies are fully explored later in this chapter.

Institutions

These early experiences had a significant impact on Ireland's political and diplomatic elite, who viewed foreign policy as closely linked with state formation and national independence. Many members of the elite involved in the early development of Ireland's foreign policy remained in key positions until the late 1960s, thereby ensuring continuity in policy development and outlook. Irish foreign policy was framed and led by key political figures such as Desmond Fitzgerald (1922–27), Éamon de Valera (1932–48, 1951–57), Seán MacBride (1948–51) and Frank Aiken (1951–54, 1957–69), as well as by successive secretaries general, including Joseph Walshe (1922–46), Frederic Boland (1946–50), Seán Nunan (1950–55), Seán Murphy (1955–57) and Cornelius Cremin (1957–63). Éamon de Valera – who combined the roles of Taoiseach and Minister for External Affairs for sixteen years – defined the parameters of Irish foreign policy: emphasising independence and sovereignty, supporting Ireland's role in the League of Nations and espousing a policy of military neutrality during the war years. His successor as Minister for External Affairs, Seán MacBride, followed a different path, being a stronger supporter of European unity and favouring the development of the OEEC and Council of Europe.

The responsibility for the formation and development of foreign policy has been vested in the executive branch of government, reflecting the traditional Westminster model of government, with relatively limited oversight by the Oireachtas and the judiciary. The Minister for Foreign Affairs is normally responsible for the day-to-day conduct of foreign affairs, with the Taoiseach, as head of government, representing and speaking on behalf of the state in international fora and at major international events. Other relevant ministers and their departments have been involved to varying degrees in international affairs, depending on the issues under discussion. At the cabinet level, a range of ministers participate in discussions on foreign policy matters, especially where such matters are of importance to their departments and where they are responsible for policy development (for example trade, agricultural policy, justice, defence). Notably the Minister for Finance holds a pivotal position in many such discussions, given the importance of economic policy and the primary role of the Department of Finance in providing the resources required to implement policy. It is, however, the Taoiseach who speaks on behalf of Ireland at international gatherings and ultimately is usually present at the conduct of the final stages of international negotiations and agreements. This has been especially the case in relation to Anglo-Irish relations, where the Taoiseach has usually taken responsibility in key discussions. In so doing, the Taoiseach and his department usually work in close collaboration with the Minister for Foreign Affairs and his department.

The Department of External Affairs (renamed Foreign Affairs in 1971) was at the outset a small department with limited influence in the formation of government policy and with very few resources at its disposal. As a department it had an inauspicious start, having incorporated the publicity department of the Dáil government which had been the proponent of the 1921 Treaty and was therefore not seen as 'part' of the government. In the early years the department was managed by Joseph Walshe, who was given the title Secretary General in 1927 at a late stage reflecting ongoing tensions with regard to the standing and role of the department. During this period Ireland had a limited but active diplomatic network, with offices in the Holy See, Berlin, Washington, Geneva, Paris, Madrid, Brussels and London, plus representatives at a number of international organisations including the League of Nations and then the

OEEC (1948), the Council of Europe (1949) and the UN (1955). The development of the diplomatic network was largely a reflection of political considerations, and later, by the 1960s and 1970s, of economic interests and EEC membership.

The underlying institutional structures and resource base of the Department of Foreign Affairs remained limited between 1922 and 1949, especially in light of the role played by de Valera. It was the appointment of MacBride that led to administrative changes in the department, with a significant increase in budgetary resources and personnel, including the appointment of press attachés and information officers (Keatinge, 1973). During this period the department's remit was extended to include management of the European Recovery Programme, with an increased staff in Washington and Dublin. A number of new sections were established including trade, political affairs and information and two additional assistant secretaries were appointed (Keatinge, 1973). Later, Aiken was particularly active in promoting Ireland's interests overseas, focusing principally on the UN, where his efforts on disarmament and peacekeeping went far beyond interests intrinsic to Ireland. Under his guidance, the department's diplomatic network expanded to Nigeria (1960), Denmark (1962), India (1964) and the EEC (1966), ensuring that Ireland was represented in key regional locations around the world. In practice, however, the department found it difficult to argue for resources, which in turn had consequences for the way it developed up to EEC membership. The small size of the department – only 400 personnel prior to EEC membership – ensured that officials had close ties with each other, but limited the degree of specialisation, with much of the focus being on day-to-day issues as opposed to policy development. The department was organised at this stage on functional rather than geographical lines, given the limited resources available, with four main sections in 1972: administration; economic, political and cultural; Anglo-Irish; and information.

Global, European and domestic pressures for adapting Irish foreign policy

In looking at how Irish foreign policy changed after EEC membership, it is possible to distinguish three phases of development associated with treaty reform and the growing role of the EU into the foreign policy domain. What has evolved is a complex system of foreign policy cooperation among the EU member states, reflecting a mix of high-level EU foreign policy coordination and joint action. For example, the member states have carefully coordinated their approach towards Iran, following the Iranian decision to engage in uranium enrichment, which the EU along with the US strongly opposed. In this instance, three member states – France, Britain and Germany – have taken the lead in negotiating with Iran, with the EU's High Representative, Javier Solana, playing a leading role. This example also highlights the risks for small states, such as Ireland, who can find their influence limited in such situations, as well as being under pressure to support a particular EU position on an issue. In this sense the adaptational pressures have been growing since the 1990s, reflecting treaty changes, whereas in the 1970s the pressures were relatively low as the following illustrates.

1973 to 1986 – Low adaptational pressures
In the lead-up to and immediately following EEC membership, adaptational pressures to change the manner and way in which Irish foreign policy was formulated and implemented were low, reflecting the EEC's limited role in international affairs during the 1970s. The EEC remained a fledgling political actor, with its primary roles in external affairs focused on trade negotiations (GATT) and aid to Third World states (Yaounde and later Lomé). Indeed, Ireland was a key player in completing the negotiation of the first Lomé agreement during Ireland's first Council presidency in 1975 under the leadership of Garret FitzGerald, the then Minister for Foreign Affairs. This also impacted on Irish foreign policy, with the state developing its first bilateral aid programme in 1974 ahead of the presidency.

In the more general area of political relations, the development of the European Political Cooperation (EPC) process was a significant milestone. EPC was largely aimed at trying to ensure a degree of coordination among the nine EEC member states on issues under discussion in arms control, oil, the Middle East and the Third World (see Nuttall, 1992). In practice, this largely depended on intergovernmental coordination through the member states' representatives, with common agreement proving difficult to achieve. The limitations of the intergovernmental process were highlighted by the oil crisis, whereby states broke ranks with their EEC counterparts and largely pursued national interests. Global pressures combined with strong domestic concerns undermined the possibility of achieving a common European interest. Moreover, a weak European political structure meant that the states were largely free to do as they wished, unconstrained by a strong regime of rules, norms and expectations.

Irish foreign-policy-makers were therefore under relatively little adaptational pressure from Europe to change the manner in which Irish foreign policy was formulated and conducted. The original fear voiced during the 1972 referendum, namely that EEC membership might threaten

Irish neutrality and jeopardise Ireland's independence, proved unfounded (Keatinge, 1984). In this period the only major instance in which the Irish government claimed that Irish neutrality was compromised by EPC related to the Falklands War in 1982, in which the state refused to support Britain's actions. The government did, however, seek to protect Irish neutrality, recognising that public opinion was in favour of this policy, leading the government to impose caveats on European attempts at further cooperation in the sphere of foreign and security policy. Notably, the government added a footnote to the report of the Ad Hoc Committee on Institutional Affairs (1985, also known as the Dooge Report, see Chapter 12), in regard to security and defence matters. In practice, EPC imposed very little in the way of constraints on Ireland, while offering up far more in the way of opportunities to Irish foreign-policy-makers. The development of the machinery associated with EPC ensured that Irish foreign-policy-makers had access to far more information and intelligence on areas and issues in international affairs than was previously the case.

The pressure for adaptation came from within the state and was largely associated with a policy elite that viewed this as an opportunity to bring Ireland in from the cold and to reposition the state in Europe and international affairs. It also led to significant institutional and policy changes in the way in which Irish foreign policy was formulated and conducted, which are discussed in the next section.

1986 to 1993 – Moderate to medium adaptational pressures
The changing nature of the EU's foreign policy regime, whereby the member states agreed that the EU should play a more prominent role on the international stage, was reflected in the Single European Act (SEA) (1986) and then the Maastricht Treaty on European Union (1993). In the case of the SEA, the codification of EPC procedures (Title III of the Act) and the commitment to the formation of a European foreign policy and closer European cooperation on the political and economic aspects of security raised increasing concerns in Ireland about the implication of these changes for Irish neutrality, where opponents of the Act actively campaigned against its approval. The process of ratification was blocked by a legal challenge undertaken by anti-EC campaigner Raymond Crotty, who argued that the Act required a constitutional amendment. The case was rejected by the High Court, but that judgment was overturned by the Supreme Court. As a result, the Act was delayed and a referendum was held in May 1987, where it was approved by 70 per cent of voters. The focus of the Single European Act, however, was largely on the removal of barriers to free movement and the completion of the single market (see Chapter 4). The move towards increased coordination on foreign policy

matters contained in Title III of the Act still remained a matter for intergovernmental cooperation and there was no binding legal obligation on the member states.

The end of the Cold War in 1989 and the lead-up to the formation of the Maastricht Treaty on European Union marked a critical phase for the Irish government, given the Irish presidency was responsible for the early stages of the negotiations in the first six months of 1990. The Irish government's focus in the negotiations was largely on the structural funds, reflecting a desire to ensure any commitment to EMU would be offset by economic benefits. It did not, however, strongly oppose the provisions in the treaty relating to a Common Foreign and Security Policy (CFSP), which remained relatively modest, especially when linked in Article J.4, which sought to protect existing national prerogatives to act in this arena (see also Chapter 12). In Ireland the Maastricht Treaty was passed in a referendum by 69.1 per cent to 30.9 per cent, with a turnout of 57 per cent, despite claims by opponents that this might lead to a European superstate and the formation of a European army.

In practice the adoption of provisions for the development of a CFSP seemed far distant from the reality of European foreign policy on the ground, where the divisions over the Gulf War (1991) and the crisis in Yugoslavia (1991) highlighted the inability of the EU to develop an agreed European position or action on these critical issues. Europe remained, as in the Cold War era, dependent on the US to undertake military action, and the EU was divided over what to do, reflecting differing national positions and the lack of common agreement. These issues, however, were distant from Irish shores, and the Maastricht Treaty appeared relatively unthreatening, albeit with some domestic disquiet. Nevertheless, Ireland's foreign policy position, especially in relation to neutrality, was becoming increasingly irrelevant in the post-Cold War era. There was also a growing risk that by not participating in the new European initiatives that emerged in the 1990s, such as Partnership for Peace, that Ireland could become isolated on the periphery of Europe and play less of a role in international affairs.

1993 to 2007 – Medium adaptational pressures

The adoption of the Maastricht Treaty in 1993, the Amsterdam Treaty in 1997 and the Nice Treaty in 2001 further enhanced the powers and role of the EU as a political and security actor. The absorption of Petersberg tasks[1] (and the Western European Union) into Union and the explicit treaty

---

[1] The Petersberg tasks, as listed in the treaty, include humanitarian and rescue tasks, peacekeeping tasks and tasks of combat forces in crisis management, including peacemaking.

commitments to form a CFSP, based on the adoption of common positions and actions, as well as new articles on development cooperation, enhanced the EU's capacity to act. The establishment of new institutional structures in the military/security area, namely the political committee, military committee and military staff plus the adoption of headline goals around civilian and military capabilities (made up of national contributions) significantly enhance the potential of the EU as a security actor.

The degree of change, some of which was precipitated by treaty change and some by intergovernmental agreement, was remarkable in such a short period of time given the reservations that some members had about the EU developing as a political and security actor. This has placed increasing pressure on member states to adapt their policies, processes and actions to support European-level policy development and to meet these requirements. A practical illustration of this is evident in the way in which national military capabilities are being developed in response to EU (and NATO) force requirements, reflecting a commitment by the members to participating in European-level common actions and European Security and Defence Policy (ESDP) missions. However, while the adaptational pressures are evident, they are still largely based on the voluntary commitment of the members to act on an intergovernmental basis, with some states choosing in what areas they wish to participate. There are, in fact, strong domestic adaptational pressures among policy elites that seem to favour enhanced cooperation on security matters, whereas public opinion in some member states lags behind that of the policy elite.

In Ireland the adaptational pressures arising during this period highlighted the limitations of Ireland's declared position as a military neutral state, which seemed increasingly irrelevant in the post-Cold War period. It also left Ireland 'sitting on the fence' in relation to security developments in Europe, adding ambiguity and uncertainty about Ireland's position on international issues, such as Bosnia and Herzegovina, as well as the NATO intervention in Kosovo (Rees, 2000). The problem for many politicians and most of the diplomatic service was that the Irish public remained committed to such a policy, given that it had historically been interwoven with Irish nationalism and independence, asserted as a core value, and was used to distinguish Irish foreign policy as highly moralistic. The government's 1996 White Paper on foreign policy, the first ever such paper, carefully restated Ireland's commitment to military neutrality, while opening up the possibility that Ireland might eventually seek to join the Partnership for Peace (Government of Ireland, 1996).

The practice of neutrality, of course, had been very different, with many observers suggesting that Ireland did not meet any of the international standards associated with neutrality and that participation in the EU had already undermined that position (see Sharp, 1990; Salmon, 1989). Indeed, senior politicians across most of the major political parties were cognisant that Irish neutrality meant very little outside of Ireland, and had become increasingly irrelevant in the 1990s. It did, however, remain important to a range of minority groups opposed to aspects of further European integration, such as the Peace and Neutrality Alliance (PANA), as well as to segments of the public, surfacing usually at times when referenda were held on European treaty changes.

The adaptational pressures associated with the EU's growing involvement in foreign and security affairs did not formally require that the Irish state change its position on neutrality, given that several other European states also had similar reservations. Rather the pressures for adaptation came from within the state, where the policy preferences of the majority of the political and diplomatic elite cautiously favoured increasing Ireland's involvement in political and security affairs. At a political level, Irish leaders were able to 'punch above their weight', and were at times in influential positions whereby they were able to play a significant international role in the EU and at the UN in shaping events. Notably, Ireland's European presidencies afforded Irish political leaders an opportunity to use their negotiating skills to pursue agendas that were closely linked to Ireland's early principled stance in the UN. For example, during Ireland's EU presidency in 2004, the state was able to place development and HIV/AIDs in Africa firmly on the EU's agenda and was heavily involved in the dialogue in support of the roadmap for peace in the Middle East.

In contrast, the military/security area has been the most problematic for the policy elite, where a desire not to be excluded from participating in European operations and action has to be balanced against traditional Irish concerns about being 'dragged' into operations to which the state is opposed. As a result, Ireland has often adopted an ambiguous position on actions such as that of NATO in Kosovo and the US-led coalition attack on Iraq. Ireland continues to participate actively in UN peacekeeping operations, such as in Liberia (UNMIL) and Lebanon (UNFIL), as well as becoming increasingly involved in ESDP peacekeeping missions in Bosnia-Herzegovina and Kosovo. The triple lock procedure, whereby Irish troops cannot participate in such a peacekeeping mission unless it is within the context of a UN authorised operation and on the basis of cabinet and Dáil approval, could be viewed as either a limitation or a safeguard. Nevertheless, there has been a maturation of the Irish position, with the state's representatives participating in European discussions of military issues and in ESDP operations.

The pressure for adaptation has tended to come from within the state, given that Ireland is not a significant security actor, and there has been little pressure from other European states for Ireland to participate. Ireland has tended to be in the position of trying to 'catch up' with developments in this arena, given that it was slow to commit to participating in the 'battlegroups' identified by the EU's Defence Ministers as part of a rapid European reaction force that might be required to be deployed at short notice to address a crisis. Ireland has, however, chosen to participate in the Nordic battlegroup, which is led by Sweden, and has agreed to contribute personnel with an expertise in mine clearance. In order to facilitate this role, which required training outside the state, amendments to the existing Defence Act (1960) had to be made in the Oireachtas. At the same time the government took the opportunity of changing the Act to allow Ireland to send troops overseas to respond rapidly to humanitarian crises, such as the tsunami that occurred in the Indian Ocean in December 2005.

Impact of Europe on Irish foreign policy – Institutional and policy change

The impact of Europeanisation on the manner in which Irish foreign policy is formulated and conducted and on the policy content over the last thirty plus years has been immense, reflecting the fundamental repositioning of the state inside the EU and its move away from its traditionally neutral position, which was increasingly irrelevant in the post-Cold War era (Keatinge, 1996). The distinction between domestic and foreign policy matters no longer exists, in so much as Europe impacts on all aspects of the Irish political process, economy and society. The challenge for Irish leaders is to play a meaningful role in shaping the development of EU foreign policy in a way that is consistent with the underlying principles of Irish foreign policy, which can be difficult when negotiating with large states with different outlooks and interests in international affairs. It requires considerable diplomatic and bargaining skills, which Ireland is credited with having used effectively on many occasions in European negotiations and on behalf of the EU in external affairs.

Attitudinal and institutional change
At the heart of this process, the core executive and machinery of Irish government have been responsible for providing the interface between Europe and the Irish state. The pre-existing domestic structures and processes had to be adapted and changed to manage Ireland's relationship with Europe and to ensure that the state was able to benefit at an early

stage from European policies and subsidies (see Chapter 10). In most cases the machinery of government was adapted to ensure that Ireland was able to take on board the body of EC law and policy. In general the approach was incremental, piecemeal and pragmatic, reflecting a feeling that the existing system of public administration could handle European matters and that there were limited resources of people and money available to change the existing system radically (Laffan and Tannam, 1998). Underlying this was a generally supportive attitude towards Europe, with support strongest in those areas – such as the Departments of Foreign Affairs and of the Taoiseach – where Europe was seen as critical to Ireland's future prosperity and role in international affairs.

At the heart of this system the government and ultimately the cabinet have been responsible for managing the relationship with Europe, with the Taoiseach and Minister for Foreign Affairs playing the leading roles. At a relatively early stage, following Irish accession, the cabinet established a sub-committee comprising the Taoiseach, Tánaiste and the Ministers for Foreign Affairs, Finance, Agriculture and Fisheries, and Industry and Commerce to coordinate EC policy (Burns and Salmon, 1977). The establishment of this sub-committee was also in preparedness for Ireland's EC presidency in 1975. In practice this committee did not play the role that had been envisaged for it, namely that of coordination, and, as Table 7.1 illustrates, it evolved over the years with a number of title changes. In effect, the then Minister for Foreign Affairs, Garret FitzGerald, provided the focus for much of the coordination and was the leading proponent for Ireland inside the EC. EC membership significantly raised the profile and the importance of the role of the Minister for Foreign Affairs and of the Department of Foreign Affairs. Prior to EC membership, the Department of Finance was the leading ministry, and while this did not change after membership, the Department of Foreign Affairs was given the leading role in handling the coordination of European matters.

In the Irish system of government the role of the legislature in foreign affairs has been limited, especially prior to EC membership. The European Communities Act 1972 provided the Oireachtas with a limited role in relation to the EC, principally through the monitoring of EC legislation (see also Chapter 11). The government was required on a twice-yearly basis (Section 5, EC Act) to submit reports on developments within the EC to both houses.[2] In practice, these reports, while informative, did little to stimulate debate and certainly did not make the government accountable to the Oireachtas for its actions.

---

[2] Following enactment of the 2002 European Scrutiny Act, the twice-yearly reports were replaced by an annual report.

Table 7.1: *Key committees in the Irish system*

Committee	Chair	Dates
European Communities Committee	Department of Foreign Affairs	1973–1984
European Communities Committee	Department of the Taoiseach	1987–1990
Ministers and Secretaries Group	Department of the Taoiseach	1988–1990
Ministerial Group on the Presidency	Taoiseach	1989–1990
European Communities Committee	Department of the Taoiseach	1992–1997
Ministers and Secretaries Group	Taoiseach	1994–1999
Senior Officials Group	Department of the Taoiseach	1994–1998
Expert Technical Group	Taoiseach	1998–1999
Cabinet Sub-Committee	Taoiseach	1998–
Senior Officials Group	Department of the Taoiseach	1998–2002
Interdepartmental Coordination Committee on Europe	Department of the Taoiseach	2002–

Source: Laffan, 2005a

Notably, an Oireachtas Joint Committee on Secondary Legislation of the European Communities was set up by the government to scrutinise legislative and other EC proposals, although it had a limited impact on community policy or in generating much interest or knowledge about the EC.[3] It was the principal watchdog in the early period of Ireland's membership, i.e. during the 1970s and 1980s. It mainly focused on examining secondary legislation, although its terms of reference were extended to allow it to examine all Commission policies and proposals, EC regulations and other acts, as well as Irish legislation flowing from the European Communities Act 1972. Its role in practice proved to be far more limited, given its remit, limited resources and the overall weaknesses of the Oireachtas committee system (for an early assessment of the functions of the joint committee, see Robinson, 1979).

In the mid-1990s a new Joint Committee on Foreign Affairs (1993) was established, along with a Joint Committee on European Affairs (1995), both of which provided a forum where international issues could be debated and reports presented to the Oireachtas for consideration. The existence of the two committees, both of which have been renewed following elections in 1997, 2002 and 2007, provide the Oireachtas with a greater opportunity to debate and examine international European matters. They also offer a forum in which outside experts, professionals and interested parties may give evidence and contribute to discussion on topical issues of concern to the Oireachtas. As in the past, however, attendance at meetings is patchy, reflecting the continuing problems of the parliamentary committee system.

---

[3] It comprised twenty-five members: eighteen TDs and seven senators.

In general, however, there was limited interest in ensuring that the Dáil and Seanad scrutinised or in any way played a role in relation to European matters up until the outcome of the first Nice Treaty referendum in June 2001. The outcome of the Nice referendum, in which a narrow majority of voters opposed the adoption of the treaty in Ireland, prompted a far-reaching reappraisal by the government of the manner in which EU matters are debated and communicated in Ireland (O'Mahony, 2001).[4] It was strongly felt that Irish people were detached from EU developments, with EU business, and more generally European affairs, having slipped down the agenda. Similarly, many Irish officials felt that Ireland had become complacent and was not in tune with developments in Europe, perhaps focusing inwardly on national economic and social developments, and absorbed by a number of domestic scandals. Even prior to the result the government had decided to convene a National Forum on Europe (2001) to stimulate debate and discussion regarding Ireland's relationship with Europe and to look at the future of Europe in light of the upcoming European Convention.[5] However, following the referendum result, and in a context where a further referendum was likely, Taoiseach Bertie Ahern and Minister for Foreign Affairs Brian Cowen placed Europe centre stage on the government's agenda. Thus, the National Forum on Europe took on an added prominence, with the government ensuring a continuing presence of senior ministers and officials at its meetings.

The government also sought to improve the Oireachtas's role in the process by establishing a Sub-Committee on European Scrutiny of the Select Committee on European Affairs under the terms of the European Union (Scrutiny) Act 2002. The sub-committee, comprising eleven members, was given a broad remit to scrutinise all aspects of EU affairs across the principal EU and Irish institutions. In recent years the Taoiseach, the Minister for Foreign Affairs and other ministers have briefed the Oireachtas on European developments, especially on the outcome of European Council meetings, treaty reform proposals and major international events, such as the crises in the Middle East peace process (see Chapter 11 for further details on parliamentary scrutiny of European activities).

---

[4] See the All-Party Oireachtas Committee on the Constitution (2001) for a review of the factors leading to a 'no' vote.

[5] The National Forum on Europe, which is chaired by former senator Maurice Hayes, comprises representatives of all the Oireachtas parties, as well as an Observer Group made up of representatives of civil society. See Reports of the Chairman of the Forum on Europe, available at www.forumoneurope.ie

There has been some restructuring of the Department of Foreign Affairs, reflecting the need to reorganise the department's functions to cope with the demands of EC membership. In 1967 the department was organised along the lines of three divisions: administration; economics; and politics. The principal division responsible for relations with the EEC was the economics division, which also handled all matters relating to the GATT, EFTA and foreign trade. By 1977 the department was structured around six divisions: administration; legal; Anglo-Irish; political; economic; and overseas development assistance. There was a significant expansion in the overall size of the department, with the number of staff based in Dublin growing from 68 in 1972 to 94 in 1977, and overseas from 85 to 120. The political and economic divisions were charged with handing European matters.

In the early stages EC membership clearly placed a considerable burden on the department, especially in the run-up to Ireland's first EC presidency in 1975, and the overall increase in staff numbers was inadequate to cope with the increased workload and the complexity of dealing with EC business. The budgetary realities of the 1970s, however, limited the resources available to support its activities. In any event, the department was placed at the centre of European affairs, and was responsible for coordinating Ireland's position on European issues with the Irish Permanent Representation in Brussels. Critically, the Secretary of the Department of Foreign Affairs was given the responsibility for chairing the interdepartmental EC committee, despite protestations from the Department of Finance. In practice, however, the department was not responsible for the initiation policy, which tended to rest with other functional departments. The most important of these were the Departments of the Taoiseach and of Finance, followed at the time by the Departments of Industry and Commerce, of Agriculture and Fisheries, of Lands, of Social Welfare, and of Labour.

The Department of Foreign Affairs continues to play the leading role in European affairs, where it remains the main conduit and interlocutor between Brussels and Dublin. There are now more divisions and units within the department than at the start of Ireland's membership, although most European matters are still handled by the EU and political divisions, and while staff numbers have grown it still depends on other functional departments, who initiate policy, offer technical advice and provide personnel for the staffing of the Irish Permanent Representation in Brussels (see Table 7.2). Over the period the staff of the department acquired a highly regarded reputation for their knowledge of European affairs and their ability to negotiate skilfully on behalf of the state. They have also been acknowledged for the smooth running of the EU presidency when they have been in the chair.

Table 7.2: *The Irish Permanent Representation*, 2004*

Grade	Numbers
Permanent representative	1
Deputy permanent representative	1
Representative on PSC	1
Military representatives to EUMC/PSC	8
Deputy secretary general	1
Counsellors	20
Adviser	1
First secretaries	40
Third secretaries	24
Total	97

* includes representatives to the Political and Security Committee (PSC) and the EU Military
Committee (EUMC).
Source: EU Inter-Institutional Directory, available at www.Europa.eu.int/idea

The key point, however, is that EC membership placed Irish political leaders and diplomats at the heart of international affairs. Prior to membership, Ireland had already made its mark in the UN system by supporting decolonisation, arms control and the rights of all sovereign states. It was, nevertheless, still a small state with a limited ability to influence events. As a part of the EU, however, Irish officials are privy to a wealth of information and intelligence that has placed the state's governmental leaders and officials in a position to play an important role in world affairs. They have access through the COREU telex network and regular working group meetings to privileged information (Tonra, 2001). For example, the monthly meeting of the General and External Affairs Council means that the Minister for Foreign Affairs and his or her counterparts from the twenty-six other EU states have a regular opportunity to examine both internal EU affairs and major international issues such as the Middle East peace roadmap, the war in Iraq, Afghanistan, terrorism and a myriad of other topics. At a lower level, Irish officials sit on a range of Council working groups that examine these issues and try to agree EU common positions and actions in advance of ministerial meetings.

Similarly, in the UN structure the EU seeks to coordinate through the EU presidency its position on major international issues. In October 2001 Ireland, as an elected member of the UN Security Council, chaired the meetings and led the UN's response to the 9/11 attacks in the US. In this role it also sought to ensure that all the other EU states were briefed on developments in the UN Security Council and it aimed to ensure that the US response to these events took place within a UN context. Irish leaders, therefore, have access to world leaders, international organisations and multilevel talks, which place the state in a position to pursue and advance its own foreign policy objectives.

Policy change

A key issue in terms of Europeanisation is the extent to which Europe has impacted on the central elements of Irish foreign policy. In foreign policy, Ireland had built a niche as a reasonably principled contributor to world affairs prior to accession. Primarily through its work in the UN, it acquired a reputation for supporting a range of 'progressive' policies in areas such as nuclear disarmament and arms control, decolonisation, peaceful resolution of disputes and a broad commitment to international economic justice. These did not disappear from Irish foreign policy on joining the EU. Indeed, Sharp (1990, p. 239) suggests that successive Irish governments 'maintained a distinctive approach to arms control, disarmament and peacekeeping, and extended the projection of an Irish role into the issues of development assistance and a Middle Eastern peace settlement'. EU membership, however, did involve a significant broadening of the range of issues under consideration by Irish diplomats and required in some areas the formation of policy positions on a range of issues which Irish foreign-policy-makers had previously had little knowledge or involvement with.

In the 1970s the EU's role in foreign policy, as distinct from its part in trade and aid-related areas where the role of the European Commission was significant, was underdeveloped and posed little challenge to the core tenets of Irish foreign policy. The EPC process was a framework for information exchange and loose policy coordination. It did not involve security matters, which might have prompted greater opposition from groups and individuals concerned with Irish neutrality. In general, EC membership gave a significant boost to Irish foreign policy, leading the state to broaden its involvement in international affairs and slowly expand its diplomatic representation to ensure that it had embassies in key regional locations. Another noteworthy development was the establishment of a bilateral aid programme, thereby ensuring that Ireland had moved from being a recipient of funds to one which provided support and assistance to a group of the least developed and poorest Third World states (see Holmes *et al.*, 1993).

The challenge for Irish foreign-policy-makers has been to balance Ireland's principled stance in international affairs alongside its pragmatic economic interests. Ireland has also to meet the challenge of making its voice heard in a group in which the larger states, such as Britain, Germany and France, can dominate EU fora and decision-making. Irish political leaders and diplomats have proved to be skilled at defending Irish interests while supporting more general common European policies and positions in international affairs. This was particularly notable in the various rounds of the GATT negotiations, where the Commission was charged with leading the negotiations on behalf of its member states, but in which its negotiating mandate was subject to the control of those same states. In the case of Ireland, the issue of agricultural policy was always of major concern in such negotiations, given the sensitivity of the issue in Ireland. Irish negotiators were usually strongly allied with France and the Mediterranean countries, who were opposed to liberalising the market and making concessions to developing states. The dilemma for Irish negotiators was that the pursuit of Irish economic interests was not always consistent with Ireland's principled approach to development issues and support for developing states. Similarly, in relation to climate negotiations over CO_2 emissions Irish government policy was supportive of a reduction in emissions, which was in line with EU policy, but at a practical level the government was reluctant to put in place a carbon tax that might have adversely affected Irish economic competitiveness.

The impact of Europeanisation on Irish foreign policy has been largely positive, ensuring that the state is in a position to shape and participate in EU foreign policy actions. At a policy level, this means that Irish officials and politicians are now embedded and involved in international relations in a way that is very different from the 1950s and 1960s. Ireland, as an EU member state, has a much stronger voice in international affairs, especially on those occasions when it holds the presidency and speaks for Europe. It has played a critical role in international negotiations, ranging from the concluding of the early Lomé agreements on European aid to developing countries, to negotiation in the Middle East peace process and conflict resolution in Africa. It has also become involved in EU ESDP peace operations, deploying the military and police, as well as civilians, in support of such operations. Ireland has, nevertheless, been able to maintain an independent foreign policy. For example, through the Irish Aid programme, the state has provided aid to a number of bilateral partners largely in Africa. It has also been able to use its position in Europe, such as during the Irish presidency in 2004, to prioritise Africa on the EU's agenda. Ireland's role in Europe has matured and this is reflected in the ability of the state to change its foreign policy outlook, largely dropping references to neutrality, while positively accentuating its commitment to using its defence forces for humanitarian and peace operations.

European foreign, security and defence cooperation and Ireland

The Irish experience has been that pressures to adapt Irish foreign policy to emerging developments in European foreign, security and defence cooperation came from both domestic and European sources, with global pressures having a limited effect on policy formation and institutional development. Irish foreign-policy-makers, especially officials in the Department of Foreign Affairs, welcomed EU membership, seeing it as an opportunity for the state and for Irish foreign policy. In general, European developments were used as means of adapting and changing Ireland's foreign policy in order to meet the needs of a progressively modernising state. At all times foreign-policy-makers were aware of the key issues for Ireland inside Europe, whether they related to EU treaty negotiations or more general international affairs. In some ways the development and maturation of EU foreign policy over a lengthy period suited Ireland, given that early concerns around neutrality and economic interests influenced everything that the state did inside Europe. Ireland was, by any standard, cautious about supporting and playing a part in a more developed European foreign policy. On any issues related to defence and security matters there was deep reluctance to engage at an early stage with Europe, given domestic sentiment that favoured neutrality. There was also a concern about the role of large states, which justifiably remains today, given the tendency for mini-summits and the reluctance of some large states to take on board the concerns of small states.

The state's participation in Europe, and the development of elements of a European foreign policy, afforded many opportunities to Ireland that would not have been available previously, and Irish foreign policy matured and changed to accommodate the post-Cold War environment. Ireland is still a small player on the international scene, but the state's foreign-policy-makers are now better informed and in a much stronger position to play a role on the world stage. This is reflected in the manner in which Ireland is valued as a partner in peace operations and for its support for UN reform. Ireland has also been able to extend its diplomatic network across the globe and has focused its activities on developing trade links in Central and Eastern Europe and Asia. It has also maintained a strong focus on aid to poor states, supported initiatives on HIV/AIDS and provided support to meet humanitarian crises as and when they arise. The key point in all of this is that Ireland's place in Europe has assured it a stronger role in international affairs. There are, of course, times when Irish foreign-policy-makers have found themselves at odds with their European counterparts, but for the most part Irish politicians and officials have usually been able to play the European game to Ireland's advantage.

In this case the learning that has occurred has largely been driven from within the Irish foreign policy elite, who have striven to change and shape Irish foreign policy in light of the changing international environment (Rees and Holmes, 2002). Nevertheless, the underlying principles that have guided Ireland's approach to international affairs since the 1950s, and which were reiterated in the 1996 White Paper (Government of Ireland, 1996), are still evident today in the formulation and conduct of Irish foreign policy. For example, the renewed commitment in the 2006 White Paper on development aid, leading to a number of new policy developments in this arena, reflects Ireland's fundamental support for developing states (Government of Ireland, 2006). Ireland remains strongly committed to international peacekeeping, as evident in its recent commitment of troops in Liberia and Lebanon, as well as in Europe, where it has contributed to ESDP missions such as in Kosovo. At times Irish foreign policy was slow to adapt to Europe, given domestic political concerns around neutrality, but this no longer seems as relevant today as it did in the post-Cold War era. Irish foreign policy is firmly embedded in European foreign policy, but is still distinctive, reflecting core underlying Irish foreign policy principles, with the state having gained immensely from coordination and cooperation with other EU states in the foreign and security policy arena.

8

Cooperation on Justice under the Third Pillar: Propping up a Shaky Consensus?

Barry Vaughan

Introduction

Talk of justice or police cooperation in Europe through its official designation as the third pillar of Europe can beguile us. It suggests some classically constructed edifice erected with attention to symmetry and detail. In reality, the third pillar is more akin to a strut used to prop up a building constructed in haste whilst the owners argue about appropriate renovations. Although circumstances seem to demand closer cooperation between the law enforcement agencies, immigration bureaux and judiciary of member states, individual governments often make the running and try to align others to their views. Sometimes this works but, since decisions have to be forged from consensus, grand ambitions are often thwarted for the sake of functional compromises. Despite increases in migration and asylum claims in Europe in the 1990s and the urgency of counter-terrorism in the new millennium, agreement on justice matters has not been easily won since member states still prize their capacity to arrest, prosecute and sanction in matters of criminal justice and to admit and expel in affairs of asylum and migration. As Max Weber foretold, one of the defining features of the state is its legitimate monopoly on physical violence and member states are reluctant to relinquish this capacity.

Allowing for the primacy of member states should not obscure the scale and scope of developments that have occurred under what has become known as the third pillar. This chapter begins with an overview of the genesis of justice and police cooperation in the 1970s and its reliance on informal working groups. This emphasis on what has been called 'intergovernmental' working arrangements has been somewhat curtailed by developments in the 1990s and beyond but the very designation of police and judicial cooperation as a third pillar indicates that it is not a core competence of the European Union. Situating it thus has meant that, despite agreements on matters such as expedited extradition procedures, there is no clear infringement procedure to invoke against those countries which are tardy in their implementation or whose courts resist EU developments on the ground of inconsistency with national constitutions (Leczykiewicz, 2007). An inability to devise harmonious policies across all member states, a problem that only increases with enlargement of the EU, has led some countries to revert to intergovernmental arrangements with little reference to the EU. This is not the end of the story, for the Commission has recently won a criminal competence in the area of environmental protection, a capacity which it wishes to extend into other core objectives. It remains to be seen how well the third pillar resists these twin pressures of intergovernmental processes and supranational procedures in matters of security and criminal justice.

Cooperation behind closed doors – 1970s to 1990s

To appreciate the incremental approach to the construction of what has become known as the third pillar, we need to reach back into its origins in the 1970s as an ad hoc arrangement between governments to combat terrorism. Despite greater formalisation over the years, the third pillar has been characterised by uncertainty and incrementalism as governments have been slow to cede powers in this most delicate of areas.

Although cooperation in policing matters amongst European nations extends as far back as the nineteenth century, it was not until the 1970s, after several countries had experiences with domestic terrorism, that European Ministers for Justice and Home Affairs formed the Trevi group – named after the venue of the first meeting – to coordinate their anti-terrorist efforts (Anderson *et al.,* 1995). The group operated on a 'wholly intergovernmental and confidential basis and was responsible solely to national ministers' (Tonra, 1997, p. 51). A number of working groups developed from this initial meeting: the first, created in 1977, dealt with anti-terrorism; the second dealt with policing and later enveloped public order concerns such as football hooliganism in the mid-1980s; and the third dealt with serious crimes such as arms and drug trafficking. The evolution of these groups was largely reactive in nature, as perceived crises became matters of public concern.

Developments in justice and home affairs were prodded along by the decision of five governments (Belgium, France, Germany, Luxembourg and the Netherlands) to sign the Schengen Agreement, which abolished border controls between their countries. The slow emergence of a 'single European space' gave rise to a series of 'compensatory measures' to maintain internal security within a single market, as enunciated at a European Council meeting in 1989. In 1990 the Schengen Convention specified what these measures would be, including a common visa regime, an electronic database termed the Schengen Information System (SIS) and policies on asylum and immigration. Schengen has been fundamental both in setting a cast for the future development of immigration policies and for aligning immigration with security concerns and blurring the boundaries between borders. As Guild comments, 'the border of the Netherlands for the admission of aliens is to be found at the edge of the frontiers of all the Schengen states. Thus Germany, France, Italy etc. are part of Dutch sovereignty for the purpose of the borders for persons' (cited in Mac Éinrí, 2002, p. 41). A country's borders are now found not at the limits of its own geographical territory but at the extremities of the area of free movement. And this has decisive consequences for those countries outside the 'security zone' of Schengen:

> As the system developed most of the EU members 'outside' became not only worried about being excluded from the political dynamic of the 'core' which Schengen claimed to be but also about becoming a sort of buffer zone for unwanted aliens and criminal activities outside of the new 'security wall' erected by the Schengen members. Italy's decision, for instance, to join Schengen in 1992 was very much motivated by these considerations. As a result most of the EU 'outs' struggled hard to meet the standards set by the 'ins', and the more former 'outs' joined the stronger this dynamic of inclusion became (Monar, 2000, p. 8).

Also in 1990 the Dublin Convention established that the state in which an asylum seeker first lands has the responsibility of examining the claim for asylum. Its function was to prevent multiple applications for asylum in several member states (so-called 'asylum shopping') and restrict the uncontrolled circulation of asylum seekers. Due to lengthy ratification procedures, it only entered into force in September 1997. One of the most important mechanisms for ensuring the efficiency of the Dublin Convention has been a fingerprinting system known as EURODAC, which stores details on all individuals over fourteen years of age.

Migration became a fulcrum of concern, much to the disgust of many academics who see a tendency to transform 'social relations into security relations' (Huysmans, quoted in Loader, 2002, p. 135). Bigo (2002) claims that a self-interested coterie of security professionals have identified the problem of immigration as one to be resolved by greater recourse to security measures – more surveillance, border control etc., what Loader (2002) has termed the 'securitisation of Europe'. Whilst it is not the purpose of this chapter to adjudicate on these claims, they are nevertheless important for drawing attention to how the 'problems' of migration and security have become more central to a European order and identity, as articulated through the third pillar. I will return to this point in the conclusion.

Erecting the third pillar – Maastricht and Amsterdam

It is undeniable that towards the end of the 1980s and the beginning of the 1990s there were significant concerns about the phenomenon of migration. Some of this concern was stimulated by the completion of the single market in 1992 and the subsequent spillover effect on the movement of people. The collapse of communism led to fears, particularly within Germany, of a swathe of people moving westwards. In the run-up to the Maastricht Treaty on European Union, the German government was committed to incorporating justice and home affairs fully into the business of the EU. Other governments were more protective of state sovereignty and were unwilling to accede to a Community competence in this area; the end result was an awkward compromise between allowing the institutions of the EU to have extensive responsibilities in the area and continuing with closed discussions between representatives of national governments. Minor 'concessions to an input from the essential community institutions such as the Commission, the Parliament and the Court of Justice' were made whilst the primary emphasis on 'co-operation between member states and collaboration between the relevant departments of their administrations' remained (Walsh, 2000, p. 24).

The Maastricht Treaty on European Union (TEU) explicitly recognised the sphere of justice and home affairs as a third pillar of the EU to be managed by intergovernmental processes (also known as Title VI of the TEU). Most areas of European cooperation were provided for under the first pillar (or community pillar), while the foreign and security policy made up the second pillar. The treaty listed nine policy areas as matters of common interest: asylum policy, the crossing of external borders, immigration, combating drug addiction, combating international fraud, judicial cooperation in civil matters, judicial cooperation in criminal matters, customs cooperation and police cooperation (Barrett, 1997).

Title VI established four legal instruments. *Joint positions* elaborate the Union's agreed position on a matter of common interest. For example, the first joint position related to the definition of the term 'refugee' as expressed in the 1951 Geneva Convention to ensure that the same criteria were being used across the EU. *Framework decisions* aim to ensure that the laws and regulations of the member states approximate to each other. Like directives (the instruments used in the first pillar), framework decisions are binding upon the member states as to the result to be achieved but leave the choice of form and methods to the national authorities. *Decisions* are used for purposes other than the approximation of laws and regulations. These decisions are binding and the Council, acting by a qualified majority, adopts the measures necessary to implement them at EU level. Neither framework decisions nor decisions have direct effect, i.e. are enforceable by citizens of the member states. The fourth instrument, the *convention*, reflects a joint undertaking and is recommended to member states for adoption in accordance with their own constitutional requirements. Unless they provide otherwise, conventions enter into force once they have been ratified by at least half of the member states that adopt them. For example, the idea of a European Police Office or Europol was aired under German bidding at the Luxembourg European Council in June 1991, although the outcome did not meet German expectations of a European FBI. Instead, it acts as a conduit for information between different countries and undertakes intelligence analysis. The convention setting up Europol was not signed until July 1995; it entered into force in October 1998 and has been implemented only since July 1999.

Despite admissions of common interest, officials within individual jurisdictions had become used to working to domestic agendas and found it difficult to shift to a more cooperative mindset (Lavenex and Wallace, 2005). Tonra (1997, p. 55) likened the attempt to drive forward a common security policy as being hampered by having 'twelve [the number of member states in 1992] pairs of hands at the wheel – and twelve feet on the brake'. Apart from the difficulty of getting unanimity, the input by the Court of Justice and European Parliament was also lamented. Unsurprisingly then, in a review in 1996, the operation of the third pillar was found to be 'clearly defective' (quoted in Tonra, 1997, p. 55). Three principal defects were evident: ambiguity about the legality of many policy proposals; the low level of accountability attaching to these proposals, reflecting the original nature of the Trevi group; and the lack of any means of ensuring that agreed policies were being implemented (Lavenex and Wallace, 2005).

Several views were canvassed as remedies. An initial proposal was to develop justice and home affairs as a Community competence, in effect to transfer it into the first pillar. This was an incursion too far for some but a compromise was reached whereby matters pertaining to free movement, asylum and immigration were transferred to the first pillar. The United Kingdom, Denmark and Ireland were apprehensive about this move which was further complicated by the decision to incorporate the Schengen *acquis*, even though this had no definitive text but consisted of a set of working arrangements. Schengen arrangements became the template for EU border management, which had the unforeseen result of blurring the lines between internal and external security as borders between countries became permeable.

The provisions that were agreed under the Amsterdam Treaty of 1997 have been described as 'unprecedented in their complexity' and as involving a 'patchwork of opt-ins within opt-outs' (McDonagh, 1998, pp. 181–182) for the three aforementioned countries depending on the position in question. Since the UK chose to opt out of the incorporation of the Schengen *acquis*, Ireland followed suit in order to preserve the Common Travel Agreement with the UK. Yet both countries secured an 'opt-in' policy to cooperate on particular aspects of Schengen, a prerogative that they would both later exercise. Ireland confessed that it would strive to adopt the measures to the 'maximum extent compatible' with preservation of the Common Travel Area, which shows how Ireland was 'torn between its commitment to maintain the Common Travel Area and its wish to participate in deeper integration in EU justice and home affairs' (Monar, 2000, p. 10). To avoid the repetition of exclusive intergovernmental collaboration on the lines of Schengen, Title VI of the TEU now provides that member states intending to establish closer cooperation may be authorised to do so within the EU framework.

Towards an area of freedom, security and justice

The other major outcome of the Treaty of Amsterdam was the aspiration to develop the first and third pillars (the latter was formally redesignated as 'Police and Judicial Co-operation in Criminal Matters') into an area of freedom, security and justice as a way of ensuring that Europe became 'more relevant to its citizens' (cited in Lavenex and Wallace, 2005, p. 464). Freedom was defined in terms of the provision of free movement within the EU for those legitimately residing there. This internal freedom was complemented by the existence of intensified external controls, which were justified as providing security for those residing within the EU's borders. Justice was defined primarily in terms of 'improving links between prosecuting authorities in pursuing cross-border criminals' (den Boer and Wallace, 2000, p. 497) and increasing judicial cooperation.

Adjustments were also made to the manner of decision-making. Joint actions were replaced by framework decisions. All conventions would have effect once they have been ratified by half of the signatory member states. The Commission, together with the member states, gained the right of initiative that was extended to cover all areas under the third pillar. The Treaty of Amsterdam also allowed for enhanced cooperation amongst some member states when their desired objectives could not be attained by agreement with all member states. The Treaty of Nice later specified that this mechanism should only be activated as a 'last resort'.

Despite this concession to flexibility, efforts were still made to advance cooperation in a uniform fashion. In 1998 Jack Straw, the British Home Secretary, contended that further alignment in criminal law was needed (den Boer and Wallace, 2000). The British government was talking openly about the abolition of extradition and the need for arrest warrants enforceable throughout Europe. In July 1998 the Commission President suggested it would be useful for the heads of state to devote a European Council meeting to justice and home affairs. The Finnish government took up this proposal and embarked on a tour of capital cities to generate enthusiasm and proposals for the meeting in Tampere in October 1999. Although there was ambitious talk of generating a work programme comparable to that which accompanied the single market, one Finnish diplomat was more downbeat, commenting that the purpose of the Tampere Summit was 'to make sure that our heads of government at last understand what they signed up to at Amsterdam' (den Boer and Wallace, 2000, p. 517).

The Tampere Accord listed a series of objectives dedicated towards a 'Union of Security, Freedom and Justice'. The first objective pertains to the harmonisation of laws so that behaviours contrary to common European values, such as human trafficking and money laundering, should be prosecuted and punished in the same way everywhere in the EU. Moves to approximate certain aspects of criminal procedure, for instance the standing of victims, also began to germinate. The second objective relates to mutual recognition which was acknowledged as the mainstay of judicial cooperation. Mutual recognition arises when a member state agrees to recognise as valid a decision taken in another jurisdiction even if that decision might have been taken differently or had another outcome in the first jurisdiction. This allows for a greater recognition of the diverse ways through which different jurisdictions can secure justice but does run the risk of inconsistencies in procedural justice arising. For example, a European evidence warrant that allows for the acquisition of objects or data may be issued by a judicial authority that may in some jurisdictions include police officers. Some deem mutual recognition more appropriate than a harmonisation of laws since it is based on a 'tolerance of diversity on the basis of mutual confidence and trust in others' legal systems, as opposed to insistence of uniformity for its own sake' (quoted in Ryan, 2006, p. 8). The third objective has been fulfilled by the creation of coordination bodies. Perhaps one of the most notable is Eurojust, composed of one judge from each of the twenty-seven member states, whose aim is to improve the cooperation between national personnel investigating and prosecuting serious crime.

Cooperation before terror?

The Tampere Accord was accelerated and augmented by the terrorist attacks of 9/11 and later bombings in Madrid and London that resulted in significant fatalities. Previously, terrorism was viewed largely as a matter of domestic concern but the perceived transnational nature of Al'Qaeda instilled a desire to have more effective methods of prosecution across borders. At the Laeken European Council in December 2001, a call was made for 'better management of the Union's external borders'. The Commission made an original proposal for a European border police in 2002, which ran foul of member states' desire to maintain their sovereignty; instead, countries agreed to cooperate on joint operations maintaining border controls.

A five-year review of the Tampere programme was explicit about the reluctance of member states to 'co-operate within this new European framework when their interests are at stake' (European Commission, 2004a, p. 4). Moreover, their right of initiative, shared with the Commission, ensured that national concerns were often given priority over the Tampere programme. Despite the misgivings about the level of progress achieved, developments within and outside the EU demanded a fresh impetus. One of the most important developments within the EU was the extension of membership to ten new member states in May 2004. Enlargement required the strengthening of external borders and the preparation of the new member states for the removal of all internal border controls and the setting up of a second-generation SIS. Requiring new member states to submit to the Schengen regime may well cause resentment given that Ireland, the UK and Denmark have secured an opt-out clause with the option to opt in when they deem it necessary (an option which the UK and Ireland exercised in 2000 and 2002 by participating in SIS and by agreeing to strengthen police cooperation).

The process of enlargement also required efforts to ground the principle of mutual recognition and establish confidence in the propriety of the workings of individual justice systems. These aspirations were realised in the Hague programme which set objectives to be achieved in the period from 2005 to 2010. With the aim of strengthening freedom, the document urged a coordinated migration and a common asylum system. Managing migration flows was also identified as a priority and the implementation of the Schengen *acquis* was seen as pivotal. Information systems incorporating biometric information from the visa application stage to entry and exit were also deemed necessary for both migration and crime control. A significant output of the Hague programme has been the establishment of the European Agency for the Management of Operational Cooperation at the External Borders (FRONTEX) in 2005. FRONTEX's functions include coordinating the management of borders, the establishment of common training standards for border guards and the conducting of risk analysis. Perhaps the greatest innovation of FRONTEX is the proposal to create Rapid Border Intervention Teams (RABITs) that could be assigned to locations faced with a large influx of third-party nationals. These teams would be under the command of the requesting member state.

Security was to be strengthened by a greater priority granted to the exchange of information concerning threats to all member states. Information should not be held back by individual member states if evidence of a threat to another member state emerged – the so-called 'principle of availability' of information. Furthermore, it envisaged by 2008 the interoperability of national databases and access to existing information systems such as SIS. In March 2005 the Luxembourg Council presidency entered a note on efficient information exchange: 'The aim is obviously that as large a list of information categories as possible is exchangeable with as little effort as possible (ie: requiring a minimum of formalities, permissions, procedures, *if any*)' (quoted in Statewatch, 2006, p. 3 – emphasis added).

Justice was to be augmented by 'the progressive development of a European judicial culture based on diversity of the legal systems of the Member States and unity through European law' (Council of the European Union, 2004, p. 27). This would be achieved by the certainty that all European citizens have access to a judicial system meeting high standards of quality. To ensure the full implementation of the principle of mutual recognition, a system for evaluating the achievement or otherwise of EU policies in the field of justice was deemed necessary. An action plan arising from these commitments was adopted in 2005 and a review published in 2006. To understand why such a move is necessary, it is instructive to examine the fate of the European arrest warrant.

Nations obstructing justice

In 2002 the European Council assented to a European arrest warrant (EAW), which came into force in Ireland on 1 January 2004. One of the most high-profile cases in which the EAW has been used has been the forced repatriation of Hussain Osman, a suspect in the 7/7 bombings, from Rome to London. However, the operation of the EAW has experienced obstacles in terms of member states' compliance (House of Lords, 2006a), which underlines some of the difficulties of making progress in this area. In April 2005 the Polish Constitutional Tribunal annulled implementation of the EAW framework because it conflicted with the constitutional prohibition on extraditing Polish nationals. The tribunal held that the individual liberties contained within the Polish constitution 'indicate a minimum and unsurpassable threshold which may not be lowered or questioned as a result of the introduction of Community provisions' (quoted in Komarek, 2007, p. 3). The Federal Constitutional Court of Germany argued that the strict principle of mutual recognition 'cannot restrict the [national] constitutional guarantee of fundamental rights' (quoted in Komarek, 2007, p. 13) and found implementation of the EAW to be unconstitutional. The Polish case touched on the matter of the primacy of EU law under the third pillar, whereas the German case challenges the very principle of mutual recognition, since it refused to take on trust the bona fides of foreign judicial systems. Instead, it insisted that in every individual case a review of the requesting country's judicial system must be made to see if it conforms with German constitutional requirements. Treating this as an act of self-exclusion from the European system of judicial cooperation, the Spanish courts began to treat German requests for surrender of nationals under the EAW as conventional requests for extradition even though the conventions governing extradition were replaced by the framework decision introducing the EAW.

The German case is symptomatic of the difficulties of building a European judicial culture based upon the criminal and civil systems of twenty-seven different member states. A recent ruling from the European Court of Justice (C-303/05 *Advocaten voor de Wereld*) would seem to differ from the German interpretation. It considered that the framework decision establishing the EAW 'does not seek to harmonise the criminal offences in question in respect of their constituent elements or of the penalties which they attract' (para. 52), which counters the German demand that there be complete congruence in the definition and prosecution of offences. Yet the court also insisted that, by virtue of Article 6 of the TEU, member states are bound to observe the rule of law and ensure that they respect fundamental rights as articulated in the European Convention on Human Rights (ECHR). Whether this entails a convergence upon recognised standards in terms of procedural protections remains to be seen (Jackson, 2005). If this is achieved by reference to the ECHR, upon which the EU has increasingly relied, then it is not necessarily of benefit since the ECHR may, in some respects, fall short of the protection afforded by the Irish constitution (O'Mahony, 2000). The fundamental difficulty is of reconciling practices and principles of different legal and judicial systems, of which the distinction between the adversarial system of common law countries such as Britain and Ireland and the inquisitorial system of many continental countries is the most vivid.

The difficulties surrounding the implementation of the EAW and the lack of an effective redress procedure against refractory member states (Leczykiewicz, 2007) has led the Commission to propose a new modus operandi for the third pillar in order to avoid individual member states holding a veto over future developments.

Beyond blockages?

One of the most striking features of the proposals was the evident frustration with the 'recurrent difficulties leading to numerous blockages' in the area of freedom, security and justice (European Commission, 2006c, p. 5). Progress proved impossible on a decision to enable cross-border investigation and prosecution whilst there had been no unanimity on the European evidence warrant. Agreement has been sparse on the subject of procedural rights throughout the EU whilst the definition and criminalisation of the offences of racism and xenophobia had been stalled for two years. The Commission compared this tardiness to the progress in the first pillar, where a directive on data retention had been produced within three months. The Commission suggested that further progress could be achieved by the invocation of bridging clauses whereby policy areas can be governed by the Community method, subject to a unanimous vote of the Council of Ministers, without an amendment to existing treaties. Applying the Community method to the third pillar would, according to the Commission, allow the use of Community legislative instruments such as regulations and directives; favour consensus under qualified majority voting; and bringing the area of justice, security and freedom under one legal framework would allow more legal certainty and efficiency.

The Finnish presidency from July to December 2006 labelled these problems as ones of deficient efficiency. But it also spoke of deficient implementation, whereby national implementation of framework decisions has been slow with the Commission powerless to initiate infringement proceedings against member states for failure to implement third pillar decisions. And the cumbersome method of decision-making was also said to impair legitimacy, given the limited involvement of the European Parliament and the Court of Justice. Finland proposed invoking Article 42 of the TEU (the so-called 'passerelle clause') that makes provision for the policy areas of the third pillar to migrate to the first pillar where the Council will determine the relevant voting procedures, which can include the loss of the national veto. A majority of countries were fiercely opposed to these proposals. In response, the Commission (2006b, p. 14) cited a judgment from 1996 calling for the abolition of 'certain sorts of police and judicial protectionism' and reasserted that 'this demand is still top of our agenda'.

Despite this strong defence of nation-state sovereignty, national agendas may be undermined in another way. In February 2005 a European Court of Justice (ECJ) ruling found that the Commission can impose criminal sanctions for breaches of European environment law. The Council had contested this initiative on the grounds that to seek the harmonisation of criminal sanctions was a matter for the third pillar even if the objective – protection of the environment – was laudable. The Commission contended that since the protection of the environment was one of the core competencies of the EU, and as it considered that legislation would only be effective with the backing of criminal sanctions, the EU institutions should be able to legislate for criminal sanctions through the first pillar. Although the court agreed that the EU did not possess a general competence in criminal matters, this should not

> ... prevent the Community legislature, when the application of effective, proportionate and dissuasive criminal penalties by the competent national authorities is an essential measure for combating serious environmental offences, from taking measures which relate to the criminal law of the Member States which it considers necessary in order to ensure that the rules which it lays down on environmental protection are fully effective (Case C-176/03, judgment of 13 September 2005, para. 48).

Despite the lack of clarity surrounding the implications of this judgment, it now forms, in the words of former Irish Minister for Justice Michael McDowell, an 'immovable part of their [ECJ's] jurisprudence' (House of Lords, 2006b, Q165). Whilst member states have insisted that this competence only applies to the policy area of environmental protection dealt with in the case, the Commission considered that the judgment laid down principles 'which "go far beyond the case in question" and which may apply to other Community policies and to the free movement of persons, goods, services and capital' (cited in House of

Lords, 2006b, para. 42), a point of view supported by many legal experts. In fact, McDowell complained that the ECJ ruling 'asserts a general competence without in any way being sharp as to where the edges of that competence lie' (House of Lords, 2006b, Q173).

In February 2007 the Commission proposed that the new directive specify a list of serious environmental offences, a similar level of liability as well as a level of penalties incurred. This would ensure that 'serious cases of environmental crime are dealt with in a similar manner in all Member States and that perpetrators cannot take benefit from the existing differences in national legislation' (European Commission, 2007b, p. 3). The proposal outlines a minimum basis for sanctions and member states are 'free to maintain or introduce more stringent measures than those foreseen in the directive' (European Commission, 2007b, p. 3).

Despite this communitisation of criminal justice, some member states have become dissatisfied with the rate of progress on security matters and have forged their own agreement. Seven countries (Austria, Belgium, France, Germany, Luxembourg, the Netherlands and Spain) signed the Treaty of Prüm to engender greater cooperation in combating crime, migration and terrorism. Measures included the exchange of information such as DNA and vehicle registrations, the deployment of air marshals in civil aviation, the seconding of advisers to countries that have been the source of illegal migrants, and closer police cooperation involving joint patrols and other operational matters. The treaty entered into force between Austria, Germany and Spain in November 2006 and Luxembourg in December of that year and the remaining countries hope to ratify the treaty in 2007.

Some have characterised Prüm as continuing in the experimental spirit of Schengen, whereas others have countered that it has neglected twenty years of development of the third pillar and risks undermining it by setting up a club within a club. Post-Schengen developments can be read as trying to pre-empt precisely this possibility, even at the cost of introducing a Byzantine system of complexity the implications of which are unclear to many. The Treaty of Prüm might legitimately be accused of undermining the coherence of the system by reintroducing variable arrangements. In doing so, it risks undermining trust between member states, which, as illustrated by the EAW, is still fragile. And, by reverting back to intergovernmental arrangements, it has diminished the transparency of arrangements, which has been a fundamental criticism of the third pillar since before it was formally constituted (Balzacq *et al.*, 2006).

Conclusion

Monar (2000, p. 5) offers the following judgement on the effects of the third pillar upon the EU:

> A 'fortress Europe' may well emerge, with higher and more homogeneous external walls, but internally it will continue to be a system of interlocking but separate national security zones. The exclusive effects of the 'fortress' are therefore likely to continue to vary from one zone to the other in spite of the common rationale.

It is curious that Monar does not note how this fortress mentality has sprung from efforts to develop the freedoms enunciated within the Treaty of Rome (1957). As noted above, the elevation of the third pillar coincided with the completion of the single market and the abolition of many border controls between countries. To compensate, countries have tried to establish a common security zone by linking up the various systems used to manage security, asylum and immigration. Mathieson (2006) prophesises that there is increasing horizontal integration of these systems whilst the level of vertical integration into national states is being weakened as their operation is being decoupled from any scrutiny at this level. Another, perhaps more significant, consequence is that this horizontal integration may introduce an element of 'function creep' as systems designed to monitor asylum, for example, are being increasingly used for security purposes. Mitsilegas (2007) argues that as a result of the Hague programme's emphasis on the availability and interoperability of databases, the very nature of the SIS is being changed:

> ... with the system being transformed from an alerts mechanism accessed for specific immigration control or law enforcement purposes on a hit/no hit basis, to a general law enforcement database, to be accessed for a wide range of purposes. A related concern involves proposals to enable the interlinking of alerts in SIS [Mark] II. Interlinking of alerts may thus lead to a detailed profiling of individuals and the change in the nature of the SIS. This development, along with broadening the purpose of SIS and extending access to the database to a number of authorities, may lead to the collapse of the current distinction between SIS 'immigration' and 'police' data. The European Data Protection Supervisor has also noted that the introduction of links between alerts is 'a very typical feature of a police investigative tool'.

Heeding how a policing mentality may pervade other functions only returns us to the issue of police cooperation. Its improvement was one of the purposes in establishing the Trevi group but it is an issue that has not been resolved despite the decades of institutional reform. Taking Europol as an exemplar of this, it has been criticised for 'inefficiency, cumbersome procedures and has been plagued by intra-institutional and political expediencies' (Mitsilegas, 2007). Of course, these deficiencies should not be laid at the door of Europol since its effectiveness depends almost entirely on the willingness of member states to contribute to an organisation that may lack the legitimising credentials of a national entity.

This is indicative of the wider problem of legitimacy within the EU about which so much has been written in recent years (Schmidt, 2006). It is acknowledged that without a European demos, affiliation to the European order will always be tentative and recalcitrant as developments in the sphere of justice have shown. Canvassing for an alternative to the strong bonds of nationalism, it has been suggested that the EU should recognise solidarity whilst embracing difference, what has been called a cosmopolitan order (Beck and Grande, 2007; Vaughan and Kilcommins, 2007). The determination of the original Treaty of Rome to 'lay the foundations of an ever closer union among the peoples of Europe' affirms the diversity of Europe whilst seeking to strengthen solidarity amongst its constituent member states, what has been more specifically enunciated as 'border-transcending solidarity based upon the recognition of the rights of others' (Offe and Preuss, 2006, p. 27). This form of solidarity:

> ... can only mean the denationalization of rights. While democracy, as we have demonstrated, is inevitably tied to the demos of a nation state, solidarity as the endowment of others with rights and claims is an achievement that supranational agencies specialize in and derive their legitimacy from. To the extent that the EU (as a special case of a supranational agency) is able to free rights, including social and economic rights, from their national containers and make them available to all Union citizens, it gains access to the same kind of legitimacy (Offe and Preuss, 2006, p. 28).

The Commission has striven to reform the decision-making process to avoid the national veto and to free rights from their 'national containers'. The customary interpretation is that they have been rebuffed, with the result that countries determined to accentuate security procedures have collaborated amongst themselves by signing the Treaty of Prüm. But the example of the criminal law competence granted to the EC in the case of environmental protection shows how rights might be enforced in spite of the wishes of nation-states. The third pillar has always been a shaky edifice but it may become more unstable in future years as member states set up exclusive arrangements in security matters and the Commission employs the criminal law to achieve many of the EU's core objectives. The Treaty of Rome set itself the achievement of certain fundamental freedoms yet this aim went largely unrealised until the advent of qualified majority voting allowed Europe to escape the sovereignty trap of the national veto. It may be that the development of justice policies requires similarly courageous and creative thinking to inspire member states to forsake treasured practices and to meet new challenges.

9

The View from the Minister's Chair

Alan Dukes

The background

When Ireland first joined the European Economic Community (as it was in 1973), relatively few of the fifteen members of the cabinet had a close involvement in decision-making on European affairs. At that time EEC legislation was the preserve of the Council of Ministers, which was (and still is) composed of ministers from each of the member states meeting to make decisions and to pass laws. In the interests of effective functioning, the Council had (and still has) a number of 'formations': Foreign Ministers meet in the General Affairs and External Relations Council (GAERC), Finance Ministers meet in the Economic and Financial Affairs Council (ECOFIN), Agriculture Ministers meet in the Agriculture Council, and so on.

In the 1970s the Ministers for External Affairs, Agriculture, and Finance, as well as the Minister for Industry and Commerce (who then dealt with transport questions), were the Irish government members most deeply and frequently involved in EEC decision-making in the Council of Ministers:

- The Minister for External Affairs dealt with 'high policy', such as over-seas development aid (where the EEC was already a major player), and the very few world-level issues that impinged on the EEC, which had no foreign policy to speak of and no treaty competence to speak of it
- The popular perception of the job of the Minister for Agriculture was to bring home as much money as possible through the mechanisms of the Common Agricultural Policy (CAP)
- The Minister for Finance was popularly perceived to have the function of making sure that Ireland paid out as little as possible to the Community budget
- The Minister for Industry and Commerce, operating in the transport field, had very little Community business. The Common Transport Policy, as it then was, affected Ireland only through regulation of truck drivers'

hours of work. Provisions relating to inland waterway transport did not affect Ireland, little of what the Community did about rail transport affected Ireland's isolated rail system, and the Community had not yet developed any real policies in the aviation sector. There were demands on this minister in relation to trade issues, since the member states still had a wide range of ingenious ways of trying to protect their national markets against competition from other member states (through devices usually referred to as 'technical barriers to trade'). In addition, the Community, which still had appreciable tariffs on imports from third countries, was frequently in conflict with trading nations elsewhere, requiring attention on the part of ministers dealing with trade issues.

Other ministers were occasionally involved in 'informal' meetings with their counterparts in the other member states. These meetings usually took the form of rather polite and academic exchanges of views on common concerns which were only tenuously related (if at all) to any identifiable treaty competence.

The European Council (in which the heads of state or government of the member states meet) had not yet been set up, so the Taoiseach had very little involvement in 'Brussels' and its doings. This was due to some extent to the fact that the Community had made only modest progress in the policy areas (other than agriculture and, to a lesser extent, transport) set out in the Treaty of Rome.

Things have changed enormously in the last thirty-four years. The Community – now the Union – has pressed on with the common policies provided for in the Rome Treaty. The most evident of these have been:

• The single market programme
• Economic and monetary union and the euro
• Liberalisation of utilities sectors previously dominated by national monopolies (energy, telecommunications, postal services, aviation).

In addition, the European Council has increasingly taken a leadership role in setting out the broad directions of Union action.

The Single European Act of 1986 opened the way to European Political Cooperation, and the Treaty of Maastricht, concluded in 1992, brought a foreign policy dimension to the Union's activities.

International crime, illegal immigration and trafficking of women and children for sexual purposes have all obliged the Union to take concerted action where action by individual member states will inevitably be inadequate. This has led to a significant range of actions in the area of justice and home affairs.

Another major change affecting the role of ministers has been the development of the codecision procedure, which makes the European Parliament an equal legislative partner with the Council of Ministers over the greater part of Union decision-making. This effectively puts an extra duty on ministers, either to anticipate the mood of the Parliament on given legislative proposals or to engage in negotiation and conciliation with the Parliament in the (not uncommon) event of a divergence of views.

When Ireland joined the EEC, the members of the European Parliament were appointed by their national parliaments and, apart from some important functions in relation to the Community budget, were either 'consulted' or merely 'informed' about legislative proposals. As an institution, the European Parliament hardly figured on the ministerial radar.

The EEC and the Union have, since Ireland became a member state, developed a series of actions in relation to social and labour market policies. Together with the development of the actions in the 2002 Lisbon Agenda to improve the Union's competitive capacity, these moves have widened the scope of common action in these fields.

The changing security environment, the prevalence of both 'frozen' and 'hot' conflicts in the Union's neighbourhood and in areas of concern to the member states, together with the threat of international terrorism, have led the member states to develop appropriate security policy responses. As in so many other fields, they have concluded that concerted action offers better prospects of effectiveness than dispersed actions by individual member states. This has led to new forms of cooperation, both among member states and between the Union and other agencies, in the areas of defence, security and peacekeeping.

The upshot of all of this is that there is hardly a minister in today's Irish cabinet whose work does not have some EU dimension.

Parallel worlds

Irish ministers inhabit up to five parallel worlds simultaneously. That may seem a big claim, but there is nothing fanciful about it. These are respectively: the minister's constituency world, membership of the Dáil, membership of the cabinet, the EU dimension to the minister's work and the contact a minister might have with other international fora.

With only one exception,[1] every Irish minister over the last thirty-four years has been a TD, which brings with it all the considerable constituency pressures of Ireland's peculiarly intimate political system. It involves a

---

[1] Senator Jim Dooge as Minister for Foreign Affairs in 1981 and 1982.

frequency and intensity of personal, face-to-face contacts with constituents, which takes place in 'clinics', meetings with a wide variety of civil society groups and at social and recreational gatherings of every kind. These contacts with constituents have few, if any, parallels in the political systems of the other member states. This is world number one.

Each minister also has to participate in the Dáil, both as the proposer of legislation in her or his portfolio area and as a party member in the same way as other TDs in relation to other ministers' portfolio areas and in relation to the other business of the Dáil. This is world number two.

The work of the cabinet is world number three. Depending on the portfolio, and assuming that the cabinet is working in a reasonably coherent and 'joined-up' way, an individual minister will be involved in some substantive work outside his or her immediate portfolio area. Life in cabinet can be very pressured and demanding. Ideally, every minister will bring to the cabinet table not only the insights and information needed to carry out portfolio duties in a satisfactory manner, but also a fund of political insight and common sense to be applied to the rest of the cabinet's business.

On top of that comes the EU dimension: world number four. Depending on the portfolio, this can constitute a significant extra block of work. The Irish ministers with the heaviest European portfolios are:

- Foreign Affairs
- Finance
- Environment, Heritage and Local Government
- Transport
- Communications, Energy and Natural Resources
- Agriculture, Fisheries and Food
- Enterprise, Trade and Employment
- Justice, Equality and Law Reform (a relative newcomer to the pressure points).

Thus, over half of the members of the cabinet have a heavy involvement in EU affairs. All of the other ministers have some involvement.

The development over the years in the role of the European Council has led to a commensurate increase in the level of the Taoiseach's involvement in EU affairs.

In addition to all of that, EU enlargement (from nine member states when Ireland joined in 1973 to twenty-seven in 2007) has increased both the volume and complexity of work in this world.

The ministers with the heaviest involvement in EU affairs would typically be called on to attend nine or ten full meetings of the Council of

Ministers each year. In addition to that, a number of the Council formations hold informal sessions, although the proliferation of such sessions is now frowned upon.

Preparation for a meeting of the Council of Ministers (see below) will typically involve briefing and tactical analysis in relation to at least one important matter for decision. This, in turn, will frequently involve contact with the Commissioner and with several colleague members of the Council in order to coordinate positions and tactics. In the normal course of events, preparations will also involve a check on previously agreed items being presented to the Council for formal approval and progress reports on matters still in the process of being examined at technical working-group level.

Given the pressure on their diaries, most ministers prefer to cover a meeting of the Council of Ministers in one day, leaving Ireland early in the morning and returning on the evening of the same day. This, of course, is where the much-criticised (but much-prized by busy ministers) 'government jet' really proves its worth.

Some Council meetings can turn into marathon sessions, sometimes lasting through the night into the following day. The annual December meeting of Fisheries Ministers to set quotas and other rules is a case in point. So, for many years, was the annual meeting of Agriculture Ministers on the fixing of support prices and mechanisms (this arduous meeting has now fallen out of the calendar since the MacSharry CAP reforms).

The demands of EU involvement increase enormously for the member states holding the EU presidency. In this connection, it is interesting to note that there is a fairly common acceptance of the view that small member states tend to run rather more successful presidencies than many of the larger ones. The very 'smallness' of their administrations accustoms them to networking and to fluidity of communication. The habits thus acquired are very useful on the EU stage.

World number five consists of various contexts of action on the wider international stage: the UN in the case of the Minister for Foreign Affairs; the International Monetary Fund and the World Bank in the case of the Minister for Finance; the World Trade Organization (WTO, where issues of importance for several ministers are dealt with), OECD, OSCE and various bilateral relationships for all ministers and, indeed, for the Taoiseach. In many cases, an EU dimension (if not a formal agreement to support an agreed position) has to be taken into account.

It is not at all unusual for an individual minister to spend time in three or four of these parallel worlds in the space of a given week. This obviously calls for a significant element of mental toughness and adaptability, not to mention physical stamina. It requires the ability to master and absorb a variety of briefs, positions, modes of thought and modes of action in quick succession. The greatest challenge is to reconcile all of these diverse demands and to construct a coherent personal concept of an integrated political mission.

A diversity of contexts

It will be seen that the scope of most ministerial portfolios has expanded greatly since the 1970s. In 1973 meaningful policy contact with the world outside Ireland (London, the UN in New York and the Vatican) was relatively limited. Most ministers had only limited reasons to look outside this circle in any real policy sense. External Affairs, Industry and Commerce and Agriculture were almost the only ministries to have a significant international dimension. EU membership and, more recently, the increasing pace and scope of globalisation, have changed all this.

The EU context is the most important of the non-domestic contexts. It has changed considerably since Irish accession. This is as a result of successive EU enlargements from nine to 10, 12, 15, 25 and now 27 member states. The process of change from nine to fifteen was challenging enough but the 2004 enlargement, which brought in ten new member states at once, constituted a step change in every conceivable way. It has required a new way of managing relationships, involving every member state and not just the presidency.

Enlargement means that ministers preparing for EU business need to have a grasp of a wider range of national positions than they did previously. They need to expand their personal networks of close working relations and understandings with counterparts from other member states. Simply keeping in touch with their counterparts has become a much more demanding task. All of this is, of course, complicated by the fact that electoral cycles are different in all the member states, so that there is frequently a need to restructure networks and understandings.

Ireland's relations with the rest of the world are substantially affected by EU actions. The clearest example is in the field of trade. The Commission is the designated negotiator for the Union in WTO talks. While the Council of Ministers writes the basic negotiating mandate, it is the Commission which carries out the negotiations.

Aid policy provides another example. The EU has a well-defined and resourced aid programme (the largest in the world), which coexists with a range of bilateral policies run by the member states. Common sense dictates that these different elements should at least be handled in a way which avoids conflicts or inconsistencies – ideally, they should be complementary in order to maximise synergies. This can give rise to some ticklish political issues.

Inconsistencies between the expressions of national interests in member states' policies can create tensions in the Union. At the time of writing in 2007, for example, a number of member states feel somewhat aggrieved by the fact that the German government has entered into an agreement with the Russian government to build a gas pipeline through the Baltic, bypassing Estonia, Latvia, Lithuania and Poland. Others feel that this German move is an invitation to Russia to make a series of bilateral deals with EU member states which will be less advantageous to the EU than an EU–Russia deal. Fears have even been expressed that the several pumping stations proposed to be located in the Baltic along the route of the pipeline will also house Russian 'listening posts' and compromise the integrity of some member states' security systems.

Peacekeeping and peace enforcement are also areas where the variety of contexts can raise some difficult issues. Ireland, for example, cannot participate in an EU mission in Macedonia because of a Chinese veto in the UN Security Council, which means the EU peacekeeping mission does not have a UN mandate. Macedonia recognises Taiwan, China refuses to agree to a UN mandate for action in Macedonia, and this in turn means that Ireland cannot participate: the 'triple lock' remains firmly bolted even though Ireland fully supports the EU position in the matter.

The Council meeting

Preparation

Preparation for a Council of Ministers meeting can be a demanding process.

In respect of issues requiring decisions, most of the angles will have been combed through exhaustively at earlier stages in the process. Before a proposal is actually put to the Council and the European Parliament, the Commission (the initiating authority for virtually every Union initiative) will already have carried out a fairly extensive process of consultation with the member states and will have a clear idea, from the very wide range of contacts which it maintains, as to where the main lobby groups concerned actually stand. When the proposal goes to the Council machine, it will first be examined by an expert working group and by one of the two formations of COREPER (Committee of Permanent Representatives, effectively the member states' ambassadors to the EU) (for details on the preparation work for ministerial meetings carried out at COREPER and working-group levels, see Chapter 10). It is the outcome of this examination that will be reported to the Council. If a satisfactory agreement has been reached, the matter will figure on the Council agenda as an 'A' point, requiring only the formal endorsement of the Council to be recorded as the Council's position.

In respect of important proposals, ministers will normally have engaged with their civil servants in an examination of the implications at national level, and will have been given at least an outline of the positions adopted (or expected to be adopted) by other member states. Where the proposals are complex, or more than normally contentious, they will have considered a series of possible scenarios based on the interplay of positions likely to be adopted in other member states and in the European Parliament.

In the Parliament, the proposal will be referred to the appropriate committee. The committee will report to a plenary session in due course, where it may or may not be the subject of amendments. The product of this process is the European Parliament position.

Where proposals are subject to the codecision procedure and require agreement of both the Council and the European Parliament, the Parliament's position is then compared to that of the Council's. If there are significant differences between the two positions, the matter then goes into a process of conciliation between the Council and the Parliament, with the Commission 'holding the ring'. Depending on the issue, these negotiations can be difficult and contentious and the member state holding the Council presidency can find itself called upon to make judgment calls on delicate issues. There are clear rules for the conduct and conclusion of the conciliation process which are designed to preclude indefinite standoffs between the two legislative institutions.

Both before and during this process, MEPs and ministers are the targets of lobbying by the relevant interest groups at both national and EU levels.

Up to 2002, individual Irish ministers could often go to Council discussions at something of a disadvantage, not having been exposed to detailed expressions of political views outside the range of those put, examined and reported by the national civil service. National civil servants cannot always or reasonably be expected to be fully *au fait* with the variety of views coming through the national political system. It was only with the adoption in 2002 of the practice of ministers appearing before Oireachtas committees in advance of meetings of the Council of Ministers that Irish ministers began to relate to the national parliament in a way analogous to the practices in Denmark, Finland, Estonia and the Netherlands. Up to then, the Oireachtas had only rudimentary provisions for examination of EU legislative proposals before positions had to be adopted by Irish ministers in the Council of Ministers.

The meeting

If the Irish minister is making an 'over and back' visit in one day, there will be an early departure from Dublin Airport or Casement Aerodrome (depending on the transport arrangements). If such an 'over and back' visit is not logistically possible, departure will be on the evening preceding the Council of Ministers meeting. Whatever the logistical arrangements may be, there will be a briefing on arrival in Brussels by the Irish Permanent Representative to the EU or by some of the specialised staff of the Irish Permanent Representation (many of them on secondment from their home departments). This briefing will be intended to supplement the briefing already carried out at departmental level and to give a final update on any late developments in the positions of the other member states or of the Commission. This is when the finishing touches are put to the opening positions to be adopted in relation to issues to be decided at the meeting or when the parameters are finally set out for contributions to any orientation debates scheduled for the meeting.

The minister will normally be accompanied at the meeting by one or more senior departmental officials and by the Irish Permanent Representative or by a specialist from the Irish Permanent Representation. The Council occasionally goes into restricted session to reduce the number of officials in the room when particularly sensitive issues are discussed. Usually the formula is 'minister plus one'. Occasionally it is 'ministers only'.

The first business of the meeting is to agree the list of 'A' points – these are matters which have already been agreed at COREPER or expert working-group level and simply require the formal assent of the Council. This is normally a matter of course – second-guessing by ministers at this stage goes down very badly with their colleagues.

The meeting then moves on to the substantive points on the agenda. In respect of items requiring a decision, the positions of the ministers will usually be fairly well known. COREPER or the appropriate expert working group will have painstakingly combed through the issues. The Council secretariat will have clarified any (or most) of the points of obscurity in member states' positions. The object of all this preparation is to ensure that the Council can concentrate on any differences of substance between the member states and on political sensitivities.

In the normal course of events, discussion continues until a position emerges which all member states can accept. This, of course, is essential in matters requiring unanimity. It is also the norm in matters which can be decided either by qualified majority voting (QMV) or by simple majority. All ministers are keenly aware of the fact that those who might be tempted to force the pace on a given issue could find themselves on the receiving end of a similar approach by others on another issue. Notwithstanding the provisions in the Council's rules of procedure, voting is the exception rather than the rule.

Most debates in Council take place in a spirit of give and take, since the work is output-driven. Technical difficulties will normally have been ironed out before a dossier arrives on the Council table so that the Council discussion is purely political. The Commission participates in all Council debates and has the dual role of watching out for the overall Community interest and of proposing (wherever necessary) amendments to proposals designed to facilitate ultimate agreement.

The process has become more complex and time-consuming with the development of codecision involving both the Council and the European Parliament – whereby both institutions must accept the final outcome. Where a difference emerges between the Council's position on a dossier and that of the Parliament, a conciliation procedure comes into play. Here again, the Commission has the dual role of guardian of the Community interest and facilitator or broker of agreements. The system has worked much more effectively than many critics predicted at its inception. It was initiated in the context of the single market programme, and doubters predicted that giving this role to the Parliament would significantly slow down the process. To the surprise of many, the Parliament proved to be a good deal more agile than was expected and showed a capacity to concentrate its attention on matters of real substance. The result has been that the codecision process, while it has increased the volume of work in the Council, has not significantly added to the political difficulty of decision-making.

Presiding over the Council

The presidency of the Council of Ministers and of the European Council rotates every six months in an agreed order. For a six-month period, ministers of the designated member state chair meetings of the Council of Ministers, take charge of the preparation of the agenda, advance the programme of work, promote legislation and seek to broker agreement. The head of state or government chairs meetings of the European Council. Ireland last held the presidency (its sixth since accession) for the first half of 2004.

The functions of the presidency have inevitably become more arduous as the number of member states has increased successively from the original six to the current twenty-seven. The problems of 'minding mice at a crossroads' sometimes come to mind. Keeping track of the views and positions of twenty-seven member states as they evolve and develop during the course of a debate on a politically sensitive issue is no small task. The presidency is greatly assisted by a very professional Council secretariat (which makes no claim, however, to have a monopoly of wisdom). The Commission too can be very helpful, but a wise president is always keenly aware of the fact that the Commission – understandably and properly – has its own agenda.

It was not unusual, in the era before the 2004 enlargement, for the presidency to undertake a 'tour of capitals' to explore the prospects and avenues for reaching agreement on knotty issues. With twenty-seven member states, that is a demand on time that exceeds the capacities of any presidency under the current dispensation. There is clearly a temptation to call on the member states and colleagues presenting the greatest difficulty, but selective tours can be seen to be discriminatory and run the risk of creating more difficulties than they resolve.

The presidency needs a great deal of patience. In the nature of things, there is always an element of 'grandstanding' in Council debates (and this would inevitably be increased if recent proposals to make Council debates public were to be accepted). The presidency has to be able to distinguish between grandstanding and the expression of a genuine difficulty. The former is best let pass without unnecessary comment, while the latter must be met with an adequate degree of understanding. The business of reaching a consensus is rarely speedy and attempts to force the pace can be counterproductive, whatever the rules provide. The Council secretariat and the members and experts of COREPER will always counsel caution and patience.

The presidency's functions include the maintenance of relations with the European Parliament. The importance of this function has, of course, increased substantially with the expansion of the codecision procedure to new areas of policy-making. This relationship, just like the working relationship within the Council, is strongly consensus-oriented. While the presidency's relations with the Parliament are necessarily less intimate than an Irish minister's relationship with the Oireachtas (the Irish Parliament) and its committees, they are nonetheless demanding. The European Parliament's committee system is a much more central part of that Parliament's life than is the case in the Oireachtas. The level of expertise and the depth of analysis that go into European Parliament draft reports go considerably beyond most of what is normally seen in the Oireachtas. Dialogue with a European Parliament committee is not for the faint-hearted. A Council president engaging in debate with a Parliament committee will frequently encounter a wider range of views and positions than in the Council itself.

The relationship between the Council and the Parliament, particularly with the development of codecision, is vastly different from the national executive to parliament relationship normally encountered in individual member states. It is now a debate between institutions on a basis of equality rather than the kind of majority versus opposition debate frequently found in the member states (although it must be admitted that party loyalty or affiliations frequently do not guarantee ministers a comfortable passage in Oireachtas committees).

Parliamentary questions

The president in office of the Council is also required to attend the European Parliament to answer parliamentary questions. The size of the Parliament, the rules of debate and the necessity of translation all conspire to make these questions a less sharp and less lively affair than can be witnessed in some national parliaments, even if the exchanges can frequently become fairly robust. The six-month period of the presidency means that ministers do not relate to MEPs in the way that they relate to members of their respective national parliaments. This robs question time in the European Parliament of much of the edge that characterises exchanges in national parliaments. Moreover, time limits in the Parliament make it virtually impossible for MEPs to pursue ministers in the manner seen in many national parliaments.

A word about voting in Council

As noted above, voting in Council is the exception rather than the rule.

There are, of course, some occasions when corners need to be cut in order to arrive at the manifest destination. In my experience as a member of five different formations of the Council and two periods as president (one of them brief but unexpectedly action-packed), I participated in only two QMV events, each of which I provoked from the chair against the advice of the Council secretariat and of COREPER. Each was a case of blatant grandstanding by a minister who knew that he was isolated. In each case, the issue affected a number of member states and a broad consensus had emerged, from which there was only one dissenter. In neither case was the dissenting member state in danger of being seriously prejudiced by the emerging consensus. In each case there were clearly no hard feelings afterward. Each case happened in a Council of twelve member states: the presidency's calculation might have been different in a council of twenty-seven members.

Implementing Council decisions

For the most part, EU legislation is implemented by the member states. The Union has, in general, no implementation machinery of its own and the obligation falls on the member states. This is where ministers come into the picture again, since it is they who have the responsibility of implementation. Normally, one would expect this to make ministers rather cautious in their approach to legislation, since mistakes can come back to haunt them! Since, however, the Council of Ministers shares the legislative function with the European Parliament, ministers are not in control at EU level to the same extent as they are at national level.

Even though legislative responsibility is shared by the Council and the Parliament, it is ministers who receive the unpleasant notifications from the Commission in cases in which the Commission is contemplating legal proceedings where it considers that implementation of EU legislation appears to be faulty or lacking.

There are certain widely held but mistaken beliefs about EU legislation. A couple of examples deserve mention.

The first is the proposition that there is something significant and somehow objectionable in the alleged 'fact' that some 75 per cent of national legislation 'comes from Brussels'. It is not clear how that calculation is made and the figure varies from one commentator to another. The implied criticism ignores the fact that 'Brussels' does not legislate: that function is jointly exercised by the Council and the European Parliament. The implied criticism suggests that this 'Brussels' legislation is, to some extent, unnecessary. It therefore suggests that, in some way, the Council and the Parliament are being induced to do things that they should not. Most ministers, one suspects, would be happy to reduce the level of their activity in 'Brussels', so the idea that they are somehow engaging in unnecessary or otiose activity is not very convincing. One more often hears the demand that 'Brussels should do something' than any suggestion that it should not.

Every piece of legislation that emanates from 'Brussels' has either been debated by ministers or debated by their delegated experts and reported to the ministers, or has been enacted under rules agreed by ministers. In a real sense, all members of all member state governments have a collective responsibility for EU legislation. This collective responsibility is shared by all MEPs for legislation passed under the codecision procedure (which today applies to almost all EU legislation).

In truth, one suspects that much of the legislation in question would figure on national agendas even without 'Brussels', but that separate and uncoordinated bodies of national legislation would give rise to more problems, especially in trade between member states, than Community-based legislation.

There was indeed a time, before the single market enterprise was undertaken, when it might have appeared that we were being bombarded by a constant stream of directives on apparently obscure – not to say frivolous – matters such as noise standards for lawn mowers and other vexatious and nit-picking details. In truth, the problem was not so much that EU legislation was concerning itself with trifles – it was rather the case that the business of creating a truly unified market was being tackled piecemeal and without any obvious overall plan or framework. The single market programme (not yet fully completed) gave us that framework and a more methodical approach.

As is frequently the case with legislative programmes, however, some pieces of nonsense creep in. Happily, a draft proposal to require employers to provide sun-block cream for outdoor workers was treated with the derision it deserved. While some unfortunate Brussels bureaucrat had the job of developing this proposal, I suspect that some politically correct trade union influence lay behind it.

Regrettably, many ministers and governments seek to distance themselves from legislation which proves to be domestically unpopular, without acknowledging the part they played in its origination.

Another of these mistaken beliefs is that we are more diligent Europeans than the others and we apply the rules more strictly than others. In logic, not everybody can be right about this. In Ireland's case, we may well be among the better member states in implementing EU legislation, but we certainly have not got the best of records. There have been cases in which we have been over ten years late in the implementation of important pieces of legislation. Examples include the Nitrates Directive and parts of the complex of measures associated with the Waste Water Directive.

The fact is that no member state is consistently either the best or the worst in implementing EU legislation. In the nature of things, performance varies from one member state to another and from one sector of activity to another. Much of this variation can be attributed to differences in political and administrative cultures between member states. In addition, it is fair to say that, even where purely domestic legislation is concerned, all member state governments have a readier appetite for legislation than for implementation.

The personal element

Working with other politicians in a pressured environment has its lighter side. Even though personal contact tends to be rather limited by the demands of ministerial diaries and by the fact that most ministers spend as little time as possible in Brussels, there are opportunities to form friendships. Informal meetings, which take place in a more relaxed environment than the formal Council sessions, give some space for the formation of friendships. It was at one such informal session in Ireland in 1984 that many Finance Ministers first learned that the then President of the Commission, Jacques Delors, is no mean jazz pianist.

The dynamics of personal relationships in the Council make an interesting study. Some friendships emerge from political alliances on contentious issues. Some political alliances emerge from personal friendships. Yet other friendships persist despite significant political differences. Nigel Lawson, for example, had many friends among other ministers who unsuccessfully tried to persuade him that the UK should join the European exchange rate mechanism (ERM) in the mid-1980s. Hans Tietmeyer, then Secretary of State in the German Finance Ministry, still has friends among ministers whom he criticised for what he characterised as financial laxity. Many such friendships persist despite the vagaries of the different electoral cycles in the member states.

In my own case, I have friends going back to the Agriculture Council in 1981 and 1982, ECOFIN from 1982 to 1986 and the Transport Council in 1997. On one occasion Edith Cresson and I worked through the night in Lancaster House in London as Ministers for Agriculture making sure that high-level civil servants, acting under the orders of heads of state and government, did not damage French and Irish interests by seriously reducing expenditure on the CAP. The night and early morning were all the more agreeable for the fact that our first meeting some months earlier had been rather frosty.

Ministers (or rather ex-ministers) who remain active in political life when they are no longer members of the Council tend to meet again in other political circles. Friendships formed in the Council of Ministers can therefore be important in other aspects of political and professional life.

Holding the presidency of the Council presents more opportunities for contact with other ministers. The presidency frequently finds itself mediating difficult issues between ministers from other member states. In the process, the president inevitably gets insights into the pressures on colleagues and into their ways of dealing with these pressures.

In the nature of their duties, European commissioners and Commission presidents have to lobby and cultivate ministers. There can often be a very close working relationship between commissioners and Council presidents, leading to a certain complicity in manoeuvring other ministers towards agreement – or, indeed, in finding tactful ways of circumventing what some ministers would like to achieve. I can remember spending some time as president of the Transport Council with then Commissioner Neil Kinnock in setting up a discussion over lunch so that the Transport Minister of a large member state would, without feeling crushed, realise that there was no point in pursuing a favourite project. We succeeded and that minister and I remain friends.

The ministerial experience

What is it really like to be a member of the Council of Ministers?

For any minister with a portfolio affected by globalisation (and there are very few that are not so affected), work in the Council of Ministers adds a valuable dimension to the effectiveness of the office. Participation in EU decision-making is, for most ministers, both the essential framework for and an essential complement to work at national level.

10

Managing European Dossiers in the Irish Civil Service: Living with the EU System?

Brigid Laffan

Introduction

Ireland joined the European Union on 1 January 1973 and since then thousands of dossiers have wound their way from Brussels into the Irish civil service and domestic system of public policy and back again to the Brussels arena. Commission recommendations and communications, Council working party reports, instructions from Dublin to the Irish Permanent Representation, and Council and European Council agendas are part and parcel of the flow of work through the Irish system. The EU operates on a calendar basis: six-monthly presidencies, annual Commission and Council working programmes, sittings of the Parliament and multi-annual action plans are all part of the rhythm of Irish governance and government. Day by day, month by month and year by year, Irish civil servants act as 'boundary managers' between Dublin and Brussels. They track developments in Brussels, determine Irish preferences and approaches and represent Ireland within the myriad committees that populate EU decision-making. They work closely with their political masters (the Taoiseach, ministers and ministers of state) to determine what approach should be adopted, dossier by dossier and meeting by meeting.

The objective of this chapter is to provide a broad overview of Ireland's management of EU dossiers since membership in 1973. The dynamic and evolutionary nature of the EU's system of governance is crucial to understanding the engagement of the Irish civil service. Since 1973 both Ireland and the EU have been transformed. The civil service has had to navigate a changing Ireland and a changing EU. The nature and depth of change in the EU is particularly striking since the relaunch of integration in 1985 with negotiations on the Single European Act and the launch of the single market programme. The EU has become far more significant as a source of regulations, financial transfers and foreign policy during the intensive period of treaty reform that still continues. Moreover, policy frameworks such as state aids, competition policy and economic governance under economic and monetary union (EMU) limited the scope for independent, domestic policy-making. The Irish civil service found itself working in a framework that was decided in conjunction with its partners in the other member states. Sometimes the restrictions emanating from Brussels were welcome as they enabled the civil service to restrict the freedom of ministers – 'Brussels does not allow this'. Sometimes the restrictions were irksome as the final agreement emanating from Brussels did not always suit Ireland's circumstances.

This chapter firstly traces some of the key developments in Ireland's approach to managing European dossiers from the initial negotiations leading to membership to the present day. It subsequently examines the work of the Permanent Representation (including within COREPER and Council working groups) as an integral part of Ireland's management of EU business. The extent to which Ireland possesses a European cadre of officials, and the Irish approach to European negotiations and coordination between government departments, are then assessed. The final section identifies a number of the strengths and weaknesses of the Irish approach.

The Irish system for managing European dossiers: Major shifts

Three relatively distinct phases in the development of Ireland's management of European business can be discerned. These include: the early years of Ireland's membership, the period between the adoption of the Single European Act and the Maastricht Treaty and the period after the first referendum on the Nice Treaty in Ireland.

Learning to live with Brussels

The period from July 1970 to January 1972 was dominated by the accession negotiations and by an interdepartmental battle within the Irish civil service about which department would take the lead in managing European dossiers. As the prospect of Ireland's entry became manifest, a battle was fought between the Departments of Foreign Affairs and of Finance as to who would lead the negotiations. Foreign Affairs' victory on this issue set the tone for its post-membership role. Because of the focus on the membership negotiations, little attention was paid to the challenge of living with the European system after accession. Unlike the UK and Denmark, the question of how best to manage EU dossiers was left to one side. The circular (CH/177/35) that established how EU business should be managed was issued by the Department of Foreign Affairs in September 1973, nine months after accession.

Accession also altered the career prospects for high-performing Irish civil servants. The first Irish *fonctionnaires* that joined the EU institutions as employees succeeded in European competitions or formed part of the first cabinet of Commissioner Patrick Hillery. Others got expert contracts, while yet others were assigned to the Irish Permanent Representation, a cross-departmental body that was a mini-Irish civil service in Brussels. An Irish presence evolved in Brussels with its own closely knit community, club, pubs and cultural networks. Flights from Dublin to Brussels were full of civil servants on their way to Council and Commission working groups, instantly recognisable by the papers they carried.

The Irish system put in place structures and processes for managing European dossiers by the end of the first year. Adaptation went with the grain of how Ireland managed its domestic policies. The key features of the system were:

- Responsibility for day-to-day coordination on EU matters was assigned to the Department of Foreign Affairs. This constituted a break with the past, as the Department of Finance was the lead department in the period leading up to membership
- Although responsibility for day-to-day coordination was given to the Department of Foreign Affairs, the Department of Finance continued to play an important role as any EU proposals that might lead to a cost to the Irish exchequer required the prior approval of the Department of Finance
- The principle of the responsibility of the lead department was firmly established. However, the dominance of the lead department was framed within the parameters of a political and administrative culture governed by collective responsibility and an ethos of consulting 'all interested' departments
- Processes and guidelines were established for the writing of reports and the circulation of EU documents throughout the administration and to the Joint Oireachtas Committee on the Secondary Legislation of the European Communities (on the role of this committee, see Chapter 11)
- The key structure with responsibility for overall policy in relation to the Union was the newly established Interdepartmental European Communities Committee, which replaced the Committee of Secretaries that charted Ireland's original engagement with the system. This committee was chaired by the Department of Foreign Affairs. Its membership – the Departments of Foreign Affairs, of the Taoiseach, of Finance, of Agriculture and Fisheries and of Industry and Commerce –

highlighted the key ministries on EU matters in the original phase of membership. It met in two formats, at the levels of secretary general and of assistant secretary. The latter format was intended to prepare the work of the secretaries' committee. In practice, the committee began to meet only at assistant secretary level after the initial phase. Eleven interdepartmental policy groups were also established

- The cabinet was responsible for the broad political direction of Ireland's engagement with the Union. A minute from the Department of the Taoiseach in 1974 instructed that the Departments of Foreign Affairs, of Industry and Commerce, of Agriculture and Fisheries and of Finance should be consulted on all memoranda to the government that had a bearing on Ireland's membership of the EU. A Cabinet Sub-Committee on the European Communities was also established at this time. It was envisaged that it would make recommendations to the government on EU matters and decide on matters referred to it by the full cabinet.

The Irish administration faced the challenge of adapting to the Brussels system with limited human resources, a recurring issue in the management of European dossiers. One year into membership, Minister for Foreign Affairs Garret FitzGerald (1973) concluded that:

> The first ten months of Community membership have placed an enormous strain on this country's human resources in the public service and in many vocational bodies whose interests are affected by membership. We were simply not prepared for all that membership entails. In my own department the number of staff hitherto available for EEC work has fallen short by one-third of the absolute minimum to undertake this task in a manner that will safeguard Irish vital interests.

New posts were created in the Irish civil service to accommodate the demands of EU membership. However the increase in the number of full-time, non-industrial civil servants as a result of membership was relatively small. In 1980 it was estimated that a total of 1,391 new posts had been created to manage the work arising from EU membership. The total civil service complement in that year was 53,822.

The period between January 1973 and the end of Ireland's first presidency in December 1975 was Ireland's apprenticeship in the Brussels system. The preparations for the 1975 presidency were critical to Ireland's adjustment to the EU. The demands of running a presidency ensured that departmental responsibility for different policy areas was clearly delineated and management of Council business meant that government ministers and officials became *au fait* with the nuts and bolts of the

Union's policy process. The Irish government prepared extremely well for the presidency, and was determined that as a small and relatively new member state it would be seen to manage the Union's business successfully. The experience of the presidency also had a very beneficial effect on the psychological environment of national policy-makers. Thereafter, the Union became an accepted feature of national decision-making. Within three years of membership, Ireland had earned its first star in the Brussels system. The culture of running high-quality presidencies persisted in the Irish civil service.

The end of the apprenticeship period however did not mean that Ireland had such a well-oiled machine for managing EU business or that all problems were addressed. In 1978 the Department of the Public Service carried out a review of the management of EU business and, although it did not produce a final report, some of its deliberations later appeared in an OECD report (1981) entitled *Adapting Public Administration for Participating in Supranational Bodies*. Four problem areas were identified:

1. Organisation – There were disputes about who should play the lead role in some policy areas
2. Policy – There was scarcely any attempt to review systematically the effects of EU policies, and there was a need to develop and document clear policy guidelines so that delegates could effectively participate in EC meetings
3. Coordination – There was a failure in some cases to engage in effective consultation with other departments. The limited role of departmental coordination units and the diffusion of coordination responsibility within certain departments was identified
4. Procedures – There was some evidence that there was a certain failure to observe procedures concerning the circulation of reports of meetings, a lack of coordination concerning attendance at meetings and an inconsistency in the grading levels decided on by different departments.

The OECD report also highlighted the fact that although the broad parameters of how Ireland managed EU business were institutionalised between 1973 and 1975, some of the structures and procedures established by the 1973 circular did not become operational. The cabinet sub-committee rarely met and gradually fell into abeyance, as did the interdepartmental policy groups. An ad hoc, agenda-driven approach to managing EU dossiers took root, which allowed for consider-able departmental autonomy and an informal manner of dealing with Brussels.

Upgrading the role of the Department of the Taoiseach

The second important period in the development of Ireland's approach to EU matters was between 1987 and 1992 – a period that included landmark developments such as the Single European Act, the Delors I package, the 1990 presidency and the Maastricht Treaty on European Union (TEU). The referendum on the Single European Act, the work arising from the single market programme and the negotiations and implementation of the first national development plan (NDP) placed new demands on the Irish civil service. These events coincided with a new government and a Taoiseach, Charles Haughey, who adopted a strong leadership role in cabinet when he took over in February 1987. His administration made three important changes.

First, the European Communities Committee which was chaired by an assistant secretary from the Department of Foreign Affairs was transferred to the Department of the Taoiseach and the chairmanship was given to a new political role, the Minister of State for European Affairs. Second, Haughey set up a high-level Committee of Ministers and Secretaries that met once a week in the period leading up to Ireland's submission of the NDP to the Commission in March 1989. The committee met frequently in the Taoiseach's home and was attended mostly by departmental secretaries, with the intermittent participation of ministers. A restricted version of the committee planned the 1990 presidency. When the presidency was over in July 1990, the interdepartmental coordination machinery fell into abeyance. A new Taoiseach, Albert Reynolds, reactivated the European Communities Committee in February 1992 with a political chair. The third change initiated in the Haughey era was the establishment of seven regions in 1988 in response to Commission demands for consultation and partnership in the planning and implementation of the NDP.

The Nice I shock

The third period of significant review and evaluation of how EU business was handled in Ireland resulted from the deep shock to the Irish political system following the 'no' vote at the first Nice referendum in June 2001. Prior to this Ireland portrayed itself as a constructive player in the Union, with a relatively *communautaire* approach to the EU. Successive governments could pursue their European policies in a benign domestic environment. The 'no' to Nice and the low turnout in the referendum (34 per cent of the electorate) highlighted the fact that the government could no longer take its electorate for granted. Ireland's European policy was loose of its moorings, which in turn led to considerable soul searching at official and political levels about how EU business was managed and how

Europe was communicated at national level. EU issues were ratcheted up the political and administrative agenda as the government and the civil service sought to determine how best to respond to the crisis. One senior civil servant interviewed in 2002 claimed that:

> The whole way we were conducting our business in Europe was uncertain and in transition. There is a need to go into a new mode, organise accordingly and change mindset. Departments don't always see where they fit into the bigger picture. We have gone a bit tired. Losing the referendum has brought it all into focus.

Politically, the government established the National Forum on Europe to generate a debate on Ireland's place in the Union. There was widespread acceptance that there was a gap between those who were involved in Ireland's European policy (the EU 'insiders') and the wider public, and that the public had not engaged with European issues.

Within the civil service, a number of responses were evident. First, the Economic Division in the Department of Foreign Affairs was renamed the EU Division and the new Director General of that section was recalled to Dublin. He was one of Ireland's most experienced Brussels hands with strong links with EU institutions and extensive experience in high-level EU negotiations. A number of organisational changes followed in the department and new guidelines were issued for Irish embassies concerning the kind of intelligence they should gather in order to strengthen Ireland's management of EU dossiers. A new Permanent Representative was appointed, who in turn introduced a number of new processes in the Irish Permanent Representation.

Second, all of the political and interdepartmental mechanisms for dealing with the Union became more active. The cabinet sub-committee, a committee that waxed and waned since 1973, began to meet regularly and deal with work sent to it by the Senior Officials Group (SOG). The tempo of work undertaken by the SOG was greatly enhanced. The SOG represents the core of the EU cadre in that all members have substantial EU responsibilities and are sent by their departments to influence future strategy. This group began to assume responsibility within the domestic system for the establishment of priorities concerning EU policy and for plotting Ireland's future position in the Union. One result of this was the publication of a document in April 2002 on *Ireland and the European Union: Identifying Priorities and Pursuing Goals* (Department of the Taoiseach, 2002). The report identified the need to engage fully with the complex decision-making processes of the EU by:

- Cultivating ever better relations with Ireland's partners in the EU, the accession countries and the institutions of the EU
- Developing better domestic systems for enhanced coordination, coherence and priority-setting internally
- Promoting greater public awareness of the importance of the EU to individuals' lives.

Three important factors were identified: interaction with the EU system, better domestic management of EU business and sensitivity to the public dimension of Ireland's relations with the Union.

The weakness of parliamentary scrutiny of EU business was also highlighted as a serious problem during the Nice I referendum. In response to this, the government developed a system of enhanced Oireachtas scrutiny of EU affairs. This in turn had an impact on the management of EU dossiers. One senior civil servant interviewed concluded that the new guidelines would 'force Europe up the agenda of departments'. The proposals for Oireachtas scrutiny were approved by the government in January 2002 and entered into operation in July 2002, following the May general election. A set of guidelines for the new processes was prepared by the administration. The parliamentary link for the new procedures is the Select Committee for European Affairs.

The guidelines establish the main mechanism of reporting to the Oireachtas as the preparation of a 'note' by the department with lead responsibility for the policy area. The notes identify the importance of the particular proposal to Ireland (major significance, some significance, purely technical) and give an assessment of the implications for Ireland, consequences for national legislation and the EU budget, and the likely timetable for negotiations and implementation. They also provide information on the legal basis for the proposal, the voting rule that applies and the role of the European Parliament. The new arrangements also make provision for extensive engagement between the Oireachtas, minister and civil servants. Civil servants began to give oral briefings and reports of EU meetings on an agreed basis (for further details on the 2002 arrangements on parliamentary scrutiny of EU policy-making, see Chapter 11). From an administrative point of view, the new guidelines enhanced the formality of Ireland's arrangements for managing EU dossiers. For the first time there was an accessible database of the flow of EU proposals through the Irish system.

The three significant periods of change in the management of European dossiers in the Irish civil service are characterised, in the first phase, by the establishment of formal systems and processes that were trumped by an ad hoc approach and the power of the 'lead' department. The Irish system was the most weakly institutionalised across the member states, apart from Luxembourg, a micro-state. In the second phase, we see an expansion in the role of the Department of the Taoiseach as a result of the then Taoiseach Charles Haughey's preferences, the expanding role of the European Council and the relaunch of integration. The third phase of reflection was far more dramatic because the failure of Nice I was potentially a 'black hole' for Ireland in the Union, given the extent of transfers to Ireland from the EU budget and the salience of the eastern enlargement. It led to a review of processes and procedures for managing European dossiers and Ireland's macro-relationship with the Union.

The Permanent Representation

The Permanent Representation is an integral part of Ireland's management of EU dossiers. It provides the 'eyes and ears' of the Irish system in Brussels. It is a microcosm of Ireland's core executive in Brussels. The number of staff of diplomatic rank increased from seven in 1971 to fifteen in 1973 following accession. The 1975 presidency led to the next important increase in the staffing levels to twenty-four to manage the work of the presidency. The number of staff in the representation remained relatively stable for the remainder of the 1970s and 1980s. The next significant increase in staffing came in the 1990s when a number of domestic departments felt the need for a presence in Brussels. By 1999 the number of officers of diplomatic rank had risen to thirty-five and reached forty in 2002.

The expansion of staff numbers from the mid-1990s onwards points to the growth of EU-related business in the post-TEU and Amsterdam environment and to the further Europeanisation of a number of domestic ministries. In 1973 six departments had staff in Brussels. A further three ministries joined them in the late 1970s and 1980s. Later the Departments of the Marine (1991), of Justice (1995), of Health (1996), of Defence (2000) and of Arts, Culture and the Gaeltacht (2002) were added to the list, along with the Attorney General's Office (1999). All domestic departments with the exception of the Department of the Taoiseach and one other relatively minor ministry are represented in Brussels.

The departmental breakdown of staff at the representation reflects the important role that the Department of Foreign Affairs plays in Brussels. It has fifteen staff in the representation including the three most senior staff. Several of the staff are career diplomats, including all of the senior staff. The Department of Enterprise, Trade and Employment has four staff, and a further three departments have three staff each. Eight departments have only one member of staff in the representation. No domestic ministry has more than four staff in Brussels. The staff of the representation is formally part of the Foreign Service when in Brussels, and officials from domestic departments are formally seconded to the Department of Foreign Affairs while working in the Permanent Representation. However, the domestic departments decide who should go to Brussels. The Department of Foreign Affairs has never formally attempted to direct the process of recruitment.

The Irish representation is organised along functional lines arising from the work of the Council and its working parties and the departmental presence in Brussels. In addition, it is hierarchical in that the Permanent Representative, the Deputy and the Ambassador to the Political and Security Committee carry the authority of their position at the apex of the office. The Permanent Representative is the head of the office. Since 1973 Ireland has had seven Permanent Representatives, who tend to stay in Brussels for an average of five years. The first Permanent Representative spent eight years in Brussels, which reflected the early phase of membership. Two of the Permanent Representatives had acted as deputies in the representation with the result that they came to the posts with considerable EU and Council experience. In 2001 Ireland appointed Anne Anderson to the post of Permanent Representative, the first woman member of COREPER, who served until 2005 when she was replaced by Bobby McDonagh.

The cycle of Council, COREPER and working party business sets the tempo of work in the representation. The Antici group (COREPER I) and Mertens group (COREPER II) prepare the work of COREPER with the presidency and the Council secretariat (for details on the work of COREPER and the Antici and Mertens groups, see, for example, Hayes-Renshaw and Wallace, 1997, Chapter 3 or Westlake and Galloway, 2004, Chapters 11 and 12). Meetings of COREPER act as a filter between the political and the official. Issues are pushed to the limit here to determine if they should be sent up to the Council level or back down to the working parties for further consideration. National positions are highlighted and the representatives come under pressure from their counterparts. According to one former ambassador interviewed, the 'real wearing down process goes on in COREPER' because this is where the trade-offs take place. According to this official, 'the major job of the Permanent Representative is to ask "is this something we can win" and "what will I advise the Minster"' (see Chapter 9 on the operation of the Council at ministerial level). There would be continuous and high-level contact between Dublin and Brussels during sensitive negotiations on the stance Ireland should take. The members of COREPER II and I operate at the coalface between the national and the European and between the technical and the political.

The aim of the ambassadors is to push things along and to solve the problems through negotiations. The ambassadors have a keen sense of where the eventual compromise will lie and they work to ensure that the political level can solve the outstanding political issues. They are very sensitive to each other's problems and will try to assist the state in the most exposed position. Given the technical nature of much of the business of COREPER I, the deputy ambassador requires considerable knowledge of the domestic issues that can arise. The ambassadors tend to challenge the briefing material they receive because they do not want to find themselves exposed at COREPER attempting to defend a position that was weakened through bad presentation or inattention to the evolution of the dossier.

Of course, the 'first line of negotiation' on EU dossiers within the Council takes place at working group level. It is through the myriad of working groups that proposals are examined in detail to identify broad points of agreement, as well as problem areas. In the Irish case, working groups are either attended by staff from the Permanent Representation dealing with the policy area, or by departmental civil servants flying over for a day or two, or both.

The boundary managers: Few in number but distinctive in policy style

Participation in EU policy-making alters the working environment of national administrations. In order to live with the Brussels system, member states need a cadre of European specialists (Brussels 'insiders'), who combine technical/sectoral expertise with European expertise. European expertise rests on deep knowledge of how the EU system works, its legal framework and the personal skills to work in a multinational and multicultural environment. It also requires the stamina to make the early flights to Brussels, to work effectively in interminable meetings and to analyse the discussion and direction of the negotiations. EU expertise is honed at meeting after meeting in the Commission and Council. There the norms and protocols are learned and judgments are formed about how to approach European negotiations. Networks and friendships are made that in turn lubricate difficult negotiations. Many member states have EU fast tracks and highly specialised training to ensure that they have an adequate supply of EU insiders.

The core of the EU cadre in any member state can be found among those officials for whom EU business takes up more than 50 per cent of their time. They gain their initial experience at working party level and later find themselves at more senior levels with substantial EU responsibilities. The most experienced of them spend time in the representation or one of the EU institutions. Extensive exposure to Brussels brings the added bonus of contacts with counterparts in other member states or in Brussels. This cadre act as 'boundary managers' between the national and the European. They develop and transmit national preferences in the course of EU negotiations and later filter Brussels outcomes back into the national.

A substantial proportion of Ireland's EU cadre can be found in the Departments of Foreign Affairs, of Enterprise, Trade and Employment, of Agriculture, of Finance and of Justice. In all of the other departments, there are significant EU-related posts but these are few in number. The small size of the EU cadre, relative to the size of the civil service, is striking. Internal civil service estimates prepared in 1980 concluded that 151 officials at assistant principal grade or above spent the greater part of their time on EU-related matters, and a further 111 officials had significant EU involvement. The total number of officials at this level was 2,217 (Internal Note, September 1980). An incomplete estimate, prepared in 2002, that analysed those involved at higher executive officer grade or above suggested that the numbers have increased, but not dramatically. Only three departments – Foreign Affairs, Enterprise, Trade and Employment, and Agriculture – had over fifty staff working on EU matters for more than 50 per cent of their time. In many departments, the number was five staff or less.

The cult of the generalist is very strong in Irish administrative culture. Irish civil servants are expected to handle any post that they are placed in and to move to radically different work in the course of their careers. It is thus exceptional in the Irish system that an official would work only on EU matters for his or her entire career. That said, there are a small number of officials whose careers are largely EU-related in the diplomatic service and in the key EU departments. These are officials who might have served on high-level EU committees for long periods because their EU knowledge became a key resource in the system. There is no specially trained EU cadre in the Irish system and no EU-related fast track. Training on EU matters is ad hoc throughout the system. In 1974 there was extensive training for the first Irish presidency which included considerable exposure to how the EU worked. The training effort for subsequent presidencies was geared more towards meetings management as it was felt that EU knowledge in the system was adequate. Lectures on the EU form part of induction programmes for young diplomatic staff and administrative officers. Officials assigned to the representation in Brussels would not receive training before leaving for Brussels and would not shadow the area of responsibility before taking up their new positions.

Language training in the Irish system is also weak. Consequently EU expertise is built up 'on the job'.

The approach to negotiations

The manner in which Irish officials do their homework for negotiations in Brussels and conduct negotiations is influenced by a number of factors. Size matters. The relatively small size of central government, coupled with the small size of the country, and the fact that Irish delegations tend to be smaller than those of other member states, all influence perceptions of how the Brussels game should be played. Irish civil servants have an acute sense of the constraints of size. They work on the basis that, as a small state, Ireland has a limited negotiating margin and should use that margin wisely (see also Chapter 12). One Department of Finance civil servant interviewed suggested that 'Ireland has fewer guns, and not many bullets so it must pick its fights carefully'. In 1985 the then Taoiseach Garret FitzGerald identified Ireland's negotiating strategy in the following terms, 'As a small country we must ensure that we do not create problems for our partners save in the case of issues that are of vital importance to us. Only when our case is strong – so overwhelmingly strong that in logic others should objectively accept it, should we press our interests in a way that can create problems for other people'. This approach was confirmed by an interviewee from the Department of Enterprise, Trade and Employment, who suggested that in negotiations Irish officials will not raise difficulties unless they have a real problem.

Irish officials try to avoid isolation in negotiations and are largely successful. In the five years from 1996 to 2000, Ireland abstained in one vote and registered a negative vote seven times. This was out of a total of 75 abstentions and 206 votes cast in the Council. Ireland, Austria, Finland and Luxembourg are among the member states that rarely find themselves on the losing side of votes in the Council (Peterson and Shackleton, 2002). One Irish diplomat remarked to this author that 'very rarely are we without a negotiating margin and without room for manoeuvre'. In the end the minister will decide if he or she wants to go out on a limb, but would be told 'minister, you are totally isolated on this and a lot of people will come down heavily on you in Council'. The aim is to avoid this if at all possible and to negotiate solutions to problems.

The approach to negotiations is to seek to shape or reshape the five or six problem areas in any proposal for Ireland. This tactical approach stems from Ireland's size, limited human resources and pragmatic culture. All proposals are scanned and assessed in terms of problems. Problems are

identified on the basis of an informal checklist of the kinds of issues that
need watching. Those that surfaced most frequently (Laffan, 2001)
include:

• Existing national law or policy
• Departmental policy
• Likely impact on the public purse in terms of either the cost to the
  national budget or erosion of the tax base
• Where relevant, constitutional licence
• Views and concerns of relevant interests
• Administrative capacity to implement.

This strategy was likened to 'shooting ducks in the arcade' by one of
Ireland's leading EU specialists. The problem-solving approach to
negotiations means that Irish officials tend to intervene on specific issues
and would have little to say on the broad thrust of policy. When looking for
solutions, Irish officials will seek to deal with problems at the lowest
possible level (usually at working group level) and will rely on a drafting
solution in the first instance. The logic of this approach is that issues
become more politicised, and thus more difficult to solve, as you move up
the hierarchy. Links are maintained with colleagues in other member states
but on a less systematic basis than in some other administrations. Given
the changes in the EU, more attention is again being paid to bilateral
contacts at all levels in the system. Tactical rather than strategic thinking is
prevalent in Ireland on EU matters. Considerable attention is paid to the
negotiating positions of other member states.

    Personalism is a dominant cultural value in Ireland arising from late
urbanisation and the small size of the country. Civil servants working on
EU matters meet frequently in Brussels and Dublin and have an ease of
contact. Officials throughout the system can easily identify the necessary
contacts in other departments. Hayes (1984) concluded that the high
degree of interdepartmental contact owed much to the small, personal,
centralised nature of Ireland's central administration. The telephone and
email are the main channels of informal contact. While hierarchy matters,
the need to get business done means that there is a facility to meet across
levels that is more difficult in more formal and hierarchical continental
systems of administration. The intimacy of the Irish system can be gleaned
from the fact that when a particular set of negotiations is mentioned, the
names of the four or five relevant officials are offered immediately.

    There are several well-entrenched norms in the Irish system that
influence how EU dossiers are handled. First is the norm that Irish
delegations should 'sing from the same hymn sheet' and should not fight

interdepartmental battles in Brussels. Delegations would not engage in conflict in front of other delegations. Second is a norm of sharing information about developments in key negotiations. However, there are pockets of secrecy left where departments will not share information that they believe is of primary interest to themselves. The Departments of Agriculture and of Finance have been known to guard EU-relevant information from the Department of Foreign Affairs. Third is a high level of collegiality within the Irish system and a high level of trust between officials from other departments. This is accompanied by an understanding of different departmental perspectives and styles. A high level of trust is particularly prevalent among the EU cadre who see themselves fighting for 'Ireland Inc' in the corridors of the Council and Commission. Fourth is the norm that Ireland should be as *communautaire* as possible within the limits of particular negotiations. As stated above, Irish officials/politicians do not oppose for the sake of opposing. That said, the Irish would aim to be constructive players in the EU system, rather than deploy the rhetoric of the European project. Protecting domestic space is an important goal of Irish participants in the EU arena. This stems from Ireland's relative underdevelopment until the 1990s, from its common law tradition and from the character of its political economy.

Coordinating the 'national line'

A 'holy trinity' comprising the Departments of Foreign Affairs, of the Taoiseach and of Finance forms the inner core of the Irish system for managing European dossiers. The relationship between the Departments of the Taoiseach and of Foreign Affairs is particularly important. All departments have coordination units and some have internal European affairs committees reporting to the departmental management committee. The system of interdepartmental committees has been subject to considerable flux since membership, but in the post-Nice period became more stable and institutionalised. Overall responsibility for day-to-day coordination remains with the Department of Foreign Affairs. Its *Strategy Statement 1998* stated its ambition to develop 'with the Irish administration as a whole, a strategic, co-ordinated and coherent response to the protection and promotion of Ireland's interests in the EU' (Department of Foreign Affairs, 1998, p. 21). A number of actions relating to this objective were identified:

- To stimulate maximum awareness in the Irish administrative system of EU issues and to work to ensure that these receive appropriate priority

- To develop, in coordination with other departments, detailed strategies for the promotion and protection of Irish interests
- To keep under active review and seek to improve as necessary the mechanisms for EU coordination within the department and between departments.

These aspirations identify the Department of Foreign Affairs as an advocate of EU awareness in the Irish system and as a joint custodian of Ireland's management of EU business. The objective is to ensure that EU matters receive adequate prioritisation within the Irish system, that the system develops detailed strategies and that coordination mechanisms are reviewed periodically. The ability of the Department of Foreign Affairs to achieve these aims is, however, limited because it has to rely on the engagement of other officials.

National policy styles differ in terms of the ambition to coordinate and manage the interaction with Brussels. Two styles predominate: containment and internalisation. Under the containment model, a nominated central body adopts a gatekeeper role between the EU and the domestic. This style involves horizontal management of issues such as the appropriate legal basis, inter-institutional relations, comitology committees and so on. The national systems of this type have a central focal point that places a premium on control and coordination. The archetypical states that fall into this category are the UK, France and Denmark. The internalisation style is characterised by the dominance of the lead department or ministry, little formal tracking of interaction with Brussels and less formal systems of coordination. Germany, the Netherlands, Luxembourg and Ireland fall into this category.

The coordination ambition depends on the nature of the issue on the Brussels agenda, the phase of the policy process and the national style in managing EU business. A fourfold distinction between routine sectoral policy-making, major policy-shaping decisions within sectors, cross-sectoral issues and the big bargains is apposite. In Ireland, departments handle the routine business of dealing with Brussels within clearly defined sectoral areas without engaging in too much interdepartmental consultation and coordination. In addition, the Irish system gives individual departments considerable autonomy within their own sectors, even on the major shaping issues, provided the wider system is kept informed. When it comes to cross-sectoral issues and the big bargains, processes that go beyond consultation are required, and here the Irish system has put in place structures and processes to ensure coordination. The coordination ambition in Ireland could be defined as a high level of coordination on selected issues of high politics.

The member states can achieve their coordination ambitions in a variety of ways. Bartlett and Ghoshal (1989) offer a threefold categorisation of coordination styles: centralisation, formalisation and socialisation. All organisations deploy a mix of the three processes of coordination but one approach will usually dominate. A highly centralised system involves 'top down' processes of coordination with issues pushed up the hierarchy for deliberation, arbitration, resolution and strategic analysis. A highly formalised system would be procedurally strong with extensive rules and guidelines. A system that rests on socialisation relies on the development of common understandings and norms. The Irish system utilises all three approaches but the dominant mode of coordination on a day-to-day and week-to-week basis is undoubtedly socialisation. On the key national priorities, however, the Irish system engages in 'selective centralisation' (Kassim, 2001). The system will channel political and administrative resources on the big issues. Two examples, from very different eras, illustrate the capacity of selective centralisation.

In 1983 Ireland had a major problem with Commission proposals on the introduction of a milk superlevy (see also Chapter 6). The Irish government and administration effectively transformed into a task force to ensure that the outcome was not too detrimental to Irish interests. Taoiseach Garret FitzGerald toured all of the capitals of the member states prior to the December 1983 Athens European Council. This was augmented by a number of bilateral visits by the Agricultural Minister. The Ministers for Foreign Affairs and for Finance attended joint Councils on the issue. Special briefing material on the importance of this issue to Ireland was prepared and circulated to all member states and EU institutions. There was thus a high level of political prioritisation and commitment to the issue. The European Communities Committee met frequently on the superlevy and an ad hoc policy group was established to service the work of the senior civil servants and political office holders. In this instance, the outcome was better than would have been achieved if a passive approach had been adopted to the dossier.

The 1997–1999 Agenda 2000 negotiations offer a second example of selective centralisation in the Irish system. An interdepartmental Agenda 2000 group established in 1997 was the main vehicle for the development of the Irish approach to the negotiations. The ministers and secretaries group met eight times in 1998 on the issue. There was daily contact between the two Finance attachés in Brussels, the Permanent Representative and Dublin-based officials. The Department of Foreign Affairs coordinated briefings for COREPER and Council meetings on these negotiations, with input from the Departments of Agriculture and of Finance. A practice developed of written briefs for all EU meetings on

Agenda 2000. Excellent links between Dublin and the Permanent Representation led to a high level of coherence in the management of the Irish negotiating position. Throughout the negotiations there was extensive monitoring of the positions of the other member states, and Taoiseach Bertie Ahern engaged in a very intensive round of bilateral meetings with his counterparts in other member states. The management of the final phase of the negotiations was in the hands of an expert technical group that consisted of the Taoiseach and officials from the Departments of Foreign Affairs, of Finance, of Agriculture and of Enterprise, Trade and Employment. This was unusual in that it comprised the government's most senior member and four line officials from the relevant ministries. Essentially, the Taoiseach brought together the four most informed officials on the Agenda 2000 negotiations and met with them seven times between January and March 1999 when the negotiations concluded in Berlin.

The issues that are dealt with on the basis of selective centralisation are the most salient issues for Ireland but are limited in number. Coordination in the Irish system relies heavily on mutual adjustment and informal processes of interaction across departments. In addition to the coordination system based around the EU Division in the Department of Foreign Affairs, a number of additional poles of coordination have emerged. The first is a hub involving the Political Division in the Department of Foreign Affairs, the Department of Defence, and the General Staff of the Army in relation to the European Security and Defence Policy (ESDP). The development of ESDP brought the Department of Defence and the Army into the EU arena. Given the political sensitivity of the ESDP in Ireland, and its evolving nature, the three actors involved in this pole of coordination work extremely closely together, share information and interact on a continuous basis with the CFSP and ESDP personnel in the Irish Permanent Representation. A second pole of coordination is evident in the area of justice and home affairs (JHA). A government decision established an interdepartmental JHA committee serviced by the Department of the Taoiseach, chaired by a senior official from the Department of Justice and attended by officials from the Department of Foreign Affairs and the Attorney General's Office. This committee meets before meetings of the Justice and Home Affairs Council.

Thirty-five years – A balance sheet

During thirty-five years of EU membership the Irish civil service learned to live with the multilevel policy-making system that is the EU. For the Irish system of central administration, the EU is part of the fabric of government. The management of dossiers has been characterised by considerable strength but also weaknesses during the thirty-five years since accession.

The strengths of the Irish civil service in managing EU dossiers may be summarised as follows. First was a clear understanding of Ireland's core priorities within the Union. The big dossiers were always accorded considerable political and administrative time and attention. There was no neglect of 'high politics' such as the structural funds, CAP, EU budget and taxation. Second, the Irish system was highly adaptable and flexible when dealing with Brussels. Irish civil servants were pragmatic and problem-driven rather than ideological and doctrinaire. They carefully played the Brussels system with the resources at their disposal. Third, Irish civil servants used all opportunities available to them to act in a *communautaire* manner, particularly by running highly efficient and effective presidencies. Fourth, following the Nice referendum defeat, the system moved very quickly to review the management of European affairs within the civil service, the political system and the public. The strengths identified above enabled Ireland to deliver on its core priorities in major European negotiations since accession. The presidencies, major budgetary negotiations and the agreement on the Constitutional Treaty in June 2004 stand among the shining lights of EU membership.

The weaknesses of the Irish system must also be highlighted. First, the weakly institutionalised nature of the Irish system until the post-Nice period meant that a heavy burden was placed on the individual civil servants representing Ireland. They could not rely on a highly structured domestic system of policy preparation and development. Domestic departments differed in the time and attention that was paid to European business. The civil servants in the Permanent Representation in Brussels frequently had to rely on their personal judgment in the absence of instructions from Dublin. Second, the small size of the EU cadre meant that Irish delegations were small and heavily dependent on the calibre of the individual civil servant. Too often, Ireland was represented at levels of seniority way below those of other countries. This inevitably had an impact on the status of that individual in the negotiations and on his or her ability to influence proceedings. Moreover, not all Irish civil servants were culturally comfortable in the multilingual environment in Brussels. Speaking English is an advantage but continental European languages remain significant in the informal processes that surround EU negotiations. Third, the small size of the civil service also militates against the contacts that must be maintained in a much larger EU with many more small states. Fourth, Ireland did not always have adequate technical resources to understand highly technical regulations fully, which in turn led to implementation difficulties in Ireland. In a number of important policy fields, Ireland's implementation record is poor.

Positioning Ireland in the EU of twenty-seven member states and in the wider world poses a challenge for the Irish civil service in the decades ahead. The imperative of economic catch-up provided a road map for Ireland's policy preferences for the first thirty years of membership. Having achieved catch-up, the challenge facing Ireland today is to maintain its embeddedness within the EU while at the same time projecting Ireland in a globalised world. There are a number of strands in the external projection of Ireland that rightly go beyond the EU. First is the Asia Strategy, dating from 2000, that identifies relations with the major Asian countries as a top priority for Ireland's future. Second is the commitment to quadruple Ireland's development cooperation budget by 2012. Third is to promote Ireland's experience of conflict management and resolution as a model for other conflict situations in the world. These three major developments point to the re-emergence of a distinctive Irish identity and role in the world that goes beyond EU membership. This is possible because Ireland achieved key domestic goals through EU membership.

11

The European Union and the Oireachtas

Gavin Barrett[1]

Development of parliamentary control of the government's actions in Europe

Prior to the entry of Ireland into the European Economic Community, its parliament – the Oireachtas – had no serious role in controlling or monitoring the actions of the Irish government in European matters. This situation stood in marked contrast with the pre-entry experience of many other European countries – such as Denmark (which joined at the same time as Ireland and whose legislature had been involving itself in European matters since as far back as 1961) and later Finland, Sweden and Slovenia (see Fink-Hafner, 2007; Raunio and Wiberg, 2007). The historically subservient role of the Oireachtas was probably the dominant factor here (see generally Laffan, 2005b, for a discussion of parliamentary control of executive involvement in European Union affairs).

The relatively uncontroversial nature of the objective of Irish membership of the Community – reflected in the massive 83 per cent vote in favour of entry in the 1972 referendum on this topic – has been argued to have been a possible further contributory factor for such torpor by ensuring that there would be no pressure on the government to set up any such parliamentary body (Laffan, 2005b).[2]

On Irish entry to the Community, however, a role was finally created for the Oireachtas, in that provision was made for the creation of a Joint Oireachtas Committee on the Secondary Legislation of the European

---

[1] The work in this chapter is based on research for the IRCHSS-funded project *Ireland, Europe and the Challenge of Democracy – Ensuring Democratic Control over Government in European Union Affairs* and the themes dealt with in this chapter are elaborated upon at greater length in Barrett (2007).
[2] For an interesting study of referenda generally in the Irish political system see Sinnott (2002).

Communities. As its name would suggest, this committee, which came into being in July 1973 under the newly elected Fine Gael–Labour coalition, drew its membership from both the Dáil and the Seanad with political parties being represented in proportion to the number of their representatives in each House. The existence of the committee represented very slight progress in redressing the balance between the executive and the legislature (although in the context of membership of the Community, which meant it could be expected, given its institutional make-up, to reinforce the prerogatives of the executive). Thus it permitted the development of some expertise in European matters among that small body of parliamentarians who made up its members (see Chapter 5), with future President Mary Robinson playing a significant role in its activities (see Robinson, 1979, for details on the work of this committee).

Although the committee was to see its terms of reference gradually expanded over time (Robinson, 1979), it was nonetheless confined for the duration of its existence to playing a relatively minor role and furthermore was crippled by a range of problems, not least of which was a lack of resources.[3] Even what little advantage it had in terms of its intellectual resources and institutional memory was affected by the fact that its membership endured only as long as the relevant parliamentary term. There was certainly never any prospect of such a committee exercising any serious control or influence over the government. In 1993 – ironically, at a time when the involvement of the Labour Party in the Reynolds-led Fianna Fáil–Labour coalition resulted in an increase in the role of Oireachtas committees – an end was put to the existence of the Joint Oireachtas Committee on Secondary Legislation when it was subsumed into the Foreign Affairs Committee. As might have been expected, this effort to deal with European affairs in the Oireachtas as a kind of sub-category of foreign affairs generally was not a success, and was to be a short-lived venture.

Under the Rainbow coalition government led by John Bruton, a Joint Oireachtas Committee on European Affairs was established in 1995. In keeping with the evolution of a more favourable attitude of parties other than Fianna Fáil to committees (see MacCarthaigh, 2005, pp. 72–93), the new committee was given a wider remit than the earlier Joint Oireachtas Committee on Secondary Legislation. Notwithstanding this reform (and the retention of this new committee under the Bertie Ahern-led Fianna

---

[3] See in this last regard the revealing report relating to this topic in the *Irish Independent* of 19 July 1974.

Fáil–Progressive Democrats governments after 1997),[4] the reality of the conduct of Ireland's relations with the EU was that they remained utterly executive-dominated.

The shock defeat of the government side in Ireland's first Nice referendum campaign in June 2001 was to result in changes. The consequences of these events has been as good an illustration as any of the enduring truth of Monnet's dictum that 'people only accept change when they are faced with necessity, and only recognise necessity when a crisis is upon them' (Monnet, 1978). In this case, the necessity which made itself evident was the political necessity to redress at least to some degree the almost complete imbalance of power in Ireland between legislature and executive in European matters before another constitutional referendum necessary to permit ratification of the Nice Treaty could be held.

In one way, it was ironic that the ratification of the Treaty of Nice provided the flashpoint for the emergence of the issue of parliamentary scrutiny of the Irish government's EU activities, since the actual content of the Nice Treaty had little if anything to do with it. Nonetheless, the ratification process of the Nice Treaty provided an opportunity for the issue to be raised, which it was – most prominently in a May 2001 article in *The Irish Times* by a former Attorney General, John Rogers, in which he announced his personal preparedness to vote against enabling ratification of the Treaty of Nice in the then forthcoming referendum (Rogers, 2001). Those of Rogers' arguments objecting to the European-level institutional rearrangements which were the main concern of the Nice Treaty arguably took insufficient account both of political realities and of the institutional needs of enlargement, and the treaty was ultimately to be ratified with the relevant provisions still in place. But Rogers' objections to the fact that Ireland had 'not sought to adjust its domestic institutions and constitutional arrangements' and that 'the Oireachtas has been entirely sidelined in the context of legislation emerging from the institutions of the Community' were a different matter. These words struck an undeniable chord (although, puzzlingly, the fact that the Oireachtas had also been confined to an extremely limited role in the context of domestic legislation for the previous six decades seemed to escape the attention of almost all contributors to this debate). At any rate, after the defeat of the initial Nice referendum in June 2001, the government felt compelled to defuse the

---

[4] The most recent Joint Oireachtas Committee on European Affairs at the time of writing was established in the wake of the May 2002 general election, following Orders of Dáil Éireann on 27 June 2002 and of Seanad Éireann on 17 October 2002. Following the 2007 general election, a motion was passed in Dáil Éireann on 23 October 2007 to re-establish the committee.

issue of the limited role of the Oireachtas in European affairs before putting a constitutional referendum before the electorate again in October 2002.

Current approach – European Union (Scrutiny) Act 2002

A revised system of scrutiny and oversight was thus introduced by the Fianna Fáil–Progressive Democrats government in the summer of 2002. This was at first done informally, and then, at least in part, given a legislative basis with the enactment of the European Union (Scrutiny) Act 2002. Because, at the time of its enactment, the government was faced with the prospect of a further referendum on the Treaty of Nice, it strove for a large measure of consensus in relation to this measure. The compromise forged as a result has endured to the present. The reformed system of Oireachtas scrutiny in European affairs introduced at this time has two aspects to it (see Meenan, 2007; O'Hegarty, 2007).

In the first place, there is a system of review of EU-level legislative proposals, summarised by O'Hegarty (2007, pp. 281–282) as follows:

> ... the Government forwards to the European Union Committee all legislative proposals (across all three pillars of the Union), together with information notes outlining the purpose, significance and implications of the texts presented. The Sub-Committee [on European Scrutiny] then conducts a preliminary survey of the various proposals, with a view to prioritising them. Prioritisation means making a 'judgment-call' about which proposals are most significant in terms of policy, in order to ensure that adequate time and attention can be devoted to these. Proposals which have been identified for further scrutiny are then referred to the relevant sectoral committees to be considered in greater detail.[5]

This obviously represented a significant change in practice. The new system is also, however, a carefully restricted one. The effect of a recommendation made either by the Joint Oireachtas Committee on European Affairs or by any other committee is limited indeed. Thus the

---

[5] Note in this regard Section 2(1) of the European Union (Scrutiny) Act 2002, whereby 'as soon as practicable after a proposed measure is presented by the Commission of the European Communities or initiated by a Member State, as the case may be, the Minister shall cause a copy of the text concerned to be laid before each House of the Oireachtas together with a statement of the Minister outlining the content, purpose and likely implications for Ireland of the proposed measure and including such other information as he or she considers appropriate'.

relevant government minister is obliged merely to 'have regard to any recommendations made to him or her from time to time ... in relation to a proposed measure'.[6] The minister is thus not bound by any veto or even by a scrutiny reserve. Furthermore, even this limited obligation placed on ministers is subject to exceptions. It does not apply 'where there is insufficient time for the carrying out of the procedures aforesaid and the performance of the functions of the Houses of the Oireachtas' or in relation to 'a proposed measure which, in the opinion of the Minister, is confidential'.[7]

The second aspect of Oireachtas oversight of the executive since 2002 is one that derives from practice rather than law and that to this day remains unsupported by legislative provision; the government having declined to make provision in this regard in the 2002 Act. It consists of the arrangement that government ministers or ministers of state make themselves available (in particular before meetings of the Council of Ministers and the European Council) for discussions with the Joint Oireachtas Committee on European Affairs or the relevant sectoral committee, as appropriate. The government is understood to have suggested that the norm should be for a minister to be requested to appear before the relevant sectoral committee in the week before the relevant meeting of the Council of Ministers (O'Hegarty, 2007).

One aspect of this latter practice is that prior to each meeting of the General Affairs and External Relations Council, the Joint Oireachtas Committee on European Affairs is given an opportunity to meet with either the Minister for Foreign Affairs or the Minister of State for European Affairs to discuss the Council's agenda. In 2006 the Joint Committee held only six meetings in advance of General Affairs and External Relations Council meetings, a frequency which constituted a light legislative control indeed, bearing in mind that there were no less than thirteen such Council meetings at European level in 2006 (see Sub-Committee on European Scrutiny, 2007).

A final element of the post-2002 scrutiny or overview process which merits mention is the fact that Section 2(5) of the 2002 Act requires that every government minister make a report to each House

---

[6] Section 2(2) of the 2002 Act refers to recommendations 'by either or both Houses of the Oireachtas or by a committee of either or both such Houses'. The reference to recommendations by either or both Houses has in practice been largely superfluous to date since reference onwards by a committee of issues referred to them for full Oireachtas debates, although a theoretical possibility, does not normally occur (see O'Hegarty, 2007). The Act also provides for the possibility of ministers or officials being invited to appear before a committee.

[7] Sections 2(3) and 3(1) of the 2002 Act.

of the Oireachtas not less than twice yearly in relation to measures, proposed measures and other developments concerning the European Communities and the European Union in relation to which he or she performs functions.

Although the creation of such scrutiny mechanisms has been an improvement on the previous situation, their effectiveness in securing executive accountability remains open to doubt. With the second method of scrutiny mentioned above, as with the first, the relevant Irish minister is not bound in any way by the position taken by the Oireachtas, and the benefit of these processes has been questioned. One minister in the outgoing Fianna Fáil–Progressive Democrat coalition government in mid-2007 was prepared to assert to this author that he had never heard a useful contribution made at any committee meeting involving the deployment of the second method of scrutiny.

Meenan (2007), on the other hand, has been able to cite a small number of examples of where meetings of the Joint Oireachtas Committee on European Affairs clearly have had an impact on government policy (and indeed on European policy generally, as Ireland happened to hold the presidency of the Council of Ministers at the relevant time). In addition, it does seem likely that, as Meenan (2007, p. 318) has observed, 'specific, well-informed views, expressed in a consensual, cross-party setting' will tend to have an impact on ministerial positions. However, given the lack of research capacity on the part of Oireachtas committees, it is not clear how often well-informed views are actually made available to ministers in such meetings.

In any case, the extent to which ministers appear before Oireachtas committees has clearly varied considerably. By 2006, for example, O'Hegarty could point out, first, that all hearings of the Committee on Communications, Marine and Natural Resources (a committee chosen by that writer as a representative example) had involved detailed questioning of officials, but 'never of a Minister' and, second, that there had also been very little scrutiny of ministerial performance in the Council of Ministers (O'Hegarty, 2007, p. 290).

Analysing the performance of the Oireachtas

Various methods of classifying national parliaments have been put forward and can be used to gauge the relative strength of the Oireachtas in European affairs (i.e. compared to other national parliaments – for a summary see Maurer, 2007). Thus, for example, Mezey (1979) has distinguished between:

- Parliaments strong enough to veto policy proposals, modify them or compromise over them
- Parliaments having the more modest right to modify, but not reject, policy proposals
- Parliaments which can neither modify nor reject proposals put forward by the executive.

Norton (1984), in contrast, is prepared to classify none of the foregoing as parliaments with strong policy-making power. For Norton, a parliament is strong only if it can generate its own proposals, which it can substitute for the original government proposal. Whether one accepts Mezey's or Norton's definition of what is deemed to be strength in a legislature, it is clear that the Oireachtas, notwithstanding recent reforms, cannot be defined as a strong legislative body when judged by such criteria. Indeed, insofar as concerns European affairs, Maurer (2007) has classified the Oireachtas as a parliament which is a 'slow adaptor' to the reality of European integration, with a relatively weak involvement in policy-making at both national and European levels. Thus, according to Maurer, even insofar as concerns *national-level* policy-making on European matters, Ireland's parliament is comparatively weakly involved – especially when compared with member states such as Austria and the Netherlands. As for the participation of the Oireachtas in European-level (i.e. Brussels) policy-making, this is also weak, compared in particular with that of the parliaments of Finland and Denmark. Maurer's classification exercise was carried out before the 2002 reforms were put into effect, but those reforms do not in any case appear to have been far-reaching enough to justify a reclassification of Ireland's performance according to his typology.

Why has the performance of the Oireachtas been so weak? An inherited tradition of strong executives and weak legislatures is clearly one reason. What may perhaps be regarded as a corollary of this, the extremely weak committee structure in both Houses of the Oireachtas, also merits mention beyond that already made above. When it comes to analysing any system of scrutiny which has at its core the operation of an Oireachtas committee, there is a need to understand the context in which such committees operate.

There is frequently little if any electoral incentive for TDs to participate actively in any such committees. One government minister, who had some years earlier lost his seat in the Dáil before eventually being re-elected and gaining ministerial office, observed to this author that he had on entering the Dáil for the first time been warned by an older and more experienced politician on the opposing side of the political divide that one could 'talk oneself out of' the lower House. The accuracy of this warning had subsequently been made clear when a period of very dedicated committee work on the part of the future minister was followed by the loss of his Dáil seat, almost ending his political career and leaving him to appreciate ruefully the dangers which attend the payment of more attention to Oireachtas committee work than to servicing the (non-legislative) needs of constituents.

Political near-death experiences of this nature illustrate the reality that TDs who wish to retain their Dáil seats ignore at their peril the general lack of media interest or, for that matter, public interest in the work of Oireachtas committees. For now, constituency work – in other words attempting to assist constituents in dealing with the administration – is considerably more valuable in securing re-election. The consequences are somewhat inevitable: in such circumstances, it is simply not possible for the work of Oireachtas committees to be the top priority of their members. Necessarily, the work of such committees suffers as a result. They frequently do not use all their powers. Nor are they competitive in securing resources: hence, a large part of the increased resources made available for the benefit of Oireachtas members in recent years in the wake of the enactment of the Oireachtas Commission Act 2003 has been used – with the agreement of all of the political parties – to provide assistance which enables TDs to carry out their constituency roles, rather than to support their functions as legislators. The question of resources is considered further below.

As if such impediments to the effectiveness of Oireachtas committees as mechanisms of accountability were not enough, the usefulness of such committees is also severely restricted as a result of a rivalry between political parties which ensures that membership of such committees is determined primarily by party allegiance rather than expertise in a particular subject area. Party loyalty will also ensure that a minister can in general rely on approximately half of any Oireachtas committee having relatively little interest in showing the work the minister has done in a poor light through strong criticism. Eight members of the seventeen-member Joint Oireachtas Committee on European Affairs in place until mid-2007 belonged to government parties. Meenan (2007) has noted that this committee has traditionally operated on a bipartisan basis and seeks never to call votes, a description which might seem to contradict the image just presented of a committee handicapped by political considerations from demanding accountability. However, such bipartisanship only seems possible because virtually the entire committee – rather than merely those of its members who belong to government parties – sees its role as one broadly supportive of the Irish minister in Europe, as opposed to a role whereby the legislature imposes real accountability on the executive. As

Meenan (2007, p. 315) puts it, 'the *modus operandi* of the Joint Committee is consensual rather than confrontational'. In the context of European affairs, however, a bipartisan and broadly pro-European stance (in the 2002–2007 Oireachtas, on the part of all but one member of the Committee on European Affairs) has come, perhaps paradoxically, at the price of reducing its impact as a mechanism of executive accountability.

The situation in the Irish committee is to be contrasted with the far more challenging reception that can await government ministers in the legislatures of other similar-sized EU member states. Hence the recent alleged failure by the Danish Foreign Minister to brief the Danish parliament on the application to an Iranian opposition group of EU legislation directed at terrorist organisations led to an opposition MP drafting a formal rebuke for the minister to be voted on by the relevant parliamentary committee (Rettman, 2005 – for a critical examination of some of the reasons for the more powerful position of the legislatures vis-à-vis executives in Nordic countries, see Raunio and Wiberg, 2007). As of yet, such a confrontational approach has failed to evolve in the Oireachtas.

Lessons to be learned from home and abroad?

It is not easy to imagine a significant rebalancing of the relationship of the Oireachtas and the government in European affairs in the absence of a general rebalancing taking place in relation to other policy areas. Nevertheless, suggestions are made from time to time as to how legislative scrutiny of the executive can more effectively be carried out by national legislatures generally (not just the Oireachtas) in the specific field of European affairs. Among the various prerequisites for more effective scrutiny which have been suggested (see, for example, Jones, 2005) are:

- The need for adequate resources to be provided to enable legislatures to carry out effective scrutiny
- The need for such scrutiny to involve a real process of dialogue between legislatures and executives
- The need for intervention on the part of national legislatures at an early point in the EU policy-making process
- The need for legislatures to consult with individuals and bodies outside the legislature
- The need for national legislatures to coordinate their schedule with that of the Council of Ministers

- The need for legislatures proactively to seek information themselves rather than merely rely on whatever information is given to them by the executive
- The need for legislatures to vary their approach to scrutiny depending on the policy field or integration method at issue.

It is worth considering how well the Oireachtas has been doing by reference to each of these suggestions.

The need for resources
The funding made available to the Oireachtas and its members has increased considerably in recent years. However, in considering whether the need has been met for adequate resources to be provided to enable the legislature to carry out its largely committee-based task of scrutiny of the executive in European policy-making, it is instructive to mention that the latest published estimates of the Houses of the Oireachtas Commission foresee total expenditure in 2007 on the expenses of all Oireachtas committees as less than €1.5 million – an amount similar to that spent in 2006 – out of a total anticipated budget of over €122 million for the Oireachtas as a whole. To put this figure in context, this is slightly over half the estimated cost in 2007 of 'televising of proceedings of Dáil Éireann and Seanad Éireann and other services' and is less than the anticipated expenditure in respect of catering and bar staff employed by the Joint House Services Committee (Houses of the Oireachtas Commission, 2006).

Meenan (2007, p. 319) has described the entire Oireachtas committee system as 'woefully short of resources'. It is scarcely any wonder, given such a small, and clearly inadequate, level of investment in the committee system generally, that the system of scrutiny of European policy-making – heavily centred as it is on committee work – is also under-resourced.

The most recent annual report on the operation of the European Union (Scrutiny) Act 2002 observes that 'one of the most serious concerns the [Sub-Committee on European Scrutiny] has had during the development of Oireachtas scrutiny is the level of resources which have been available' and notes that 'concerns remain at the level of administrative support available to support this process'. Indeed the very last words of the report observe that 'adequate resources are required to facilitate the [Sub-Committee] in particular to take full advantage of technological advances. The ever-increasing recognition of the role of national parliaments and the requirement to engage citizens in European affairs requires this' (Sub-Committee on European Scrutiny, 2007, p. 73).

The need for a genuine legislature–executive dialogue
It has already been noted above that the system of legislative scrutiny introduced in Ireland in 2002 suffers from the limitation that no provision is made for government ministers to be bound by any veto or even by a scrutiny reserve. The holding of the executive to account by the Oireachtas is further hobbled by another factor – the failure to make the process of legislative scrutiny involve, in any meaningful sense, a dialogue between the legislature and executive.

In no committee does there appear to have been any meaningful practice of following-up those issues that were initially raised or discussed in a particular committee meeting. A good example of the lack of feedback may be seen in the case of the Joint Oireachtas Committee on European Affairs, which is briefed only before meetings of the General Affairs and External Relations Council, and not after. This is not untypical. Having expressed their views to ministers, Oireachtas committees generally have, to date, remained starved of information as to the outcome – if any – of their own contribution to the European policy-making process (O'Hegarty, 2007). This seems a critical lacuna in the system of legislative overview of the executive by Oireachtas committees.[8]

The need for early intervention by national legislatures
The need for national legislatures to time their intervention at as early a point as possible in the EU policy-making process in order to maximise any prospect of influencing the eventual outcome of the process is one that is frequently stressed (Raunio, 2007). This need is not being met in the Irish context. This is not necessarily entirely the fault of the executive: the reality is that even after proposed measures have been referred to the Oireachtas by the government for scrutiny, a time-lag of several months has tended to occur between this referral and the actual scrutiny by the relevant Oireachtas sectoral committee (O'Hegarty, 2007). Influence, in any case, is sometimes more usefully exercised before an individual European legislative proposal is published by the Commission – in other

---

[8] Interestingly, the Joint Oireachtas Committee on European Affairs now engages in some limited dialogue with the European Commission, which has made internal administrative arrangements to deal with observations received from national parliaments. The committee's 2006 annual report observes that it 'views the Commission's decision to consider and respond to comments from national parliaments as an important signal in the increasing cooperation between the Commission and national parliaments in EU policy-making. The Committee has for some time engaged directly with the European Commission by sending contributions to Commission proposals, white papers and green papers. The new Commission initiative, which provides an official channel of communication between national parliaments and the Commission, will reinforce this exchange and cooperation' (Joint Oireachtas Committee on European Affairs, 2007a, p. 16).

words when work programmes or Commission green or white papers are published. In this respect, although O'Hegarty has noted that the Sub-Committee on European Scrutiny has 'routinely' examined green and white papers (and to this may be added the observation that the Joint Oireachtas Committee on European Affairs has itself – albeit infrequently – made contributions in respect of Commission green and white papers), sectoral Oireachtas committees do not seem typically to involve themselves in scrutiny of Commission work programmes or other preparatory documents (O'Hegarty, 2007).

It is true that the work programme of the Joint Oireachtas Committee on European Affairs is at least informed by the work programmes of the European Commission for the calendar year, and of the presidency of the Council at least for the first half of the calendar year. But the effect of this is moderated by the need to take into account various other factors such as the Joint Committee's own priorities and work in progress, including the ongoing work of the Scrutiny Sub-Committee (Joint Oireachtas Committee on European Affairs, 2007b).

The need for consultation outside the legislature
The need for legislatures to consult with individuals and bodies outside the legislature itself is sometimes mentioned as a desideratum when it comes to matters European (Jones, 2005). Such meetings with non-members of the legislature may seek to serve a number of functions. In the first place, they may involve an effort by the legislature to be better informed about initiatives at European level and about relevant policy considerations.[9] Meetings may also involve an attempt to keep government ministers and other players in the European policy-making process (such as commissioners or MEPs) better informed of the national parliamentary perspective. Thirdly, they may involve an effort to stimulate awareness on the part of interest groups within the Irish electorate (such as farmers, trade unions or employers) of legislative or executive action proposed or being taken at EU level.

The degree of involvement of parliamentary outsiders obviously varies from one Oireachtas committee to another. The Committee on Communications, Marine and Natural Resources, for example, has invited interest groups to meetings (such as non-governmental organisations when discussing the Internet, and fisheries groups in discussing marine issues) (O'Hegarty, 2007). As for the Joint Committee on European Affairs itself,

---

[9] According to its website (http://euaffairs.ie/), the Joint Oireachtas Committee on European Affairs receives oral presentations from individuals and bodies 'in order to hear their views and perspectives on issues under consideration'.

in recent times it appears to have made considerable efforts to involve Oireachtas 'outsiders', both as invitees before and as participants in the Joint Committee. Insofar as involving them as participants is concerned, according to the relevant Orders of Reference,[10] certain persons who are not appointed to the Committee from the membership of the Dáil or Seanad may attend meetings and take part in proceedings (although without having a right to vote or to move motions and amendments). These include:

- MEPs elected from constituencies in Ireland (including Northern Ireland)
- Members of the Irish delegation to the Parliamentary Assembly of the Council of Europe
- At the invitation of the Joint Committee, other – i.e. non-Irish – MEPs.

Examples of bringing in outsiders as invitees may be seen in the list of persons invited before the Joint Committee on European Affairs in the first three months of 2007, when the committee engaged in a discussion with an admirably broad, although perhaps somewhat eclectic, selection of interlocutors consisting of the Commissioner for Fisheries and Maritime Affairs, the Foreign Minister of Armenia and the Speaker of the Slovakian Parliament. Looking at the entire period covered by its 2006 annual report (Joint Oireachtas Committee on European Affairs, 2007a), the Joint Committee records having met during this time with three Irish government ministers, two Irish junior ministers,[11] the Ukrainian foreign minister, six representatives of EU institutions,[12] three ambassadors to Ireland,[13] three delegations sent from parliaments of European countries,[14] a representative of one intergovernmental organisation[15] and of one non-governmental organisation,[16] seven Irish government department

---

[10] These are to be found in Appendix I of Joint Oireachtas Committee on European Affairs (2007a). See in this regard the Orders of Reference made by Dáil Éireann on 16 October 2002 at paragraph 2(c) thereof, and the Orders of Reference made by Seanad Éireann on 17 October 2002 at paragraph 1(c) thereof.

[11] According to its account, in the period under report the Select Committee on European Affairs met with the Minister of State for Foreign Affairs on only two occasions, which seems a surprisingly small number of meetings.

[12] Ranging from the President of the European Parliament to a head of unit within a directorate-general of the Commission.

[13] From Finland, Romania and Bulgaria.

[14] From France, Poland and Iceland.

[15] Former Commissioner Peter Sutherland in his capacity as Special Representative of the UN Secretary General for Migration.

[16] The Immigrant Council of Ireland.

officials,[17] four statutory bodies or agencies,[18] representatives of the Irish Farmers' Association, plus one academic from Trinity College. In addition, the Joint Committee held what it referred to as 'informal private meetings' with five other officials or public representatives from other European countries.[19] Committee members have also engaged in a considerable amount of travel – in the course of 2006, committee members made a total of twenty-nine individual trips abroad, of rather varying degrees of seeming usefulness, to Austria, Finland, Estonia, Belgium, Lithuania, Latvia, Bulgaria, Romania, Monaco, Italy, Russia and France (Joint Oireachtas Committee on European Affairs, 2007a).

While one cannot quibble with the fact that a reasonable level of activity is involved in the organisation or attendance of many of the above such meetings, it does seem legitimate to query how systematically linked these meetings were with the objectives of providing some input into the legislative or policy-making process at European level or with controlling government activity in this regard, and further how effective such activities have been. In other words, the Joint Committee on European Affairs may well have succeeded in better informing itself about European affairs through such meetings, but whether it has achieved any more than that seems open to question.

The usefulness of the Oireachtas as an entity for transmitting information 'upwards' to policy-making players is severely restricted by the lack of provision made for government ministers to be bound by any veto or scrutiny reserve by Oireachtas committees and, more generally, by the failure to make the process of legislative scrutiny generate a meaningful dialogue between the legislature and executive. The usefulness of the Oireachtas as an entity for transmitting information 'downwards' seems to have been hobbled by the very limited ability which the Oireachtas has had to date in attracting the attention of either the electorate or the media in the work it does. Although, according to its 2006 annual report (Joint Oireachtas Committee on European Affairs, 2007a, p. 7), 'the Joint Committee on European Affairs has given high priority in its work programme to raising national awareness of European issues and to reconnecting the people with the European Union and its institutions', it would be difficult to view the committee as having been a major success in this respect. Such work arguably continues to be

---

[17] Although it may be noted that four of these were from the Department of Transport.

[18] The Ombudsman and representatives of FÁS, the Equality Authority and the Marine Institute.

[19] Namely, the Deputy Foreign Minister of Moldova, the Bulgarian Minister for Labour, the Cypriot Ambassador to Ireland, the German Minister of State for Europe and a member of the French National Assembly.

better done by the National Forum on Europe, a body which it is noticeable that the government has felt the need to maintain in existence for several years (see Brown, 2007, and www.forumoneurope.ie for further details).

The need for coordination with the schedule of the Council of Ministers

In order to maximise the influence of the Oireachtas on the executive when government ministers participate in Council meetings, there is an obvious need for the Oireachtas to coordinate its schedule with that of the Council of Ministers. At least some effort has been made in this regard since the new system of overview was introduced in 2002, in that government departments now forward draft and revised agendas for Council meetings to the secretariat of the Sub-Committee on European Scrutiny, which then notifies all other Oireachtas committees. In addition, the 2002–2007 government is reported to have suggested that the norm be that a minister be requested by the relevant Oireachtas committee to appear before it in the week prior to the relevant Council meeting (O'Hegarty, 2007). In practice, it may be noted, such appearances have indeed become the norm for some individual ministers but certainly not all of them (see above regarding the Committee on Communications, Marine and Natural Resources).

Much, however, clearly remains to be done. Thus, for example, the meetings of the Joint Oireachtas Committee on European Affairs, although reasonably frequent and regular during the parliamentary calendar, tend to take place only during that time. This is notwithstanding the fact that the European-level activities of the government it supervises are not so temporally restricted.

The need for alternative sources of information

The need for legislatures to seek out information proactively rather than to have it provided to them by the executive has been suggested as desirable if effective scrutiny in the field of European affairs is to be assured. This need, if it is one, is not met in Ireland. In practice, what happens in Ireland is that information comes via government departments. Hence, it is the Department of Foreign Affairs which is responsible for forwarding all EU documents to the relevant government department that then forwards the documents along with an information note to the Sub-Committee on European Scrutiny (Sub-Committee on European Scrutiny, 2007). This is in line with the approach of the European Union (Scrutiny) Act 2002, according to Section 2(1) of which, as soon as practicable after a proposed measure is presented (i.e. at EU level) by the Commission or initiated by a member state, the relevant minister shall cause a copy of the text concerned to be laid before each House of the Oireachtas 'together with a statement of the Minister outlining the content, purpose and likely implications for Ireland of the proposed measure and including such other information as he or she considers appropriate'. In practice, the information note also states the anticipated negotiation period and the expected implementation date of the measure.

In this process, the Department of Foreign Affairs acts as a liaison point between the Oireachtas and the government departments, ensuring that the Sub-Committee on European Scrutiny is provided with information notes on all proposals falling within the terms of the European Union (Scrutiny) Act 2002 and on all documents that the sub-committee has requested to be examined. There is no suggestion of any bad faith on the part of anyone involved in any of this work. Nonetheless it does seem to involve somewhat peculiar institutional logic to compel a legislature seeking to hold to account a government minister to depend on that minister's department for virtually all of the information it needs to carry out this task. At the very least it would appear desirable that additional sources of information would be available to Oireachtas committees in this situation, so that a legitimately critical approach may be taken in the consideration by the Oireachtas of the executive's performance of its tasks. At present, however, the Sub-Committee on European Scrutiny appears to engage in its work on the basis only of 'detailed examination of the material presented [i.e. in the above-described manner] and the conclusions of additional enquiries made by [its] Policy Advisor in relation to these matters' (Sub-Committee on European Scrutiny, 2007, p. 7). Improvement here is clearly desirable, either at the level of the Sub-Committee on European Scrutiny or on the part of the various sectoral committees who carry out the actual scrutiny and need to acquire and deploy the appropriate information resources to ensure accountability, or both.

Two recent improvements in this regard are worthy of note. The first is that, in 2006, national parliaments gained the ability to exchange EU-related information directly via the Interparliamentary EU Information Exchange (IPEX) – a website set up as the result of a series of decisions taken by the Conference of the Speakers of EU Parliaments in 2000, 2003 and 2004.[20] Not only can the Oireachtas now benefit from information uploaded onto the IPEX database by other parliaments, but, since September 2006, the Sub-Committee on European Scrutiny has commenced uploading information onto this site in relation to Irish

---

[20] The IPEX website address is http://www.ipex.eu/ipex/cms/pid/

scrutiny of EU legislation. Another effect of this initiative is of course that badly lacking 'public visibility, accountability, appreciation and understanding of what the Houses and their Members do on a day to day basis is maintained and improved' (Sub-Committee on European Scrutiny, 2007, p. 72).

A second initiative which may lead to some long-term improvement is that, since September 2006, the EU Commission has transmitted proposals for EU legislation, and also discussion documents relating to legislation, directly to national parliaments at the same time as these are sent to the Council and the European Parliament. Interestingly, the Sub-Committee on European Scrutiny asserted in its 2006 report that the Joint Oireachtas Committee on European Affairs had for some time engaged directly with the European Commission by sending contributions to Commission proposals, white papers and green papers. The Joint Oireachtas Committee on European Affairs expressed the hope that the new Commission initiative, 'which provides an official channel of communication between national parliaments and the Commission, will reinforce this exchange and cooperation' (Sub-Committee on European Scrutiny, 2007, p. 72). It may also furnish Irish parliamentarians with at least the foundations of an alternative source of information to the administration in relation to such proposals, although clearly much remains to be done on this point.

The need to vary the approach according to policy area
Finally, it would seem barely more than a truism to observe that in order to maximise the influence of legislative scrutiny of executive action in the field of European policy-making, appropriate account must be taken of – and appropriate adjustment made for – the kind of European action which is being scrutinised. Significant EU activity now occurs in a wide range of fora – from the Council of Ministers (including COREPER), the Commission and the Parliament, to a multitude of technical committees, to institutions such as the European Central Bank. EU activity also spans an extremely broad range of policy areas (for example, from justice and home affairs to foreign and security policy to single market rules), and is subject to a broad range of procedural rules (from the codecision procedure to comitology to social dialogue to the open method of coordination). It seems clear that a sophisticated, differentiated approach needs to be taken to controlling the activities of the executive in such a context. There is little if any evidence that any such approach has yet been taken by the Oireachtas. In this author's experience, Oireachtas members' levels of awareness, even of what, to take just one example, the

deployment of the open method of coordination at European level has involved, appear to be very low even within the Joint Committee on European Affairs itself.

The future – Grounds for optimism or pessimism?

There has been considerable reform in the relationship between the legislature and the executive in Ireland in relation to European affairs, largely stemming from the time of debate over the Treaty of Nice. Notwithstanding this, however, any realistic assessment of the role of the Oireachtas in European matters must conclude that it is not much different to its role in every other area of policy-making – that is to say, the Oireachtas occupies a relatively weak and indeed subservient role in its relations with the executive.

There are historical and – at least in some respects – logically plausible explanations for this state of affairs. From the historical point of view we continue to live with an executive–legislature relationship, the main features of which were established (with the support of the members of the Oireachtas themselves) in the period just after independence was achieved and which have continued largely unaltered since then by successive administrations of every political variety. From a logical point of view, the maintenance of a situation in which the executive branch of government plays the leading role is far from indefensible. A considerable portion of the growth in power of the modern executive state stems from the need for all states to cope with the complexity of modern life, necessitating the creation of a large, expert and multidimensional civil service.

In the particular case of European policy matters, this complexity has manifested itself in the shape of the adoption at European level of a flood of necessary but highly technical legislation relating to everything from the CAP to the establishment and regulation of various aspects of the single European market.[21] There are efficiency considerations which must be borne in mind when structuring the relationship between each national executive and legislature in such circumstances (indeed, one is likely to be told sotto voce by Danish officials that the much stronger Danish system of parliamentary control of the executive is not without considerable drawbacks in terms of the amount of flexibility it leaves to representatives of the Danish government to respond to sometimes rapidly changing circumstances in discussions within the Council of Ministers). In addition, there may be some unavoidable structural reasons explaining at least some

---

[21] Buck (2007) notes the manner in which the EU has become the global pacesetter for technical regulation of various kinds.

of the relative weaknesses of the Oireachtas vis-à-vis the government. For example, in judging the failure of the Oireachtas to establish a committee system capable of holding the executive properly to account, we need to take into account arguments such as that of Meenan (2007), who asserts that because of the limited size of parliament in a country as small as Ireland, it will never be possible to develop the kind of committee system that exists in the United Kingdom. There is thus perhaps an element of advisability in being cautious about what one wishes for in arguing for a radically altered delineation of competences between the executive and the legislature.

Clearly, however, not every aspect of the lack of balance in the relationship between the Oireachtas and the government is inevitable. Ongoing policy choices are being made in this respect (and not by a disinterested party, but rather by the institution of government which, as executive, benefits the most from present arrangements). There are signs that the choice which has been made is not ideal. Opposition criticisms of the government attitude to the Oireachtas are of course far from infrequent, even if the temptation may exist to dismiss them as being made for political reasons. However, in the recent past, even government backbenchers have been occasionally prepared to express publicly their concern at their relative inability to influence policy (see, for example, Andrews, 2003). Indeed by June 2006 such frustrations were felt sufficiently strongly to result in sixteen Fianna Fáil deputies, members of the dominant party in the ruling coalition, signing a letter inviting other backbench TDs in this party to a meeting outside normal party structures (although it was ultimately decided to abandon the planned meeting when the government agreed to consider setting up a new party committee through which backbencher voices could be heard) (Brennock, 2006).

Further evidence, albeit of a different kind, that all may not be not well as regards the balance prevailing in Ireland between legislature and executive was provided by a national survey commissioned by the Houses of the Oireachtas Commission in 2006, which produced the finding that 60 per cent of respondents did not regard the work of the national parliament as important (Houses of the Oireachtas Commission, 2007a). This survey was deemed by the Houses of the Oireachtas Commission to show clearly the need to promote the work of parliament and its members, which seems a reasonable conclusion (Houses of the Oireachtas Commission, 2007a and 2007b; Donohoe, 2007). But arguably changes of substance in the role of the Oireachtas, not merely improvements in presentation, are also needed. There seems little point in trying to communicate the significance of the Oireachtas to the population at large if the reality is that it is a largely impotent institution.

The focus of this chapter is on the role of the Oireachtas in controlling the executive in the European policy-making field. In the last section above a list of desiderata has been set out, which, if met, might improve the performance of the Oireachtas in this regard. Beyond changes of the nature suggested in the section above, however, changes that would succeed in shifting the balance of power between the Oireachtas and the executive in a real sense in European affairs would require much more radical reform in the Houses of the Oireachtas. Thus, for example, it may be noted that in its control of the government's policy-making in European matters, the present role of the Oireachtas is an undeniably – and perhaps, given the electoral needs of its members, unavoidably – part-time affair, something which considerably reduces its effectiveness. In 2006 the Joint Oireachtas Committee on European Affairs succeeded in meeting on only thirty occasions. In its 2007 work programme, the committee expressed the intention to meet weekly in 2007, but fell well short of this target (one could make allowances for the fact that 2007 was a general election year – however, the business neither of government nor of the EU comes to a halt during elections).

Apart from the essentially part-time nature of Oireachtas control, and the sometimes major gaps in continuity which occur in its exercise, an intertwined difficulty in having the Oireachtas play an effective role is that the clientelistic nature of Irish politics results in the necessity for politicians to spend far more time servicing the advocacy needs of their electorate than engaging in legislative work. It is difficult to envisage any change occurring in this situation without reform of the Irish electoral system – and it is not clear that even this would be enough to reduce adequately the relative emphasis placed on constituency work rather than legislative activity on the part of members of the Dáil.[22]

By way of conclusion, it may be said that those reforms which have been introduced in the relationship between the legislature and the executive in the field of European policy-making have undoubtedly been welcome. However, a truly significant shift in power from executive to legislature in relation to the activities of the Irish state in European policy-making activities remains elusive. This is not, it must be emphasised, a phenomenon confined to the European policy-making field. It stretches across all areas of policy and law-making in Ireland. Real change in the present scenario is likely to require broad-ranging fundamental reforms, including of the Oireachtas itself, and affecting its role in all policy fields, not just that of European law and policy. Whether such reforms will ever come about, however, remains to be seen.

---

[22] For some reflections regarding the electoral system see Laver (1998) and FitzGerald (2000).

12

The Irish Contribution to 'Treaty-Making'

Mark Callanan[1]

Introduction

As well as examining Ireland's relationship with the European Union, past and present, a number of chapters in this book look at the impact the EU has had on Ireland, for example by exploring different EU policy areas from an Irish dimension. Scott, writing in 1994, turned the question 'what has the Union done for us?' on its head and considered Ireland's impact on the EU throughout its membership. Scott highlighted different aspects of Ireland's contribution to the integration process, from economic resources and trade flows, to Ireland's policy contribution, to the institutional input (for example the management of the presidency) and the human contribution that Irish nationals make in the activities of the EU institutions. This chapter examines a specific element of that contribution, namely Ireland's role in the treaty-making process and Ireland's involvement in the major changes to the Treaty of Rome since the country joined the then EEC in 1973.[2]

The treaties effectively act as the EU's rulebook, and are the fundamental basis on which all decisions are made at EU level. The treaties specify the areas in which the EU can adopt legislation and specify how this happens, including the roles of the different EU institutions. They also

---

[1] I would like to thank a number of individuals that were closely involved in treaty negotiations, including Jim Dooge, Noel Dorr, Bobby McDonagh and a number of anonymous interviewees, for kindly agreeing to be interviewed and for reviewing some of the material prepared for this chapter. Needless to say, however, the responsibility for any errors, omissions and comments rests with the author alone.

[2] It should be noted that this chapter does not enter into the debate over the merits or otherwise of treaty reforms, or indeed the ratification process and the referendum campaigns in Ireland on individual treaties, on which there is now an extensive literature (Gallagher, 1988; Holmes, 1993; Mansergh, 1999; O'Mahony, 2001 and 2004; Gilland, 2002; Hayward, 2003; Holmes, 2005b). Rather the chapter assesses the Irish contribution to the negotiation of the treaties themselves.

outline the objectives of the Union itself, as well as objectives for specific policy areas. Although in recent years there has been a debate over whether the term 'constitution' is an appropriate one to characterise the EU's basic law, the European Court of Justice as long ago as 1986 described the treaties as a 'constitutional charter' (Hartley, 1998; Weatherill, 2003; Shaw, 2000). Treaties therefore amount to the de facto constitutional framework for the EU.

These basic rules were originally established by the Treaty of Paris in 1951 and the two treaties signed in Rome in 1957. One of these, the Treaty of Rome establishing the EEC, in particular acts as the building block on which subsequent treaty reforms have been built. Subsequent 'treaties' such as the Single European Act or the Maastricht Treaty are effectively texts that amend the 'rulebook' and the Treaty of Rome itself. Cumulatively these 'treaty reforms' have radically changed the EU's primary legal framework from that of the founding treaties of the 1950s.

In assessing the Irish contribution to the 'treaty-making' process, it should be noted that there are three broad elements to the contribution that any member state can make to treaty reforms. Firstly, member states may contribute to treaty changes through putting forward submissions and suggestions for treaty reforms, usually related to particular themes, policy areas, aspects of institutional reform or changes to specific provisions or treaty articles. Secondly, a key contribution member states can make is to engage constructively in discussion and debates on the basis of ideas and proposals made for treaty changes. Finally, there is an often essential brokerage role that member states can be called on to play in mediating progress and finding compromises between different interests during the treaty-making process. Most commonly, of course, member states are called upon to play this role when they hold the presidency of the Council, although it can also arise on other occasions.

The next section of this chapter provides some background information on the process involved in amending and reforming the treaties. Subsequent sections then address the key changes to the founding treaties, particularly the Treaty of Rome. These reforms include the Single European Act, the Maastricht Treaty (Treaty on European Union), the Amsterdam Treaty, the Treaty of Nice, and most recently the abandoned Constitutional Treaty and the subsequent Reform Treaty. In each case, following a general overview of the final treaty, the Irish approach and contribution to the negotiations and the text are explained. The final section draws together a number of common themes from Ireland's track record in the treaty-making process, highlighting particular areas where Ireland has played an important role.

Background to treaty-making in the EU

The process of amending the treaties is subject to negotiation between the EU's member states, who must unanimously agree to any changes. An intergovernmental conference (IGC) is the name given to a series of meetings between representatives of each member state which are held with the purpose of negotiating the details of these changes.

Intergovernmental conferences operate at a number of levels. At political level, they involve national ministers, usually Ministers for Foreign Affairs.[3] During an IGC, ministers usually meet once a month, or more frequently as necessary, to review developments and discuss proposals for treaty changes.

More frequent meetings to discuss more detailed issues during an IGC would take place between ministerial representatives (usually senior officials). Occasional working parties of national experts might also be convened on particular issues as and when they arise.

The European Council, as the body representing the supreme political authority in each EU country, is kept regularly informed of progress being made. Ultimately, the intergovernmental conference culminates with agreement on a text (and on occasion an agreement to disagree) by the European Council. If such a text is agreed, it must be ratified in each country, either by a vote of the national parliament or by a referendum depending on the constitutional requirements of the country.

The presidency of the Council, which rotates between member states every six months, plays a particularly important role during an intergovernmental conference. The country holding the presidency chairs meetings of the IGC at all levels, and thus plays a crucial role in setting the agenda. For example, the presidency tables proposals and papers that are usually the focus of discussion at IGC meetings. The presidency is also to the forefront in searching for common ground between member states, progressing the negotiations, and to some extent shaping the content of treaty reforms, and ultimately determining whether an agreement is reached. Unlike day-to-day EU business, where the Commission sets the agenda by coming forward with proposals, at an IGC this role is largely determined by the presidency, albeit occasionally influenced by proposals coming from individual countries.

A new dimension was added to the treaty-making process during the preparation of the draft Constitutional Treaty – namely the convening of the Convention on the Future of Europe before the opening of an intergovernmental conference. This approach arose partly due to the desire

---

[3] The exception to this was the IGC on economic and monetary union leading to the Maastricht Treaty which involved Finance Ministers.

to involve national parliaments in the treaty-making process, and partly to introduce a greater degree of transparency to the process (see below). Many of the suggestions that arose from this convention were reflected in the Reform Treaty agreed in 2007. Such was the openness of this approach that many believe that the model of a convention followed by an IGC may well be used for any future significant changes to the treaties.

Some of the earlier treaty reforms did have a process of reflection that preceded the convening of an intergovernmental conference, although this tended to involve a smaller number of individuals representing national governments in a personal capacity. This approach was used, for example, in the Ad Hoc Committee on Institutional Affairs, which met in advance of the negotiations over the Single European Act, and the Reflection Group, which deliberated proposed treaty reforms before the IGC on the Amsterdam Treaty.

Single European Act

The Single European Act constituted the first major reform of the treaties and thus was a major milestone in the development of today's European Union. The reforms provided for new areas of activity at European level as well as changes to institutional arrangements. Amongst other things, the Single European Act:

- Introduced provisions on the single market, with a view to further liberalising trade and free movement of goods, services, capital and people within Europe
- Introduced a formal legal basis to allow legislation to be adopted at European level in areas such as environmental protection, economic and social cohesion, and research and development
- Provided for the use of the qualified majority voting system in the Council for decision-making in a number of areas, particularly those associated with completing the single market
- Introduced the 'cooperation' and 'assent' procedures, designed to give the European Parliament more of a say in legislation
- Introduced formal provisions to allow executive decisions to be delegated to the Commission
- Made other institutional changes, such as recognising the European Council, and establishing a Court of First Instance to deal with some of the caseload of the European Court of Justice
- Brought the arrangements for foreign policy cooperation, which had evolved during the 1970s and early 1980s, into the treaty framework.

A central part of the preparatory work for the negotiations leading to the Single European Act was the convening of a special committee of personal representatives of heads of state and government to discuss institutional reform. The European Council in Fontainbleau in 1984 had set up the Ad Hoc Committee for Institutional Affairs – usually known as the Dooge Committee as its chairman was Jim Dooge, the former Irish Foreign Minister. It was sometimes also known as 'Spaak II' because its mandate, according to the European Council conclusions at Fontainbleau, was to examine European institutions along 'the lines of the Spaak Committee' established in 1955 which had paved the way for the original Treaty of Rome (Moravcsik, 1991). In many ways, this indicated the level of importance and to some extent the level of ambition attached to the work of the committee.

The mandate given to the Dooge Committee was vague, apart from being asked to make 'suggestions for the improvement of the operation of European cooperation'. Meenan (1985 and 1999), who worked with the small secretariat for the Dooge Committee, notes that this general mandate was supplemented by further guidance from the incoming President of the European Council and Taoiseach, Garret FitzGerald, who wrote to the committee suggesting that it examine the functioning and decision-making arrangements of the institutions, the effectiveness of European cooperation in the socioeconomic sphere, and the possibility and modality of cooperation in areas such as education, culture, health, justice and combating terrorism (see also Keatinge and Murphy, 1987).

The fact that each member of the Dooge Committee was in regular contact with the respective head of state or government that had appointed them was critical and lent considerable clout to the recommendations the committee would make. A decision was made early on to try to come up with creative ideas, and the mandate of the group was essentially a political one (Meenan, 1985). According to the chairperson, this was reflected in the fact that the members of the committee would undertake most of the work themselves, to bring in fresh thinking, as opposed to having a large and perhaps cautious secretariat drawn from the EU institutions to do this (see also Keatinge and Murphy, 1987).

In fact, looking at the text of the Single European Act and the report of the Dooge Committee, it is clear that the committee heralded a large proportion of what was eventually incorporated into the Single European Act. This included proposals to complete different elements of the single market, as well as institutional reforms such as reducing the use of unanimity in the Council, giving greater powers to the European Parliament and strengthening the executive powers of the Commission. The report also proposed extending the competences of the European institutions by introducing new treaty provisions in areas such as foreign policy cooperation, social policy and research and development (Dooge Report, 1985). While some of these ideas were not entirely new, the priority attached to them by committee members in close contact with their heads of government, who would eventually have to sign off on any treaty reform, was a significant development (Meenan, 1985).

It is generally felt that Dooge as chairperson acted as a mediator between the very different views expressed within the group, particularly between those (such as the founding six member states) who were looking for ambitious reforms and those (including some of the newer members at that time) who essentially wanted to retain the status quo. Keatinge and Murphy (1987, p. 221) note that because Dooge came from a 'new' member state, 'which did not display marked objections in principle to further integration, he was perhaps in a favourable position to attempt to bridge the gap between these countries and the original six'. According to Scott (1994, p. 18), Dooge played a vital role in keeping the group together, 'eventually snatching consensus from the jaws of discord, and getting everyone to sign by allowing them to express their reservations through the device of footnotes ... Dooge's chairmanship of the Ad Hoc committee was in a sense Ireland's contribution to the Single European Act'.

The Dooge Committee met for the first time in September 1984 and took five months to complete its work, producing a 35-page report by February 1985, which was presented to the European Council the following month. At the Milan Summit in June, the Italian presidency called a vote on the central question of whether or not to convene an intergovernmental conference to revise the treaties, as recommended by the report. The episode is described first hand by Garret FitzGerald (1991).

FitzGerald's decision to support the convening of an intergovernmental conference to revise the Treaty of Rome was a graphic illustration of Ireland positioning itself with the founding six member states as opposed to allying itself with its fellow 'new arrivals' (Scott, 1994). It did not go unnoticed by many of those involved (Mitterrand, 1986). FitzGerald (1999, p. 137) has stated that he 'had no hesitation in voting with the original Six in favour of the calling of this Conference, thus marking in the clearest way possible the difference between Ireland's position as a new member state and that of the other three countries that had joined the Community between 1973 and 1981'.

Compared with some later intergovernmental conferences, the IGC to negotiate the Single European Act completed its work in a relatively short space of time, opening in September 1985 and closing in December

1985, although of course the debate over many of the issues had been rehearsed several times beforehand. Two working groups of senior officials dealt with the details of the provisions, one focusing on treaty revisions and the other largely dealing with foreign policy cooperation. Foreign Ministers met regularly to review progress.

Of course Ireland had its own priorities in the negotiations. A key concern was over cohesion and the inclusion of stronger provisions for regional and structural funds in disadvantaged parts of Europe, particularly if peripheral regions were going to benefit from the drive towards the single market (Fogarty, 1985). Ireland, working closely with the Commission, made a strong case for new treaty provisions on cohesion (see also Chapter 5). The Irish views on cohesion were submitted to the IGC in October 1985, and ultimately the Luxembourg presidency and other member states responded positively to most of the proposals made, which were reflected in the final text of the Single European Act (FitzGerald, 1991 and 1999; Government of Ireland, 1986; O'Donnell, 1992). As FitzGerald (1991, p. 600) comments, 'all this was no pious aspiration: after the ratification of the Single Act the Commission speedily brought forward proposals for a doubling of the Structural Funds'.

The Irish government also believed that the completion of the single market would be of major benefit to Ireland as an export-oriented economy and in making Ireland more attractive as a location for inward investment (Government of Ireland, 1986; Fogarty, 1985).

Ireland was also generally supportive of proposals for other new areas of cooperation at European level, such as environment and social policy (Fogarty, 1985). In the area of research and development, a specific Irish proposal emphasising the importance of involving small and medium-sized enterprises in R&D was reflected in the treaty text (Government of Ireland, 1986).

On institutional reform, Ireland strongly supported the move to qualified majority voting in most areas connected with the single market, although it favoured retaining unanimity for decisions over tax harmonisation (FitzGerald, 1991; Government of Ireland, 1986; Corbett, 1987). In the run-up to the IGC negotiations, one senior diplomat from the Department of Foreign Affairs had commented that 'we do recognise that the veto has been abused and that it must be modified so as to restrict its use to genuine, sustainable cases' (Fogarty, 1985, p. 603).

Irish negotiators were also in favour of the provisions allowing the conferral of executive and implementation powers on the Commission, and had no objections in principle to greater powers for the European Parliament (Government of Ireland, 1986; Fogarty, 1985).

The provisions on foreign policy cooperation, which were ultimately to be at the centre of the Supreme Court's decision on whether a referendum would be required in Ireland to ratify the Single European Act, were not seen as problematic by Irish negotiators. The Act provided for closer cooperation 'on the political and economic aspects of security', but made no provision for cooperation on military aspects of security (FitzGerald, 1991).

Maastricht Treaty

Like the Single European Act, the Maastricht Treaty (or to give it its formal title, the Treaty on European Union) introduced important institutional reforms and significantly expanded the competences of the European institutions. For example, the Maastricht Treaty:

- Introduced provisions on economic and monetary union (EMU), paving the way for the locking of exchange rates in 1999, the introduction of the euro notes and coins in 2002 and the establishment of the European Central Bank
- Provided for EU citizenship
- Incorporated subsidiarity as a principle of the Union
- Introduced new provisions to allow the EU to undertake activities in areas such as development aid, education, public health and consumer protection, and strengthened provisions in areas such as environmental protection, economic and social cohesion, and social policy
- Extended qualified majority voting in the Council to a considerable number of new areas
- Introduced a number of provisions to give the European Parliament more influence over legislation, in particular through the codecision procedure, as well as greater influence over the nomination of the Commission
- Made other institutional changes, such as giving the European Court of Justice the power to fine member states for failure to implement EU legislation, and establishing an EU Ombudsman and an advisory Committee of the Regions
- Provided for the 'pillar' structure of the EU, with cooperation in the areas of foreign and security policy and justice and home affairs taking place on a largely intergovernmental basis.

Two parallel intergovernmental conferences negotiated different elements of the Maastricht Treaty. One IGC was devoted to issues surrounding EMU, while a second IGC was devoted to what was termed 'political union', and effectively encapsulated other proposals for changes to the treaties, including institutional reform and proposed new responsibilities at European level.

In Irish government circles generally there was, at least initially, some caution over a major change to the treaties so soon after the Single European Act. The British under Margaret Thatcher were more conspicuously sceptical about major treaty reforms, as they had initially been over treaty reforms in the mid-1980s. That said, the European environment was changing rapidly, particularly after the collapse of communism and the fall of the Berlin Wall. It was clear that most other European leaders, including Helmut Kohl and François Mitterrand, as well as Commission President Jacques Delors, were strongly advocating a new treaty.

While Ireland did not hold the presidency during the formal negotiations over the Maastricht Treaty, it did hold the presidency in the period immediately prior to those negotiations in the first half of 1990, and this was to affect the government's initial hesitancy over embarking on a new round of treaty reforms. On the basis of a paper on treaty reform tabled by Taoiseach Charles Haughey, the decision to hold an IGC on political union to run in parallel with the IGC on EMU was taken by the European Council under the Irish presidency at its meeting in Dublin in June 1990.

This was a delicate issue that had to be handled sensitively, given the open dispute that had occurred between member states in Milan in 1985 over opening the IGC that led to the Single European Act. The presidency had to engage in considerable diplomacy to encourage restraint on both sides, with a view to reaching a consensus.

The Irish government's overall approach to the negotiations was to support the objectives of economic and monetary union, the establishment of the Common Foreign and Security Policy, extending the EU's role to new areas, and improvements to the efficiency of EU decision-making, while safeguarding particular interests (Government of Ireland, 1992). Key political actors involved included Charles Haughey, Gerry Collins, Bertie Ahern and Albert Reynolds, who were seen as good negotiators and who had good relationships with fellow leaders and ministers in the Council and with the Commission.

A key concern for Irish negotiators at the Maastricht negotiations was to strengthen the treaty provisions surrounding cohesion, in particular as a complement to market liberalisation under the single market and the Maastricht provisions on economic and monetary union, which it was felt might exacerbate regional disparities (Government of Ireland, 1992;

Laffan, 1991). As one interviewee involved in the negotiations commented, 'We worried in those days about a single market in a way that has never been justified since – in fact we've been huge beneficiaries of the single market ... If we were a bit nervous at the time, I think that was understandable. The Ireland of 1990 was certainly not like the Ireland of 2007'.

Ireland worked very closely with the Commission during the negotiations, which played an active role in mobilising the main likely beneficiaries from strengthening the EU's role in cohesion (namely Spain, Portugal, Greece and Ireland). Ireland submitted proposals to the IGC to amend the basic principles and activities of the EU set out in the treaty to reflect the objective of greater cohesion, as well as an extensive revision of the specific provisions dealing with economic and social cohesion. Maastricht made cohesion one of the fundamental objectives of the Union, stated that cohesion must be taken into consideration in the formulation of all EU policies, and provided for the establishment of a new cohesion fund, which was to make a major contribution in improving Ireland's transport and environmental infrastructure in subsequent years. The Irish government's White Paper on Maastricht argued that 'Irish proposals for a significant strengthening of the existing title on cohesion were accepted as the basis for the improvements in the title included in the Treaty' (Government of Ireland, 1992, p. 24). Naturally, as one of the larger member states, Spain also played a prominent role in this debate (Laffan, 1991; O'Donnell, 1992; Scott, 1994). But according to one of the Irish negotiators involved, Ireland 'still played an important part. We had the experience for more than a decade between 1973 and 1986 when we were the ones essentially carrying the flag of cohesion and structural and regional funds'.

Ireland was also proactive in putting forward proposals for treaty articles that would extend EU competences to new areas such as education, public health and culture. A specific proposal for a treaty text on education was submitted by Ireland, the main features of which were accepted by other member states. These provisions included encouraging student and teacher mobility and cooperation between educational bodies, and promoting the teaching and dissemination of languages. In relation to public health, the Irish government tabled proposals, drafted by the Department of Health, designed to give the EU a formal legal competence to promote cooperation in areas such as the prevention of disease and drug dependency. Ireland worked closely with the European Commission in proposing new provisions on culture. Irish negotiators also strongly supported the incorporation of treaty provisions on development aid and alleviating poverty in developing countries (Government of Ireland, 1992; Scott, 1994; Brown, 1992).

Part of the rationale behind these proposals was to engage constructively in efforts to give the EU a more 'human face' beyond purely trade and economic cooperation. As one individual involved in the negotiations pointed out, 'Ireland did have an interest in trying to broaden the operation of the treaty into areas like public health, like culture, like education – areas which would, if you had to sell a treaty [in a referendum], you could show people that the Union had a broader face than just economic and monetary union'.

A more defensive approach was taken by Ireland on some other areas discussed at Maastricht, including the new provisions on justice and home affairs. Irish acceptance of the Social Protocol was qualified by an emphasis that this should not involve increased costs for business (Keatinge *et al.*, 1991).

In terms of institutional reforms, there was some concern over changes that might upset the institutional balance between the Commission, Council and European Parliament. The Irish approach was to support the extension of qualified majority voting in the Council to most areas of decision-making, with the exception of the specific areas of taxation, foreign policy and justice and home affairs. There were initially some concerns in Irish quarters around some proposals to increase the powers of the European Parliament, given that Irish representation in the Parliament is far smaller than in the Council or Commission (Laffan, 1991; Scott, 1994). However, Irish negotiators were conscious not to be seen as opposing initiatives such as the codecision procedure or giving the Parliament a greater role in the nomination of the Commission, given that these changes were supported by a large number of member states.

Ireland was also concerned with maintaining the status of military neutrality, which required delicate negotiation, some of which even preceded the IGCs themselves. Specific aspects of the treaty provisions on Common Foreign and Security Policy reflected Irish concerns over neutrality and recognised the position of states outside military alliances. In particular, the provisions of Article J.4 of the Maastricht Treaty specifying that the policy of the Union 'shall not prejudice the specific character of the security and defence policy of certain Member States' was designed to take account of Ireland's status as the only non-member of NATO in the EU at that time. This wording has been maintained in subsequent treaty changes, up to and including the Reform Treaty agreed in Lisbon in 2007. Indeed the provision equally applies to neutral countries that subsequently joined the Union.

Amsterdam Treaty

The Amsterdam Treaty introduced a number of new provisions to the EU treaties, building on many of the changes agreed under the Single European Act and the Maastricht Treaty. The Amsterdam Treaty:

- Introduced new provisions on EU activity in a range of areas of concern to European citizens, including fundamental freedoms, non-discrimination, transparency within the EU institutions, employment and social inclusion; and strengthened provisions in areas such as environmental protection, public health, consumer protection, free movement of people, immigration and asylum, and cooperation in areas such as policing and combating crime
- Strengthened the Union's Common Foreign and Security Policy, in particular through allowing the EU to engage in joint actions in areas such as humanitarian and rescue tasks, peacekeeping tasks, and tasks of combat forces in crisis management including peacemaking (known as the 'Petersberg tasks')
- Provided for some institutional reforms designed to prepare the EU for enlargement through the accession of a large number of countries, particularly in Central and Eastern Europe. Reforms included some extension of qualified majority voting, as well as a simplification and extension of the codecision procedure giving more powers to the European Parliament, and a requirement that the Parliament vote on the nominee for Commission President. In addition, the treaty outlined new provisions on what became known as 'enhanced cooperation', which set out basic rules and safeguards allowing a group of EU states to cooperate in particular areas without having to wait for all countries to take part.

However, agreement was not possible under the Amsterdam Treaty on some of the more fundamental institutional reforms that were proposed, in particular over the size and composition of the Commission, changes to the system of qualified majority voting and the size and composition of the Parliament.

Ireland in the chair – Preparing the first draft of the Amsterdam Treaty
Ireland held the presidency of the Council in the second half of 1996, during a crucial period in the negotiations at the intergovernmental conference that led to the Amsterdam Treaty, before handing over to the Dutch presidency to finalise the text at the European Council meeting in Amsterdam in June 1997. A 'Reflection Group', comprising personal

representatives of Foreign Ministers, as well as the Commission and European Parliament, had been established in 1995, chaired by the then Spanish European Affairs Minister Carlos Westendorp. Then Minister of State for European Affairs Gay Mitchell was Ireland's representative on the group. This group set out a number of areas that the IGC could usefully address in the upcoming treaty, including institutional reform, improving the coherence of the EU's external and security policy, provisions around 'enhanced cooperation', and reforming the treaties in those areas of direct concern to citizens (Council of the EC, 1996). It was also clear from this early stage that proposals to reform the institutions were going to be particularly sensitive, as indeed it turned out (McDonagh, 1998).

The IGC originally opened in March 1996 under the Italian presidency. However, according to one actor involved, by the time the Irish presidency took over 'there was a feeling that real negotiations had not yet started'. The European Council in Florence in June 1996 had asked the Irish presidency to prepare 'a general outline for a draft revision of the Treaties' to be ready for the European Council in Dublin in December of that year. It became the focus of the work of the Irish presidency to advance negotiations on the new treaty (Svensson, 2000). If this text, which came to be known as the 'outline draft treaty', could be accepted as the basis for further discussions by December 1996, this would then allow the Dutch presidency to use that text to conduct the final stage of negotiations in early 1997.

The Irish presidency experimented with a number of innovative ideas to nudge the negotiation process forward (Svensson, 2000; McDonagh, 1998). According to one of those involved, the aim was 'to break up the set-piece formality that had characterised previous meetings ... We tried a few little things to loosen up the discussion amongst the group and we dispensed with some of the apparatus that went with the formal Brussels meetings'.

Small innovations such as these reflected the Irish presidency's view that, in the words of Svensson (2000, p. 103), it was time to 'get down to business'. The presidency decided early on that the focus of negotiation had to be on draft treaty text. This was done by first tabling presidency 'introductory notes', including legal texts on different topics, often on the basis of initial discussions either in the Reflection Group or under the Italian presidency, or on the basis of proposals tabled by different delegations.

The papers were either drafted by the presidency or more commonly in conjunction with the Council secretariat. Where papers were drafted by the Council secretariat, the Irish presidency would, in the words of one of those involved, 'work them over substantially ... And we found from experience that it would have been unwise to try to do it ourselves without the help of the Council secretariat, but it would have been very unwise to take exactly what they gave us without revision, because it was really a political judgment each time'.

Where a treaty text was introduced to negotiators at the IGC, the presidency would take note of what comments were made and how far certain ideas were being rejected or tentatively accepted. The text would be refined by the presidency in the light of views expressed by different delegations, with a view to presenting later drafts which might result in agreement. The presidency would then return a few weeks later with a revised version of that paper, this time under the title of 'Suggested Approach' instead of 'Introductory Note'. A third draft might be produced if it was felt necessary, but in most cases the presidency would take note of reactions and use these as the basis for the drafting of provisions of the 'outline draft treaty' (McDonagh, 1998; Svensson, 2000; Spring, 1997).

As Dorr (2000, p. 40) comments, this slow and sometimes painstaking process of drafting and redrafting on the basis of what was emerging as the likely point of consensus on different issues was central to the treaty-making process: 'Ultimately reaching agreement is a matter of iteration – that is to say, refining a text in the light of successive rounds of discussion'. The working method also 'put an immense workload on the Presidency to prepare and follow up meetings' (Svensson, 2000, p. 110).

The shape, length and degree of detail of the 'outline draft treaty' was not specified by the European Council, so it was effectively up to the Irish presidency to decide what the document might look like. In theory, an 'outline draft treaty' could have been simply a bare outline of a couple of pages, which some member states were pushing for, or something far more developed and ambitious (McDonagh, 1998; Svensson, 2000).

The safe option would have been to go for a relatively innocuous short framework document. However, to employ a phrase used in the context of the Irish presidency of 2004, those involved in the Irish negotiations during the 1996 IGC decided in a very quiet and unassuming way to 'have a go', privately concealing their higher ambitions for something more detailed (McDonagh, 1998; Svensson, 2000). The outcome of this process of refinement was a text (Irish Presidency, 1996) which was effectively to become the first complete draft of the Amsterdam Treaty (McDonagh, 1998; Svensson, 2000).

The text was presented by Taoiseach John Bruton to the heads of government at the European Council meeting in December 1996, and it was welcomed by all delegations as a good basis for the final phase of the intergovernmental conference, which ultimately culminated in Amsterdam in June 1997. French President Jacques Chirac congratulated the Irish for their work, reportedly declaring '*vive la Présidence irlandaise*' (McDonagh, 1998; Svensson, 2000). He was to go one better for the Irish presidency of 2004 (see below).

In many ways, Ireland's key contribution to the Amsterdam Treaty was drafting and getting a tentative agreement on what was the first draft of the Amsterdam Treaty under its presidency. A comparison of the two documents shows that much of the language and treaty text found in the 'outline draft treaty', drawn up by the Irish presidency, remained essentially unchanged and was reflected in the final Amsterdam Treaty (see also Svensson, 2000; McDonagh, 1998; FitzGerald, 1998).

This applied for example to the areas of fundamental rights and freedoms, including the provision that 'the Union is founded on the principles of liberty, democracy, respect for human rights and fundamental freedoms, and the rule of law'. Ireland also drafted the provisions that would allow suspension of certain membership rights in the event that a member state was found to be persistently breaching these democratic principles, which are a precondition for EU membership. The provisions of the Amsterdam Treaty on non-discrimination on the basis of sex, racial or ethnic origin, religion or belief, disability, age or sexual orientation also closely reflect the text of the Irish 'outline draft treaty'.

Equally, the provisions on free movement, visas, asylum and immigration in the Amsterdam Treaty closely reflected the Irish drafts, with the Irish 'outline draft treaty' suggesting that moving these areas to the first pillar would provide a more effective basis for action. In fact provisions covering a wide range of other areas drafted by the Irish presidency were, occasionally with slight nuances, found in the final text of the Amsterdam Treaty, including those relating to employment, environmental protection and sustainable development, consumer protection, transparency and access to EU documents, and the role of national parliaments in the EU.

In terms of the Common Foreign and Security Policy (CFSP), the provisions regarding 'constructive abstention', the inclusion of the Petersberg tasks within the scope of the Union, and the establishment of a policy planning and early warning unit within the Council to monitor developments in areas relevant to the CFSP, were drafted by the Irish presidency as part of the 'outline draft treaty'.

Irish presidency drafts on some institutional reforms also survived largely intact in the Amsterdam Treaty. These included those provisions relating to the simplification of the codecision procedure to place the European Parliament on an equal footing with the Council, reducing the number of legislative procedures used, as well as the provision that the President of the Commission must be approved by the Parliament.

While some of these texts did require a few minor refinements under the Dutch presidency, others did not change at all. Certainly the substantive basis for the Amsterdam Treaty texts in these areas was the detailed drafting and redrafting carried out by the Irish presidency. It should of course be emphasised that the original source of many of these provisions came from ideas suggested by individual delegations and groups of member states.[4] McDonagh (1998, p. 129) modestly describes the 'outline draft treaty' as 'the fruit not of the Presidency working in isolation, but of the collective efforts of negotiators from all Member states'.

However, it was up to the Irish presidency, in the light of the discussion on such proposals, to take ideas and shape these into treaty wording that could (and eventually in most cases did) get agreement from all member states. This was a vital contribution to the process of consensus-building as part of the negotiations on the Amsterdam Treaty.

In addition, some of the provisions in the 'outline draft treaty' also reflected stated Irish priorities going into the negotiations, for example on openness and transparency, the simplification of legislative procedures, combating organised crime and drug smuggling, and the development of planning and analysis capacity within the Council secretariat (Government of Ireland, 1996). The 'outline draft treaty' also attached particular importance to strengthening the EU's ability to engage in cooperation between police and judicial authorities to counteract organised crime and drug smuggling – this also echoed particular Irish priorities at the time (Svensson, 2000).

National proposals and submissions

As noted above, the main Irish contribution to the Amsterdam Treaty came from the role it played in the second half of 1996 in drafting the text of various articles on a wide range of issues that eventually made their way into the final version of the treaty agreed at Amsterdam. As Svensson (2000, p. 136) comments, 'when the Irish Presidency took over there was a detailed agenda, when it left office there was a draft allowing a good glimpse of what the final treaty would look like'.

According to one of the Irish negotiators, there was a conscious effort during the Irish presidency to distinguish the national position from that of

---

[4] National proposals usually did not form the basis of discussions, although of course they could influence the content of presidency documents and proposals, which tend to be regarded as more neutral (McDonagh, 1998). For example, Belgium, Denmark and Sweden had tabled proposals on employment, Finland had tabled proposals on consumer protection, France had tabled proposals involving a greater role for national parliaments in the EU, and Sweden and Finland had proposed incorporating the Petersberg tasks into the treaty.

the presidency. One Irish official was nominated to speak for Ireland, but the general approach was that the real national interest was to run a good presidency and make progress on the negotiations, rather than focusing on points of detail that were in the national interest. That said, the national interest was not ignored, and Ireland had a number of national priorities that it pursued during the IGC negotiations.

Of course, by handling the presidency well and by being seen to make progress in the negotiations, Ireland would presumably be in a better negotiating position when it came to the final stage of the IGC: 'efficiency and imagination are in short enough supply to be valued, and the effect of a small state conducting a model presidency will redound to Ireland's credit in the later stages of the negotiation and beyond' (Scott, 1996, p. 40). Certainly, as Svensson (2000) argues, Ireland in a subtle way took the opportunity during its presidency to advance proposals that it and indeed other delegations favoured – while taking care to maintain its image of neutrality and impartiality and to be fair and equitable to all delegations.

One example was a national proposal tabled by Ireland, on the basis of an initiative from the Department of Social Welfare, to introduce a specific legal basis allowing the EU to undertake activities, peer review and funding of measures to combat social exclusion (Government of Ireland, 1998; McDonagh, 1998). Again the spirit of such provisions was to illustrate that the Union is more than just a purely economic entity, it also has a social dimension.

Ireland also submitted proposals on combating drug smuggling and drug addiction, as well as on nuclear safety, although the latter was not reflected in the final text (Government of Ireland, 1996; Svensson, 2000).

Ireland had specific concerns over the proposals regarding 'enhanced cooperation', which would allow groups of countries to embark on joint cooperation without having to wait for all member states to take part, and publicly expressed its opposition to any notion of an exclusive inner core of member states (Government of Ireland, 1996). According to one of the negotiators, 'we were very concerned in the negotiations to tie down the arrangements that might be written into the treaty … and ensure that firstly enhanced cooperation was open to those who wanted to join at the start, and that the conditions for those who wanted to join later were acceptable'.

Ireland was in most cases receptive to the idea of extending both qualified majority voting (QMV) in the Council and the codecision procedure to new areas of decision-making (Government of Ireland, 1996). However, in the end it only proved possible to agree to extend QMV to a small number of areas. While many agreed in principle with the idea of extending QMV, when it came down to specific discussions about what areas would be included, difficulties emerged (Dorr, 2000).

Irish negotiators were conscious during the discussions of the need to bring the Union closer to its citizens and make it more clearly understood (Dorr, 2000; Government of Ireland, 1996). In terms of the preparation of the 'outline draft treaty', there was an attempt to present the draft in a manner that would make the document reasonably intelligible and understandable to the public at large (Dorr, 2000; McDonagh, 1998; Svensson, 2000). This was done by introducing each of the different sections with a discursive piece explaining what the issue was before setting out the proposed text for the new treaty, so that each part had an explanatory piece rather than being presented raw in treaty language:

> This made the document as a whole more readable to those who really wanted to know what was being proposed, and the text was reasonably well received. I think it is regrettable that a similar approach was not followed after Amsterdam when the final Treaty text had been agreed ... This was a matter for particular criticism in countries such as mine where a referendum was a necessary part of ratification of the new Treaty. Opponents were able to say to the electorate: "if you don't understand it, vote No" (Dorr, 2000, pp. 41–42).

This again reflected a concern from a member state that was going to have to hold a popular vote on the text. One might suggest that the principle of 'readability', or at least of making the text relatively accessible to the general public, was one taken up by EU leaders and given expression in the Laeken Declaration and ultimately adopted by the Convention on the Future of Europe (see below).

Nice Treaty

The Treaty of Nice amended a number of provisions of the treaties, but was particularly focused on institutional arrangements for decision-making, as well as amending national representation in key institutions to make room for the enlargement of the Union to bring in twelve new members in 2004 and 2007. The Nice Treaty:

- Provided for one commissioner nominated from each member state – until the Union reaches twenty-seven members, when there would be less commissioners than member states, although a system of rotation would apply on the basis of strict equality between member states
- Introduced a reweighting of votes under the system of qualified majority voting, which was designed to take account of the greater population in larger member states

- Extended qualified majority voting to a number of new areas
- Redistributed seats in the Parliament, in an effort to make room for MEPs that would be elected from the new member states
- Provided for a number of other institutional changes, for example extending the remit of the Court of First Instance to ease the caseload of the European Court of Justice, and allowing for the establishment of specialised 'judicial panels' to hear cases in areas such as patents and intellectual property
- Amended the rules on 'enhanced cooperation', in particular specifying that a minimum of eight member states must be involved and that the decision to allow a group of states to embark on closer cooperation must be approved by a qualified majority of all states.

The basis for negotiations during the IGC in 2000 was the institutional questions which could not be agreed upon at Amsterdam and which were highlighted in a Protocol to the Amsterdam Treaty – namely, the size and composition of the Commission, the weighting of votes under the system of qualified majority voting in the Council, the possibility of extending qualified majority voting and other amendments that might be seen as necessary. This relatively narrow mandate, compared with previous treaty reforms, was determined by the European Council meeting in Helsinki in December 1999, which made it clear that the IGC should focus on those issues left unresolved at Amsterdam, while leaving open the possibility of including a limited number of additional issues as the IGC progressed (Callanan, 2000). It was also clear by this time that a larger task involving more fundamental treaty changes on wider issues would be undertaken at a later stage, which in turn became the agenda for the Convention on the Future of Europe.

Ireland's main concern during the negotiations involved the debate over the size of the Commission. The overriding Irish priority was to preserve equality between member states in the right to nominate a commissioner, regardless of the size of the Commission – a guarantee which was secured in the text of the final treaty.

Ireland's opening position was that, given the Commission's mandate to represent the general interest across the EU as a whole, it was important in the interests of the Union that every nationality be reflected in the composition of the college of commissioners. The absence of a commissioner from several countries might call into question Commission proposals from those countries, and this in itself might jeopardise the Commission's standing and ultimately its influence. As one of Ireland's negotiators at the IGC put it:

It is important that the Commission, in exercising its functions, and particularly its right of initiative, should be able to count on wide acceptance throughout the Union. It is important too that in its internal discussions before it takes a decision or makes a proposal – which it does by majority vote – the Commission should be alerted to the impact of that decision/proposal on particular Member States. Both these points require that each Member State should retain the right to nominate a Commissioner (Dorr, 2000, p. 38; see also Brosnan, 2000).

Those who wanted to limit the number of commissioners argued that the Commission would become cumbersome with a large membership, and that there would be insufficient portfolios of any significance to go round.

One Irish negotiator interviewed for this chapter pointed out that Ireland was one of the leading smaller countries arguing that the Commission should contain a national from each member state. However, a number of other smaller countries came to believe that because the larger countries wanted an adjustment in the voting weights in the Council, a good deal on the Commission (particularly in terms of securing equal rights of nomination to the Commission) could be secured by trading off at a time when the larger countries were particularly concerned with voting weights. Furthermore, a lot of the smaller countries were privately becoming convinced that a large Commission would be unwieldy and would be less effective. Thus, smaller countries were ultimately able to ensure that any system of rotation of the right to nominate a member of the Commission must be based on the principle of equality between member states, whether large or small.

The Irish position at the IGC was to support proposals to extend qualified majority voting to maintain the efficiency of Council decision-making in an enlarged Union. In fact Ireland would have supported a move to qualified majority voting in substantially more areas than were finally agreed, with the usual proviso that unanimity would be retained for certain sensitive areas, in particular taxation (Government of Ireland, 2002; Cowen, 2003).

Ireland also argued for an equitable approach to the reallocation of seats in the Parliament, taking into account the need to ensure meaningful representation from all states.

On the question of 'enhanced cooperation', the Irish position was certainly not that of an advocate of change. However, Ireland was willing to support the limited changes in this area, provided that basic safeguards remained in place and that such provisions would not endanger the solidarity and cohesion of the Union (Government of Ireland, 2002).

Ireland also tabled a proposal to provide a legal base in the treaty for the establishment of a social protection committee, which would review policies to modernise social protection in the Union and promote exchanges of information, experience and good practice in this area. Ireland also proposed adding social protection to the list of areas in the employment field where the EU may support national activities and cooperation between national governments (Government of Ireland, 2002). This proposal became the basis for changes reflected in the treaty and was a development from the social exclusion provisions Ireland had proposed in the negotiations leading to the Amsterdam Treaty.

The draft Constitutional Treaty and the Reform Treaty

The Reform Treaty, the text of which was agreed and signed in Lisbon in 2007, was based on an extensive period of discussion that involved meetings of the Convention on the Future of Europe in 2002 and 2003, the negotiation of a Constitutional Treaty by an IGC in 2004, and a 'period of reflection' following the rejection of that document by referenda in France and the Netherlands in 2005. However, because eighteen out of twenty-seven member states had ratified the Constitutional Treaty by 2007, many of the innovations in that document were retained in the subsequent Reform Treaty.

Much of the groundwork in terms of drawing up the Reform Treaty was therefore laid through the work of the Convention in 2002 and 2003 and the IGC that met in 2004. Many of the viewpoints over provisions included in the Reform Treaty had only a couple of years beforehand been extensively aired. This allowed negotiators to agree on the text of the Reform Treaty in a comparatively short space of time.

From the late 1990s a consensus had developed that the Union should not be engaged in an almost permanent state of IGCs and negotiations on treaty revisions and that a comprehensive settlement of the EU's basic law should be arrived at which would last the test of time (Callanan, 2000). As one of those centrally involved in past treaty negotiations has suggested, 'it is probably not a good thing to have, as it were, a builder's scaffolding permanently around the Union' (Dorr, 2000, p. 36). The Reform Treaty was intended to bring a respite in the seemingly interminable process of 'navel-gazing' over what are for the most part fairly intricate rules and details, at least to the majority of the Union's citizens.

The Constitutional Treaty, and the subsequent Reform Treaty, included a number of new provisions. In particular, the Reform Treaty:

- Replaced the Council voting system from one of vote weightings to one which would require a proposal to receive the support of 55 per cent of states representing at least 65 per cent of the EU's population
- Introduced a new position of President of the European Council, to be elected by its members
- Provided for 'team presidencies' of most Council configurations
- Provided that the number of commissioners would be set at two-thirds of the number of member states by 2014, with a guarantee that the right to nominate a commissioner would be rotated between countries on the basis of equality between states, regardless of size
- Introduced a minimum of six MEPs and a maximum of ninety-six from any one member state, with a total Parliament consisting of no more than 751 members
- Introduced greater clarity as to what activities are determined at EU level and what is reserved to the member states (definition of exclusive, shared and complementary competences)
- Introduced new provisions in areas such as justice and home affairs, public services, public health, energy and sport
- Formalised the 'open method of coordination', based on peer review of national action plans in certain policy areas
- Extended majority voting and the codecision procedure to new areas
- Gave a greater role to national parliaments at an earlier stage of the EU policy process, including the right (as 'guardians of subsidiarity') to refer proposals to the European Court of Justice
- Incorporated a legal status for the European Charter of Fundamental Rights as a protocol to the treaties.

At the time of writing in 2007, the text of the Reform Treaty had been finalised and the European Council had stated its hope that the treaty would be ratified by each member state by 2009.

The Convention on the Future of Europe

The draft Constitutional Treaty and the Reform Treaty can trace their origins to the Laeken Declaration. The European Council meeting in Laeken in December 2001 called for a clearer definition and division of competences between the Union and the national governments, a simplification of legislative instruments and the introduction of measures to increase the transparency and democratic legitimacy of the Union. The European Council also raised the question of whether 'this simplification and reorganisation [of the treaties] might lead in the long run to the adoption of a constitutional text'.

The Laeken Declaration announced the convening of a Convention on the Future of Europe to prepare the ground for what was to become known as the draft 'Constitutional Treaty', the text of which would be finalised by a subsequent intergovernmental conference.

The Laeken Declaration also specified the composition of the Convention, which was designed to usher in a broader, more inclusive approach to treaty-making. The President of the Convention was former French President Valéry Giscard d'Estaing. The members of the Convention (the *conventionnels*) included representatives of national governments and of the (then) candidate countries that were to join the Union in 2004 and 2007, as well as of Turkey. In addition, however, the Convention also included representatives of national parliaments in the member states, as well as representatives of the European Parliament and European Commission. Each member also had an alternate or substitute member.

The Irish representatives included then Minister for Europe Dick Roche, who was the Irish government's representative (Ray MacSharry had served as the government's representative during the first period of the Convention's work). John Bruton and Proinsias de Rossa represented the Oireachtas. The alternate member for the government was Bobby McDonagh of the Department of Foreign Affairs, and the alternates for the Oireachtas were John Gormley and Pat Carey.

Two other Irish individuals were also active on the Convention, namely John Cushnahan, who was one of the alternate members from the European Parliament delegation, and David O'Sullivan, then Secretary General of the Commission and an alternate member representing the Commission. While they constituted an additional Irish flavour to the Convention's work, their specific mandate was of course to represent the interests of their respective institutions.

The Convention, which started its work in February 2002, proved to be a 'marketplace of ideas' (Cowen, 2003). It established a number of working groups to discuss specific themes such as the status of the Charter of Fundamental Rights, the role of national parliaments in the EU, economic governance, simplifying EU legislation, external action, defence, and justice and home affairs.

The concept of drafting a 'Constitutional Treaty' quickly emerged from the Convention. Given that the reforms to the Union's basic law since the 1980s have taken the form of treaties amending the original treaties from the 1950s, the treaty framework as it stands is a legal labyrinth of amending articles, virtually impenetrable to the general reader. In the words of Giscard d'Estaing, the effect of successive changes is that the treaties:

Are so complex as to be in many cases incomprehensible to the citizen
... their complexity has come about through successive diplomatic
negotiations amending or partially amending the basic texts, decking
them out with additions and exceptions, protocols and declarations, all
at the time politically important to someone, and resulting in a text now
standing at 1,045 pages (Giscard d'Estaing, 2002, p. 9).

The debate over transparency and clarity in terms of how the EU
operates, and over how to make the Union more understandable to its
citizens (see section on the Amsterdam Treaty above), led to calls for the
replacement of the earlier treaties with a single, consolidated
Constitutional Treaty, the text of which might be reasonably simple and
accessible to the public at large.

In comparison with the preparation of previous treaties, which were
largely negotiated behind closed doors, the work of the Convention was a
model of openness and transparency. Open hearings were held, with
reports, documents, proceedings, proposals and other material published
on a Convention website. Irish representatives reported regularly on the
work of the Convention to both the Oireachtas and the National Forum on
Europe (Vergés Bausili, 2005).

After some initial criticism that the work of the Convention was not
being taken seriously enough by the Irish government, it appears that a
more proactive approach was taken to the Convention as its work
continued (National Forum on Europe, 2003; Gillespie, 2002). Some have
argued that this may have been partly explained by the fact that many in
Ireland were distracted by the campaign on the second referendum on the
Nice Treaty that took place in October 2002 and which overlapped with the
work of the Convention. The two referenda on the Nice Treaty may also
have contributed to a rather cautious approach by the Irish government
representatives, at least at the initial stages, and an underestimation of the
impact that the Convention might have (Vergés Bausili, 2005). In addition,
however, at its early stages it was unclear exactly what approach the
Convention was going to take, and it was only by the end of 2002 that the
work of the Convention began to step up a gear through the contribution of
its working groups. By the beginning of 2003 there appears to have been a
realisation on the part of some governments that the Convention was likely
to reach a consensus on a number of issues, and that it would be difficult
and perhaps counterproductive to try to unravel too many of these
compromises at the subsequent IGC.

The Irish approach to the discussions at the Convention by and large
reflected the view that it was an opportunity to listen to and contribute
constructively to the debate about the Union's constitutional framework

(Cowen, 2003). A key Irish priority was to maintain the essence of the Union's institutional balance, and Ireland supported much of the work of the Convention in simplifying the treaties, bringing greater clarity in the competences of the Union, giving national parliaments a role as 'guardians of subsidiarity' and extending majority voting to most areas (Vergés Bausili, 2005). On security issues, Ireland supported the updating of the Petersberg tasks to include areas such as conflict prevention, joint disarmament operations and post-conflict stabilisation missions. Ireland also supported the view that the new treaty should 'be capable of standing the test of time, lasting a generation or more' (Cowen, 2003; Ahern, 2004; Government of Ireland, 2005).

Although there were amendments submitted by Irish government representatives on the Convention designed to protect unanimity in particularly sensitive fields (Norman, 2005), the overall approach was to avoid adopting a defensive attitude by 'drawing lines in the sand' in a host of different areas. In addition, Ireland was also keen to ensure that any reduction in the number of commissioners would follow the Nice formula of rotation on the basis of equality between member states (Norman, 2005; Government of Ireland, 2005; Cowen, 2003). While Vergés Bausili (2005) argues that the Irish approach at the Convention was essentially a cautious one, the Convention records show that all the Irish members played an active role in putting forward suggestions for provisions in the new Constitutional Treaty, as well as finding common cause with other Convention members to pursue shared objectives.

For example, Norman (2005) argues that the Irish government's representative Dick Roche 'provided the small countries with a fluent and rugged advocate' and was active in coalition-building with like-minded member states such as the group of small states that became known as the 'Friends of the Community Method'. He also tabled a large number of textual amendments to earlier drafts of the Constitutional Treaty. He introduced a joint proposal for a chapter on development cooperation and humanitarian aid from the Austrian, Belgian, German, Irish, Dutch, Swedish and British governments. Ireland was also involved in proposals jointly prepared with the Swedish and Finnish governments on improving the openness and efficiency of the EU's institutions and access to documents. Irish proposals for the Union's external objectives in the opening preamble and articles were also closely reflected in the final text.

John Bruton was an active member of the Convention's influential presidium and was considered to have played an effective brokerage role in the final compromises at the very end of the Convention's work (Norman, 2005). He also chaired the Convention's Working Group on Freedom, Security and Justice, which was charged with proposing the key features of the treaty's provisions and institutional arrangements on visas, asylum, immigration, border controls and police and judicial cooperation.

Proinsias de Rossa tabled a number of amendments to provisions on equality issues, employment, social inclusion, poverty and discrimination, racism and xenophobia, public services, and to provide for a legal basis for the 'open method of coordination' and peer review of national policies (Vergés Bausili, 2005).

John Gormley tabled a number of amendments to drafts of the Constitutional Treaty, including provisions on transparency and openness in EU decision-making, participation and the proposal for a citizen's initiative, strengthening the provisions on environmental protection and sustainable development, and emphasising the importance of the principles of the UN Charter in the Union's external policy.

Pat Carey initiated a number of amendments designed to strengthen provisions related to development cooperation, and supported a number of proposals championing a greater role for national parliaments in EU activities.

Bobby McDonagh, in addition to supporting the work of the Minister of State, was active on working groups dealing with external action, the Charter on Fundamental Rights and the future of the European Court of Justice.

John Cushnahan presented a number of amendments geared towards strengthening principles such as non-discrimination and respect for human rights in the treaty, strengthening democracy clauses in the EU's trade agreements with third countries and providing a greater role for the Parliament in monitoring common foreign and security activities and external trade agreements.

As part of the Commission's delegation, David O'Sullivan tabled a number of proposals jointly with fellow Commission representatives on a variety of subjects from institutional issues to the operation of different policy areas such as agriculture, development aid, external trade and cooperation in defence and security issues.

Irish *conventionnels* submitted a number of proposals which, although they were not always contained in the final text, reflected interesting contributions to the debate on some of the more fundamental questions being discussed within the Convention. These applied, for example, to the area of institutional reform and increasing the democratic legitimacy of the Commission (Norman, 2005; Vergés Bausili, 2005; Government of Ireland, 2005). John Bruton tabled a proposal that the Commission President should be directly elected by the citizens of the Union, arguing that this would provide for a clearer separation of powers, would help create a Europe-wide demos and political space with all European citizens voting on the same choice of candidates (Bruton, 2003). Dick Roche tabled an alternative model, whereby the Commission President would be chosen by an electoral college consisting of an equal number of MEPs and representatives of national parliaments, convened for the purpose of choosing amongst a range of candidates (who could be nominated by a minimum of five states). It was argued that such an approach would reflect the dual nature of the EU as a union of states and peoples, would be a more transparent process and would give the position greater democratic legitimacy (Roche, 2003). Although such ideas gathered some support, they were ultimately seen as too radical, and perhaps ahead of their time, and were not reflected in the Convention's text (National Forum on Europe, 2004).

A text for a Constitutional Treaty was agreed by the vast bulk of Convention members, including government representatives, who agreed to the draft as the basis for the work of the upcoming IGC. The text was presented by Giscard d'Estaing to the European Council in Thessaloniki in June 2003, which welcomed the Convention's work as an 'historic step'. A minority report, signed by four dissenting Convention members and four alternates, was also forwarded to the Council presidency along with the draft Constitutional Treaty (Norman, 2005; Vergés Bausili, 2005).

Ireland in the chair – Finalising the Constitutional Treaty at the 2004 IGC

It had been hoped by some that the text prepared by the Convention would simply be 'rubber-stamped' by the subsequent IGC – indeed the vast majority of the Convention's text had secured broad agreement, given that national governments were involved in the preparation of the draft.

It soon became clear however that most national governments wanted to make some changes, albeit to a restricted number of particularly sensitive issues in the text drafted by the Convention (Vergés Bausili, 2005). The IGC began its work in Rome in October 2003, and after a number of months it appeared as if a compromise was emerging on some issues. For example, one of the first things to be changed by the IGC was the deletion of the provisions of the draft Constitution to concentrate the Council's legislative role in a single Council formation, as it was not supported by the vast majority of countries, and had even lost the support of some of those in the Convention that had pioneered it (Norman, 2005).

The IGC also revisited the following provisions:

- The new proposed system of majority voting in the Council
- The composition and size of the Commission
- The composition and size of the European Parliament

- Whether to use majority voting or unanimity in 'sensitive areas' such as taxation, budget resources, social security, foreign and security issues and issues of judicial cooperation in criminal matters
- The system for adopting the EU's annual budget
- Reforming the system of presidency of the Council, where it seemed that most states were moving towards accepting the concept of a 'team presidency' where a group of countries would hold the presidency for a longer term than the current six months.

After canvassing the views of member states, it was decided under the Italian presidency that most of the collective negotiation on the text would take place at the level of Foreign Ministers, although each member state would also have a senior official designated as a 'focal point' to convey his or her government's views to the presidency (McDonagh, 2007).

A number of areas of progress were advanced by the Italian presidency, notably on issues such as security and defence, and on the new system of 'team presidencies' where groups of countries would hold the presidency for eighteen months. These were crucial in forming the basis of the agreement on a number of provisions in the Constitutional Treaty by the Irish presidency (McDonagh, 2007; Norman, 2005; Dinan, 2005b).

However, the European Council meeting in December 2003 failed to reach an overall agreement on the draft Constitutional Treaty. A small number of problem areas remained. A particular stumbling block was a disagreement over voting arrangements in the Council. The draft Constitutional Treaty prepared by the Convention had proposed a new voting system, whereby a proposal would require the support of 60 per cent of the EU's population and 50 per cent of the member states. This approach was supported by Germany, France and most other states. Poland and Spain, on the other hand, wished to retain the vote weighting system agreed under the Nice Treaty (whereby the four largest countries had twenty-nine votes and Spain and Poland, with considerably smaller populations, had only two votes less at twenty-seven votes).

Some other issues also remained to be resolved. These included proposals to extend majority voting (whichever system would ultimately be decided upon) to a number of sensitive areas, the size and composition of the Commission as well as the minimum number of MEPs for very small countries. While these remained difficult issues to overcome, the colourful approach adopted by Italian Prime Minister Silvio Berlusconi in chairing the discussion probably did not help matters (Norman, 2005).

When it became clear at the summit that agreement was not going to be reached, Ireland proposed that a short sentence be included in the published conclusions: 'the Irish Presidency is requested on the basis of consultations to make an assessment of the prospects for progress and to report to the European Council in March'. Taoiseach Bertie Ahern suggested this wording to his colleagues, which effectively would give the Irish presidency a mandate to 'consult, assess and report' in the early months of 2004 (McDonagh, 2007).

While the collapse of the negotiations under the Italian presidency was the focus of much negative media comment, the Irish delegation at the summit clearly looked forward to the challenge: 'This reflected a recognition of the importance of the Constitution for Europe and for Ireland, as well as a sense of the responsibility which, especially for a small country, goes with holding the Presidency' (McDonagh, 2007, p. 93). On the flight back to Dublin, Ahern privately told senior officials that he wanted to 'have a go' at resolving the impasse, believing that a protracted delay might lead to a hardening of positions and make agreement even more difficult (Staunton, 2004).

An extensive series of bilateral discussions was held at various levels, involving the Taoiseach, Foreign Minister Brian Cowen and Minister for European Affairs Dick Roche, with their respective counterparts from other member states. Discussions also continued at official level with the 'focal points'. An important early decision made by the Irish presidency was to indicate its view that a new Council voting system based on a threshold of states and population would have to be part of the final deal, but that it would have to be adapted to accommodate those who wished to retain the Nice Treaty vote weighting system.

A change of government following elections in Spain in March had also increased the prospects of success. The outgoing government had been strongly attached to the Nice formula, whereas the new government was more willing to discuss alternatives to the Nice system, while naturally seeking to protect Spanish interests. At the March 2004 European Council, the Irish presidency was able to report that following its consultations an overall agreement was possible.

It was always likely that the extremely sensitive issues of the voting system and the size and composition of both the Commission and the Parliament could only be determined at European Council level. However, the Irish presidency's strategy for the resumption of formal negotiations was to try to remove as many other issues as possible from the agenda for the final Council meeting (Dinan, 2005b). The approach used by the Irish presidency was to present two documents to each negotiation meeting during the IGC. The issues were divided into 'open issues' and 'closed issues'. The open issues contained those matters which remained to be settled in the negotiations and where further discussion was required. The closed issues dealt with 'texts on which there seemed, as we put it, to be a likelihood of a broad consensus in the context of an overall agreement' (McDonagh, 2007, p. 120; see also Norman, 2005; Dinan, 2005b). Of course, the negotiations were based on the premise that nothing is agreed until everything is agreed, but the matters included in the closed issues were those where the presidency felt further discussion at ministerial level was not necessary. Gradually, as progress was made, the 'closed issues' document got bigger and the 'open issues' document got smaller.

A number of relatively minor issues of concern were dealt with by the senior 'focal points' meeting together, and others were considered and referred to Foreign Ministers. The question of whether majority voting or unanimity would apply to areas such as taxation, budget resources, social security, foreign and security issues and criminal law was also referred for discussion by Foreign Ministers, who succeeded in reaching agreement in mid-June (McDonagh, 2007; Norman, 2005).

The Irish presidency was able to get agreement on a series of provisions of the Constitutional Treaty that were ultimately reflected in the Reform Treaty, including where unanimity should apply and where majority voting should apply in the 'sensitive issues'. For example, decision-making for proposals on social security and criminal law would be by majority voting, but an 'emergency brake' procedure would be provided for, whereby governments could refer such proposals to the European Council. Agreement was also reached on the procedure for adopting the EU's annual budget.

At the European Council in June 2004 to conclude the negotiations, agreement was secured on the provision that the number of members of the Commission would consist of two-thirds of the number of member states, and that the principle adopted under the Nice Treaty of a strictly equal rotation between states regardless of size would be retained. The European Council also agreed to an Irish proposal that the minimum number of MEPs from any country be set at six.

Critically, agreement was reached on the Irish proposal that the thresholds under the new Council voting system be revised to 65 per cent of population and 55 per cent of states. In an effort to secure a compromise, the Irish presidency also added in a number of refinements to the system, for example specifying that a blocking minority must constitute at least four member states (McDonagh, 2007; Norman, 2005; Cronin and Banks, 2004; Government of Ireland, 2005). All of these were reflected in the Reform Treaty's text.

Bertie Ahern received a standing ovation from his fellow heads of state and government, an uncommon event in the European Council (McDonagh, 2007; Dinan, 2005b; Rees, 2005). The ovation effectively signalled the end of the negotiations. Norman (2005, p. 294) quotes one official as saying 'we knew we were there, because no member state would dare to unlock the deal after that'. Ahern's experience and negotiating skills (honed in industrial relations as well as negotiations on Northern Ireland) were critical in reaching agreement. In addition, the approach he took in engaging in bilateral contacts, including a tour of capitals to meet personally with other members of the European Council (where of course the final deal would be done), was seen as crucial in building both trust and gathering information on the concerns of each delegation.

The success was a testament to the skills, dedication and extensive preparation work conducted by those involved, and the 'can do', professional, even-handed, pragmatic and problem-solving manner in which Irish politicians and officials tend to approach negotiations. There was high praise from both domestic and international quarters, particularly given the limited resources available to the Irish diplomatic corps (Rees, 2005). While not one prone to understatement, French President Jacques Chirac described the Irish term of office as the best presidency he and his officials had ever witnessed (McNamara *et al.*, 2004). High praise also came from domestic political opponents in the Oireachtas and through the media, particularly for Ahern, Cowen, Roche and the team of officials involved in the negotiations (National Forum on Europe, 2004).

The Irish government's priority objective of course was to reach agreement on a text. In terms of national priorities on the text, the government indicated that it had supported nearly every aspect of the draft Constitutional Treaty that emerged from the Convention, even if it had a small number of concerns.

These concerns included the retention of a system of decision-making that would ensure that Ireland could not be outvoted on tax matters and on police cooperation and judicial cooperation in criminal matters, with a view to decisions being compatible with Ireland's system of common law. The Constitutional Treaty provisions on cooperation in criminal matters also specify that differences in legal traditions must be taken into account, something proposed by Ireland (Government of Ireland, 2005). In the end Ireland was satisfied that in the final text 'its national concerns had been appropriately resolved' (Government of Ireland, 2005, p. 14; National Forum on Europe, 2004).

Although agreed under the Irish presidency, it was decided for symbolic reasons to sign the Constitutional Treaty on the Capitoline Hill in Rome in October 2004, the venue for the signing of the original Treaty of Rome in 1957.

The Reform Treaty and the 2007 IGC

While there are a small number of differences[5] between the two treaties, the substance of most of the innovations agreed as part of the Constitutional Treaty was incorporated into the Reform Treaty text signed in Lisbon in 2007.

In that context, the work of the Convention in 2002 and 2003, the drafting of the Constitutional Treaty by the 2004 IGC and the subsequent drafting of the Reform Treaty in 2007 can be seen as a continuous and closely linked process. The German presidency during the first half of 2007 worked hard to get as much agreement as possible on which aspects of the Constitutional Treaty should be retained in any new text, and the European Council meeting in June set out a detailed mandate to the IGC outlining the broad areas of agreement. The IGC to negotiate the Reform Treaty formally opened in July 2007 under the Portuguese presidency, and a text was agreed in October 2007.

Most of the elements of the Reform Treaty thus effectively incorporated provisions originally proposed during the Convention, and decided upon by the 2004 IGC under the Irish presidency. For example, the Reform Treaty provides for a new system of majority voting in the Council from 2014, where proposals require the agreement of 55 per cent of states representing 65 per cent of the Union's population. This system is identical to that agreed under the Irish presidency in 2004.

Conclusion

Although Ireland was not a founding member or an original signatory of the Treaty of Rome in 1957, it has certainly made its mark on the process of treaty reform since then. A number of common themes emerge from this review of Ireland's role in treaty-making and its involvement in successive treaty negotiations.

Firstly, Ireland's overall approach has generally been to seek to preserve the institutional balance within the EU, and in that context to preserve the balance between small and large member states within the institutional make-up of the Union.

---

[5] Some of these differences include: a further strengthening of the role of national parliaments under the Reform Treaty beyond that provided for by the Constitutional Treaty; dropping references to symbols of the European Union such as the EU flag or anthem which had been part of the Constitutional Treaty; and retaining the original names for certain positions and legal instruments under the Reform Treaty. Another key difference is that while the Constitutional Treaty would have replaced earlier treaties with a single consolidated text, the Reform Treaty, in line with previous treaty reforms, is not a 'stand-alone' text but rather a document amending the earlier treaties.

Secondly, and as a natural follow-on from the above, Ireland has been a traditional defender of the role of the Commission during treaty discussions. It has sought to ensure that institutional reforms do not undermine the role of the Commission as guardian of the treaties and representative of the common interest of the Union. In that light it has also sought to ensure equal representation within the Commission.

Thirdly, Ireland has generally supported moves towards greater use of qualified majority voting in the Council, subject to caveats over taxation, criminal matters and foreign policy.

Fourthly, Ireland has been relatively proactive in supporting the extension of the Union's remit to new areas of cooperation and activity, and particularly to those areas designed to give the Union a 'human face' and respond to the concerns of citizens. Examples have included: proposals for treaty articles on education, public health, culture (in the case of Maastricht) and social exclusion; combating drug trafficking; and, as holders of the presidency, articles on fundamental rights, transparency, employment and the environment (in the case of Amsterdam). Ireland also pioneered efforts to make treaty texts more readable and accessible to citizens. Some of these proposals perhaps reflect the fact that, unlike most other member states, treaty reforms of this nature have to be ratified by referendum in Ireland.

Fifthly, Ireland can be said to have taken a careful position on foreign policy cooperation and particularly on cooperation in areas of defence and security, reflecting domestic concerns over Ireland's traditional policy of military neutrality.

Lastly, Ireland has acted as a regular advocate for economic and social cohesion, particularly in treaty reforms in the 1980s and 1990s. While it may not abandon this position entirely, it would be reasonable to assume that, given Ireland's changed status, the running on this issue may be taken up by others into the future.

In the opening section of this chapter it was suggested that individual member states can contribute to the 'treaty-making' process in three broad ways:

- Through taking the initiative to put forward suggestions for treaty changes and specific provisions or treaty articles
- Through adopting a constructive approach to discussion and debate on proposed changes
- Through the brokerage or consensus-building role of mediating progress, and drafting of compromise texts, particularly in the context of the presidency.

In many ways Ireland can be said to have been most active, and perhaps most comfortable, in the mediating role. It should be emphasised that this role is particularly taxing, involving considerable skill and workload. This role could also be said to be the more *communautaire* role – that is in a general European as opposed to a purely national interest. Of course, conducting a successful presidency and building a consensus with a view to securing agreement on treaty reforms can be seen as indirectly being in the national interest, in that it generates goodwill towards the country holding the presidency, which presumably can be exploited in some intangible fashion at a later date.

The first role of putting forward suggestions and ideas for treaty changes can of course also be considered as a *communautaire* one, given that many proposals from individual member states may genuinely reflect a desire to improve the workings and scope of the EU as a whole and be in its general interest. This presumably would also give any such proposal a greater chance of success than one that is patently designed for purely national advantage. At the same time, such proposals can be and have been a way of pursuing national priorities (even if couched in 'European' terms).

It is important to remember that treaty-making is a collective endeavour. Ultimately it depends on both good ideas and a willingness to compromise amongst *all* members. In a selective review of one country's involvement in treaty negotiations there is always a risk of only covering part of the story, and thus perhaps overemphasising the role that any particular country can play. For example, the Dutch presidency in 1997 played a key role in finalising the Amsterdam Treaty and in many ways had to tackle the most difficult phase of the negotiations.

It is also true that the Irish approach to EU negotiations has been subject to some criticism. Scott (1994, p. 25) argues that Ireland has been weaker at influencing the agenda and putting forward new policy initiatives at EU level than in managing initiatives or the brokerage role:

> Ireland's role is helpful in bringing to fruition discussions that have already been some time in maturing ... Ireland is correspondingly weak in putting forward initiatives. Ireland in this way is weak at the opening and strong on the end-game, and thus has the reputation of conducting efficient presidencies, a reputation that stands the country in good stead.

This view is echoed in more recent commentary on the Irish approach to EU business, which notes that Ireland tends to be reactive and agenda driven – generally a taker rather than a shaper of EU policies (Laffan, 2000 and 2001; McAleese, 2000; Holmes, 2005a).

Such assessments are usually made on the basis of day-to-day legislation making its way through the Brussels machinery. However, as far as treaty negotiations are concerned, it is perhaps fairer to conclude that Ireland has been, relative to its size, proactive in putting forward new ideas. Ireland has found itself in the prominent and indeed highly successful position of playing the brokerage role and has proposed compromise texts that secured agreement on a number of important treaty provisions, most recently on the Constitutional Treaty, many of the provisions of which were ultimately reflected in the Reform Treaty.

One characterisation of Ireland's general strategy in major EU negotiations is to remain on the sidelines during discussions, allowing the major players to sort out the broad lines of the deal, and then to seek to secure agreement on nationally important items (Scott, 1994). Certainly such a description may have applied in the early years of Ireland's membership of the EEC, however, the approach has evolved since then to a broader input to EU decision-making and revisions of the treaties. And while Ireland might have taken a somewhat cautious approach in the early stages of the negotiations leading to the Maastricht Treaty and in the Convention, this initial hesitancy quickly gave way to more active engagement.

The Irish approach places particular importance on personal contacts and relies heavily on the ability of a small number of individuals. Perhaps this should not surprise us. As one interviewee commented, 'personalities play a central role in foreign affairs and diplomacy ... It's the person to person relationships that lead to successful diplomacy'. Ireland's EU negotiations generally tend to fall to small numbers of officials, reflecting the limited resources within the Irish public service, certainly compared with larger member states. However, O'Donnell (2000) believes this may have advantages, arguing that, while the small number of individuals involved can cause problems of overload, it can mean that because Irish officials have a wider brief they have an ability to see more of the picture, and can avoid formal and more bureaucratic approaches towards coordination.

When asked whether Ireland should be more proactive in seeking to advance new initiatives and proposals for treaty reform, Irish negotiators tended to emphasise the limits to what a small country can achieve during treaty negotiations, and the need to focus on key priorities. One interviewee argued that Ireland tends to adopt a 'Softly softly approach – opportunistic perhaps. But small countries live on their wits ... there's always complaints that we're not making proposals. But I would strongly stress the position of a small member state. You've got to be very focussed. You've got only a certain amount of negotiating capital, so you have to prioritise'.

Another negotiator conceded that, although Ireland might not have a reputation for coming up with major initiatives, 'As a small country there are limits to what you can achieve. You have to look to things that are reasonable, that can be achieved, and that you would think would be in your interest ... I don't find it strange that small countries should watch their approach and calculate when to go for something and when to go along with things'.

Certainly, the quality of a country's contribution to treaty-making cannot be reduced to a mere 'numbers game' of how many papers or submissions are made by an individual government for discussion at an IGC. Presumably making submissions on poorly thought-through ideas would be counterproductive. Equally there may also be a valuable contribution in highlighting the drawbacks of proposals that might not necessarily be in the common European interest.

Scott (1994) acknowledges that, given its small size, Ireland does play a modest if somewhat reticent role commensurate with its stature. He also offers the view however that 'such realism is the enemy of the idealism offered by the founding fathers from the smaller Member States, and it is certainly a pity if it deters a potential flow of good ideas from Ireland' (p. 38).

Of course the roles of mediator and initiator of new proposals can in practice overlap to a considerable extent. A country holding the presidency during an IGC tends to find itself in the role of putting forward compromise texts for new treaty provisions in an effort to find common ground between different viewpoints and secure unanimous agreement.

Presumably more by accident than by design, Ireland has regularly found itself in the presidency chair in the run-up to important treaty changes – this was particularly so during the negotiation of the Amsterdam Treaty and the Constitutional Treaty, and key provisions closely reflect Irish proposals. In addition to these occasions, Ireland was in the chair when the sensitive decision was taken to open an IGC on political union leading to the Maastricht Treaty. And in the case of the Single European Act, the Irish representative chaired the group to identify key areas of treaty reform.

Rather than coming up with grand conceptual designs, one interviewee argued that a key area where small member states can contribute is in effectively managing the presidency: 'I think what we give back every so often is a presidency that works, that facilitates and mediates, and delivers'. For example, in the context of the Amsterdam Treaty, Svensson (2000, p. 131) argues that Ireland contributed 'an Irish sense of realism of what might be possible to achieve in the negotiation, as set out in the Irish draft [treaty], fixed the level of ambition and as such eventually determined a fair amount of the shape of the final Treaty'.

Ireland has had a tradition since 1975 of running successful presidencies that have been noted for high-profile successes. Ireland's first presidency was described by a former British Foreign Secretary as 'a remarkable model of efficiency' (Howe, 1986, p. 16). Certainly, it appears that Irish presidencies are popular and well regarded amongst other member states (Scott, 1994; Smyth, 1996; O'Donnell, 2000; Laffan, 2004). The Irish approach tends to emphasise efficiency and getting the work done, with Irish representatives seen as constructive and good negotiators, occasionally introducing an element of pragmatism and realism into the proceedings (Cullen, 2000; Laffan, 2000; Scott, 1996). Equally, we may say that Ireland has brought a blend of innovation and workman-like pragmatism to the treaty-making process.

The input of Irish individuals, whether commissioners or MEPs, ministers or officials, is often referred to as a key contribution that Ireland has made to European integration (McAleese, 2000; Hederman O'Brien, 2000). In the words of one of the central actors in recent treaty negotiations, 'national points of view and the effectiveness with which they are conveyed are inextricably bound up with the individuals who express them' (McDonagh, 1998, p. 6). If that is the case, Ireland's record attests to the quality of Irish negotiators past and present, at both political and administrative levels.

13

Europe and Ireland:
A Two-Way Process?

Mark Callanan

Fundamental changes

Looking back on the half-century since the signing of the Treaty of Rome, it is clear that today's European Union is a very different creature to the European Economic Community founded in 1957. As Chapter 1 noted, a far wider range of countries are now involved. Starting with six founding members, the membership has expanded at different intervals to nine, then 10, 12, 15, 25 and currently 27 – and the process of enlargement is likely to continue for the foreseeable future. While this has posed many challenges, the enlarged and more diverse Union has ultimately helped reunite a continent that was artificially divided following World War II. The Union has acted as a model for reconciliation between former foes, created a continent-wide marketplace, pioneered social rights, provided financing for weaker regions and disadvantaged communities and allowed citizens to avail of job opportunities across Europe. It has in many instances also helped consolidate the democratic process, not just most recently in Central and Eastern Europe, but also in the 1980s in the Mediterranean.

Alongside this far wider membership, the past twenty years in particular have seen momentous changes in terms of an expanded mandate for the EU. Successive reforms of the Treaty of Rome since 1987 have seen the EU expand its 'policy reach' into new areas of decision-making. The original Treaty of Rome focused on dismantling trade barriers amongst members and setting up a limited number of common policies, such as a Common Commercial Policy and a Common Agricultural Policy. Later treaties built on these provisions to extend this remit to include others such as cohesion policy, coordination of foreign and security policy, justice and home affairs, environment policy, employment and social affairs, consumer protection and monetary policy (in the case of the last-mentioned, for the members of the euro-zone). Of course, many fundamental tasks are still the responsibility of national governments and the EU's budget remains modest when compared to national budgets. Nevertheless, the range of activities at European level today is far more extensive than was the case in 1957, or when Ireland joined in 1973.

Some of these developments have been captured in this publication commemorating the fiftieth anniversary of the Treaty of Rome. The authors offer interesting new insights into the debate over Ireland's relationship with Europe, and how that relationship has evolved and matured. Just as the Union has fundamentally changed, so too has Ireland: the Ireland of today is a very different place to the Ireland of 1973, let alone the Ireland of 1957. Through their analyses of different areas, the contributors to this book show some of the ways in which Europe has impacted on Ireland, but also how Ireland has contributed to European developments.

Earlier publications on Ireland and the EU have tended to focus on the impact European developments have had on Ireland. Looking ahead, we may speculate that Ireland's relationship with Europe will become more of a two-way process. In others words, as Ireland has become a more self-confident, vibrant society with a more successful economy, there will be both 'give' and 'take' in the relationship. Of course, there is far from a blank sheet in this respect, and drawing on the analysis from preceding chapters, this chapter briefly reviews a number of ways in which Ireland has contributed to European developments, as well as considering the European impact on Ireland.

Europe's impact on Ireland

There are a number of different dimensions to the EU's impact on Ireland: the historical impact, the economic and financial impact, the policy and regulatory impact, and the impact on Ireland's institutional environment.

Dermot Keogh and Aoife Keogh detail the frustrations experienced by Ireland as an applicant country in the 1960s and the obstacles to enlargement that were encountered. The authors argue that by the time the referendum on membership was held in May 1972, the government had grown much more confident in its handling of EEC policies, thanks to an apprenticeship based on a series of false starts. They argue that Ireland's experience in the process of European integration has given it greater self-confidence in operating in a far more extensive range of multilateral organisations, assisting the country to find its place among the nations of the world.

Ken Whitaker argues that a number of developments in the 1950s clearly showed that Europe was preparing to abandon trade protectionism

– these included the provisions of the Treaty of Rome itself, which dismantled tariff barriers between the six founding states, as well as other discussions over free trade in Europe. In the context of the domestic debate taking place at the time in Ireland, developments in European cooperation offered external support for a complete reversal of Ireland's traditional policy of protectionism. The change in Irish policy involved increasing exports and encouraging foreign investment. Both of these meant that Ireland could not afford to remain isolated from developments in continental Europe.

Of course Ireland was heavily dependent on the British market at the time and could not accede to the EEC in the face of the French veto on British membership (a veto which apparently was not entirely unexpected in administrative circles in Dublin). In retrospect, however, Whitaker believes that de Gaulle did Ireland a favour, as the delay in joining the EEC gave industry and government some breathing space to prepare for the obligations of membership.

Michael Mulreany, Tony Foley and Margaret Mary Malone highlight some of the benefits that have resulted from the single market project of the 1980s and 1990s, both for consumers and for businesses. They argue that even if some of these benefits may initially have been exaggerated, the benefits have nonetheless been significant to date. The authors also take the opportunity to examine the efforts under way to complete the single market, particularly in the area of services – which is now the dominant sector and the main area of employment in modern economies.

As the contemporary focus shifts to services, how well prepared is Ireland for this 'new' single market? As was the case in the run-up to '1992', Ireland depends on multinationals for a very high proportion of service exports and is reliant on a small number of sectors. Ireland's services trade performance also leaves much to be desired in that it currently has a trade deficit. Looking forward to the next big 'push' in completing the single market, Ireland has much to gain as a small, open economy. However, domestic innovation, enterprise capability, skills and competitiveness will all be crucial. Just as they were for the initial phase of liberalisation involved in the single market project, these domestic factors will be critical if Ireland is to take full advantage of new opportunities emerging.

The single market of course also spawned a significant volume of legislation designed to dismantle non-tariff barriers to trade and ensure competition across the EU marketplace, as well as ensuring that minimum standards were in place to protect consumers and the environment. Therefore, despite the limited size of its budget, the EU has been active in legislating in a wide variety of fields (Majone, 1994). The Union is a particularly strong influence on Ireland's regulatory and legal framework in a range of policy areas. Many Acts of the Oireachtas and statutory instruments have their origins in EU directives.

In terms of specific policy areas, Tom Arnold traces some of the key developments in Irish agriculture, illustrating how the Common Agricultural Policy (CAP) was an important factor even before Ireland joined the EEC in 1973, and even more so afterwards, in shaping the development of agriculture. Peter Brennan points out how Ireland benefited from significant financial transfers under the European structural and cohesion funds, and Nicholas Rees and Barry Vaughan illustrate how Ireland has had to adapt to developments at European level in the fields of foreign policy and justice and home affairs respectively.

Aside from developments in different EU policy areas, Europe increasingly impacts on the operation of domestic institutions of governance in Ireland. Alan Dukes argues that EU business has now become firmly ensconced as one of a number of 'worlds' which ministers inhabit, alongside maintaining contacts with constituents, working in the Oireachtas, working in cabinet and managing the work of a government department. He discusses the practicalities of Council meetings, including how ministers are prepared, the conduct of meetings themselves and the interplay with other institutions.

As a minister during Ireland's 1984 and 1996 presidencies, Dukes also offers a number of personal reflections on some of the additional duties of a minister when his or her country holds the presidency. These can include the skill of differentiating between fellow ministers who are 'merely grandstanding' and those that have genuine difficulties with proposed legislation, and the task of liaising with other EU institutions such as the European Parliament. A number of incidents and episodes are described, including the calling of a vote in the Council, which give an insight into how personal camaraderie and friendships (which can exist in spite of fundamental political differences) can play an important role in EU business – a factor that is often lost in more legalistic or stoic analyses of EU decision-making.

Brigid Laffan examines how the administrative system has had to adapt to the realities of EU membership and public policy-making in the Brussels arena. Laffan argues that a problem that can arise is that Irish officials tend to intervene on specific issues, but can have little to say on the broad thrust of policy. The approach to coordination between different government departments and agencies tends to be informal and largely based on personal contacts and trust, given the small size of the administration. Some of the strengths of this Irish approach have included: its flexibility and adaptability; a demonstrated ability to run efficient and well-regarded presidencies; and an ability to perform well in major negotiations and on occasions when time, effort and considerable preparation were needed. Against these are weaknesses such as: a weakly institutionalised approach (at least until recently); an over-reliance on a small number of officials, particularly those in the Permanent Representation in Brussels, who sometimes have to act without instructions from Dublin; the difficulties involved in a small administration engaging with the many more member states that now exist; and on some occasions a lack of technical resources which meant that some more technical regulations were not fully understood during negotiations and proved difficult to implement on the ground.

Gavin Barrett discusses some of the historical and operational challenges in putting in place a more active role for the Oireachtas in scrutinising the executive in European policy-making. Despite these arrangements, there is clearly room for improvement and a number of practical suggestions are advanced as a means of promoting a more effective approach to Oireachtas involvement in EU affairs.

Notwithstanding the new arrangements and improvements introduced in 2002, the analysis shows that, compared with other countries, the Oireachtas has a relatively weak role in providing democratic scrutiny of government activity in the EU arena. Attendance by ministers at Oireachtas committees in advance of meetings of the Council of Ministers is sporadic at best, although officials do attend. While the Oireachtas committee arrangements may well have helped in informing TDs and senators of developments taking place at European level, whether it has achieved more than this and extended into the realm of actually influencing the national position being taken seems much more open to question.

As noted in Chapter 1, it has not been possible within the confines of this publication to draw attention to all of the different aspects of Ireland's membership of the EU. No doubt a more comprehensive assessment would include additional matters such as the impact that European integration has had on the Northern Ireland peace process, both through financial aid to support reconciliation, but perhaps more fundamentally as a model of conflict resolution based on the establishment of institutions to reconcile former adversaries in peaceful cooperation and joint activities.

As early as the 1960s, the potential for improving Anglo-Irish relations through greater interaction and more frequent personal contact between political and administrative leaders in Ireland and Britain was recognised in Irish circles as an important potential 'by-product' of the two countries' involvement in the process of European integration. Dermot Keogh and

Aoife Keogh note that at a meeting with Harold Wilson in 1967, Jack Lynch commented to the British Prime Minister on how greater freedom in trading through membership of the Community would undoubtedly be a considerable help in Irish cross-border relations between the twenty-six counties and the North. They argue that while becoming part of the EEC, and now the EU, allowed Ireland to develop a much greater economic independence from Britain, it also obliged both London and Dublin to work more closely together.

Other aspects of Ireland's membership of the EU have received only a passing reference. The influence that the euro has had on our lives as a powerful symbol of European integration (and not least the impact decisions of the European Central Bank have on interest rates and mortgage payments) deserves to be mentioned. From a public policy point of view, so too does the powerful influence that the convergence criteria and the subsequent Stability and Growth Pact had over Irish macroeconomic policy (McAleese, 2000; Cromien, 2000). Equally, in terms of the impact on the day-to-day lives of Irish citizens, the effect of EU policies has been profound in areas such as protection of the environment, employment law, fundamental rights, non-discrimination and gender equality.

The tangible benefits are there to be seen in terms of financial transfers, assistance to the farming community, physical infrastructure, and expenditure on training programmes, supporting businesses and research and development. These financial transfers have often been the result of hard negotiations. Less tangible perhaps, but certainly no less real, has been the economic impact of the creation of the single market, providing as it did additional markets for Irish exporters, making Europe a far more attractive venue for inward investment (of which Ireland managed to secure a large proportion) and ultimately more competitive prices for consumers. While there were downsides to the elimination of tariff and non-tariff barriers in exposing Irish producers to additional competition, the effect was not nearly as negative as some expected.

Perhaps more than the tangible economic benefits, EU membership has also affected Irish attitudes and facilitated a growing confidence in the country by making it part of a wider community (Stewart, 2000).

Writing in 2000, Ryan argued that the real test of 'Ireland's love-affair with Europe will come only when we are asked to be contributors rather than recipients, when we must put away the begging-bowl and reach for our cheque-book instead' (Ryan, 2000, p. 60). In the past, those advocating a 'yes' vote frequently fought referendum campaigns on the basis of the benefits of the financial transfers accruing to Ireland. Some of the broader benefits, and indeed some of the broader drawbacks, tended to be put to one side. This approach had the advantage of being a relatively easy message to sell. But, as Ireland began to graduate out of the status of a 'poor' member state, this argument was no longer available and the difficulty in explaining the content of what was a detailed text came home to roost during the referenda on the Nice Treaty in 2001 and 2002. Of course there were numerous and complex reasons for the 'no' to Nice, some domestic, some European. But a key lesson appears to be that while some people are strongly in favour of the European project and others are hostile to the integration process, the bulk of the electorate seems to be passively supportive at most – this is particularly so for younger generations who take the achievements of the Union, from peace between former enemies to free movement of people, as a given. Passive support such as this cannot be taken for granted. A merely passive consensus on European matters is no longer a sufficient basis for legitimising future changes to the Union's mandate and operations.

Brigid Laffan comments in Chapter 10 that the historical imperative of economic 'catch-up' provided a road map for Ireland's policy preferences for the first thirty years of its membership of the EU. As it moves from being a net beneficiary to being a net contributor to the EU budget, the challenge for Ireland is to position and embed itself as part of an enlarged Union, while also projecting its place in the wider world.

The Irish contribution to Europe

While the impact the Union has had on Ireland has been profound, the chapters in this publication also highlight some of the different ways in which Ireland has played its part in the process of European integration. Again, there are a number of different dimensions to that contribution: the personal contribution that individual Irish actors have made, the policy contribution in identifying and setting priorities at European level, the diplomatic contribution in terms of handling sensitive negotiations and running presidencies, the Irish contribution as a role model and indeed the greater financial contribution Ireland will make into the future as it becomes a net contributor to the EU's budget.

For example, Tom Arnold highlights the Irish contribution to CAP reform, through key Irish actors present on the European and international stage at the time of radical and at times controversial reforms. These reforms in turn made their mark on the CAP and Irish agriculture. Perhaps the most notable personality in respect of the CAP was Ray MacSharry, who as a commissioner pioneered landmark reforms in 1992 that blazed a trail for subsequent reforms in later years. Of course other commissioners, as well as MEPs such as Pat Cox, have made their mark as part of Ireland's 'personal' contribution to Europe. So too have numerous Taoisigh and Ministers for Foreign Affairs, as Chapter 12 on treaty-making illustrates.

Peter Brennan discusses Ireland's contribution to the policy debate on cohesion policy, both during the pre-accession period in the run-up to 1973, and as a member state. He concludes that Ireland, in partnership with the Commission, led the way before the accession of Greece, Spain and Portugal in the 1980s in arguing for a redistributive mechanism at European level between richer and poorer regions. In that respect, Ireland contributed to putting in place the key foundations for a more developed cohesion policy and has had an enormous influence in shaping EU policies geared towards providing financial assistance to poorer and less-developed parts of the Union.

Nicholas Rees illustrates how, building on its ability to punch above its weight in the UN, Ireland has been able to do the same at EU level. Ireland brought its traditional concerns over arms control, disarmament, conflict resolution, peacekeeping and aid to developing countries to discussions and policy initiatives at EU level. But EU membership also offered Ireland the opportunity to broaden its involvement in international affairs and extend its global diplomatic network.

In examining the Irish approach to managing EU dossiers, Brigid Laffan argues that the Irish tend to try to be constructive in negotiations with their counterparts where possible, avoiding isolation, and will only create problems for other member states when issues of fundamental importance arise. The approach that has evolved has allowed Ireland to develop a reputation for running efficient and well-regarded presidencies. This tradition dates right back to the first time Ireland held the presidency – Nicholas Rees notes how Ireland presided over the negotiation of the first Lomé agreement providing aid to developing countries during its presidency in 1975. Equally, Mark Callanan notes how Ireland has tended to attach a particular priority to running well-managed and workman-like presidencies that deliver, as one way of 'giving something back'.

Mark Callanan also outlines how Ireland has made a considerable contribution to the negotiations over various treaty reforms from the Single European Act up to the Reform Treaty. Throughout the treaty changes since the 1980s, Ireland has displayed a positive attitude towards greater integration and extending the policy remit of the Union, has been a traditional defender of the Commission and has supported institutional reforms such as the extension of qualified majority voting. The experience of holding regular referenda on treaty reforms has also meant that Ireland has proposed and supported new provisions designed to give the Union a 'human face' beyond purely economic integration. Ireland also held the presidency at several intervals when treaty reforms were being negotiated (particularly during 1996 and 2004) and when it was called upon to mediate between different interests and propose compromise texts for new treaty articles.

Perhaps one might also say that a key Irish contribution to the EU has been through its experience of making the most of EU membership. While domestic reforms were crucial to the rapid economic growth of the Celtic Tiger years, European developments also played an important part. The single market was the basis for attracting inward investment into Ireland. The Stability and Growth Pact helped in the debate over accepting discipline in public expenditure and borrowing. Financial transfers assisted in improving the country's infrastructure, strengthening the skills of its workforce and enhancing competitiveness. Ultimately, Ireland's success in breaking out of its historic vicious circle of low growth, high unemployment and high emigration has become something of a role model for smaller, less-developed states that have joined the Union.

A genuine attempt has also been made in Ireland to create a domestic arena for dialogue and discussion on European matters within civic society, through the National Forum on Europe, which has been highlighted by some as an example for other countries. Given that it is still a young institution, it is perhaps too early to make any definitive judgments on the Forum. Early indications, however, are that it has helped significantly to widen the scope of debate over a broader range of European issues and policy areas, even if the vast bulk of the public does not engage in the debate over EU developments (O'Brennan, 2005). While permanent mobilisation of citizens in a debate on European issues might be a somewhat Utopian aspiration, there does appear to be a challenge in developing a greater understanding of the EU's activities and how it works.

In the Irish case, the electorate at large only tends to be involved in the debate during referenda on European treaties. And such debates have tended to take the form of assertive statements (on both sides of the argument), rather than actual debating. Advocates assert their positions and stick to them and, without a broader public debate on Europe, the campaign quickly descends into polarised positions or interpretations over what specific articles or provisions mean. This ends up firstly confusing, then irritating, and frequently boring, the electorate, who are in most cases left wondering 'who to believe?' (Holmes, 2005b). Referendum campaigns also seem to focus quickly upon a small number of specific elements of treaties, while broader questions about EU activity in areas such as trade, environmental protection, social policy and equality, or agriculture tend to be lost.

A challenge for the future will be to engage a wider proportion of citizens in the debate over Ireland's relationship with Europe, and to develop a broader understanding of the activities of the Union, outside of the temporary heat that is generated during a referendum campaign. This challenge of engaging citizens in EU decision-making is of course not unique to Ireland, but rather a challenge right across Europe.

Bibliography

Ahern, B. (2004), 'Ireland and Europe: Embracing Change', in J. Hourihane (ed.), *Ireland and the European Union: The First Thirty Years, 1973–2002*, Dublin: Lilliput Press, pp. 94–106

Allen, D. and M. Smith (1990), 'Western Europe's Presence in the Contemporary International Arena', *Review of International Studies*, vol. 16, no. 1, pp. 135–154

All-Party Oireachtas Committee on the Constitution (2001), *Sixth Progress Report: The Referendum*, Dublin: Stationery Office

Anderson, M., M. den Boer, P. Cullen, W. C. Gilmore, C. D. Raab and N. Walker (1995), *Policing the European Union*, Oxford: Clarendon Press

Andrews, B. (2003), 'Who Runs this Country? Certainly not Dáil Éireann', *The Irish Times*, 19 July

Balzacq, T., D. Bigo, S. Carrera and E. Guild (2006), *Security and the Two-Level Game: The Treaty of Prüm, the EU and the Management of Threats*, CEPS Working Document, no. 234, Brussels: Centre for European Policy Studies

Barrett, G. (1997), 'Cooperation in Justice and Home Affairs in the European Union – An Overview and a Critique', in G. Barrett (ed.), *Justice Cooperation in the European Union*, Dublin: Institute of European Affairs, pp. 3–47

Barrett, G. (ed.) (2007), *National Parliaments and the European Union: The Constitutional Challenge for the Oireachtas and Other Member State Legislatures*, Dublin: Clarus Press

Bartlett, C. A. and S. Ghoshal (1989), *Managing Across Borders: The Transnational Solution*, London: Hutchinson Business Books

Beck, U. and E. Grande (2007), 'Cosmopolitanism: Europe's Way out of a Crisis', *European Journal of Social Theory*, vol. 10, no. 1, pp. 67–85

Bigo, D. (2002), 'Security & Immigration: Toward a Critique of the Governmentality of Unease', *Alternatives*, vol. 27, pp. 63–92

Bradley, J. (2006), 'Imagination and Reality in a Flat World: Ireland in the Global Economy', paper presented to the *VI International Conference of the Spanish Association of Irish Studies*, Valladolid, 25 to 27 May

Breen R., D. F. Hannan, D. B. Rottman and C. T. Whelan (1990), *Understanding Contemporary Ireland: State, Class and Development in the Republic of Ireland*, Dublin: Gill & Macmillan

Brennock, M. (2006), 'Backbenchers Want to Influence Policy and Have Voices Heard', *The Irish Times*, 24 June

Bretherton, C. and J. Vogler (1999), *The European Union as a Global Actor*, London: Routledge

Brosnan, J. (2000), 'The Commission', in Institute of European Affairs, *IGC 2000: Issues Options Implications – Final Report*, Dublin: Institute of European Affairs, pp. 52–65

Brown, T. (1992), 'New Policies', in P. Keatinge (ed.), *Maastricht and Ireland: What the Treaty Means*, Studies in European Union Series, Dublin: Institute of European Affairs, pp. 34–40

Brown, T. (2007), 'Ireland's National Forum on Europe: Helping to Make Up for the Democratic Deficit?', in G. Barrett (ed.), *National Parliaments and the European Union: The Constitutional Challenge for the Oireachtas and Other Member State Legislatures*, Dublin: Clarus Press, pp. 323–346

Bruton, J. (2003), 'A Proposal for the Appointment of the President of the Commission as Provided for in Article 18 bis of the Draft Constitutional Treaty', Brussels: The European Convention, CONV 476/03, available at http://european-convention.eu.int/

Buck, T. (2007), 'Standard Bearer: How the European Union Exports Its Laws', *The Financial Times*, 10 July

Burns, B. and T. Salmon (1977), 'Policy-Making Coordination in Ireland on European Community Issues', *Journal of Common Market Studies*, vol. 15, no. 4, pp. 272–287

Callanan, M. (2000), 'The 2000 Intergovernmental Conference on Preparing the EU for Enlargement: The Contribution of the Dehaene Report', *Administration*, vol. 48, no. 1, pp. 3–17

Christophersen, H. (1994), 'Cohesion Policy Before and After Maastricht', in J. Mortensen (ed.), *Improving Economic and Social Cohesion in the European Community*, Basingstoke: Palgrave Macmillan, pp. 17–21

Coakley, J., M. Holmes and N. Rees (1997), 'The Irish Response to European Integration: Explaining the Persistence of Opposition', in A. W. Cafruny and C. Lankowski (eds.), *Europe's Ambiguous Unity: Conflict and Consensus in the Post-Maastricht Era*, Boulder: Lynne Riener, pp. 209–238

Commission of the European Communities (1973), *Regional Problems in the Enlarged Community*, COM (73) 550 final, Brussels: European Commission

Commission of the European Communities (1981), *The Regions of Europe, First Periodic Report on the Social and Economic Situation of the Regions of the Community*, Luxembourg: Office for Official Publications of the European Communities

Commission of the European Communities (1984), *The Regions of Europe, Second Periodic Report on the Social and Economic Situation and Development of the Regions of the Community*, COM (84) 40 final/2, Luxembourg: Office for Official Publications of the European Communities

Commission of the European Communities (1988), *Research on 'The Cost of Non-Europe' Project*, Luxembourg: Office for Official Publications of the European Communities

Corbett, R. (1987), 'The 1985 Intergovernmental Conference and the Single European Act', in R. Pryce (ed.), *The Dynamics of European Union*, London: Croom Helm, pp. 238–272

Council of the European Community (1996), *Intergovernmental Conference 1996: Reflection Group Report and Other References for Documentary Purposes*, Luxembourg: Office for Official Publications of the European Communities

Council of the European Union (2004), 'The Hague Programme: Strengthening Freedom, Security and Justice in the European Union', available at http://ec.europa.eu/justice_home/doc_centre/doc/hague_programme_en.pdf

Cowen, B. (2003), 'Annual Address by Brian Cowen, Minister for Foreign Affairs to the Institute of European Affairs', Dublin, 16 January

Cromien, S. (2000), 'Serving in New Spheres', in R. O'Donnell (ed.), *Europe: The Irish Experience*, Dublin: Institute of European Affairs, pp. 148–158

Cronin, D. and M. Banks (2004), 'Irish Plan to Pave Way for Constitution', *The European Voice*, 17 June

Crotty, R. D. (1966), *Irish Agricultural Production: Its Volume and Structure*, Cork: Cork University Press

CSO (2004), *Ireland and the EU 1973–2003*, Dublin: Central Statistics Office

Cullen, M. (2000), 'Sharing Sovereignty', in R. O'Donnell (ed.), *Europe: The Irish Experience*, Dublin: Institute of European Affairs, pp. 44–51

Daly, M. E. (1992), *Industrial Development and Irish National Identity, 1922–1939*, Dublin: Gill & Macmillan

Daly, M. E. (2002), *The First Department: A History of the Department of Agriculture*, Dublin: Institute of Public Administration

de Schoutheete, P. and H. Wallace (2002), 'The European Council', paper prepared for *Notre Europe*, Research and European Issues no. 19, September

den Boer, M. and W. Wallace (2000), 'Justice and Home Affairs', in H. Wallace and W. Wallace (eds.), *Policy-Making in the European Union*, Oxford: Oxford University Press, pp. 493–519

Department of Agriculture (1970), *Irish Agriculture and Fisheries in the EEC*, Dublin: Department of Agriculture

Department of Agriculture and Food (1990), *Agriculture and Food Policy Review*, Dublin: Department of Agriculture and Food

Department of Agriculture and Food (2004), *Report of the Agri Vision 2015 Committee*, Dublin: Department of Agriculture and Food

Department of Agriculture, Fisheries and Food (2007), *Annual Review & Outlook for Agriculture & Food 2006/07*, Dublin: Department of Agriculture, Fisheries and Food

Department of Finance (2007), *National Strategic Reference Framework for Ireland: Supporting and Enabling Dynamic Regions*, Dublin: Department of Finance

Department of Foreign Affairs (1998), *Strategy Statement 1998*, Dublin: Department of Foreign Affairs

Department of the Taoiseach (2002), *Ireland and the European Union: Identifying Priorities and Pursuing Goals*, Dublin: Department of the Taoiseach

Dinan, D. (2005a), *Ever Closer Union*, Basingstoke: Palgrave Macmillan

Dinan, D. (2005b), 'Governance and Institutions: A New Constitution and a New Commission', *Journal of Common Market Studies*, vol. 43, The European Union: Annual Review, pp. 37–54

Donohoe, M. (2007), 'Dáil, Seanad Plan to Blow Dust off Image', *The Irish Times*, 18 June

Dooge Report (1985), *Report to the European Council*, Ad Hoc Committee for Institutional Affairs, Brussels, SN/1187/85 (Spaak II)

Dooley, T. (2004), *The Land for the People*, Dublin: University College Dublin Press

Dorr, N. (2000), 'The IGC 2000 Agenda: An Irish Perspective', in E. Best, M. Gray and A. Stubb (eds.), *Rethinking the European Union: IGC 2000 and Beyond*, Maastricht: European Institute of Public Administration, pp. 29–42

Economic Development (1958), Dublin: Stationery Office

European Commission (1987), *Memo to the Heads of State and Government*, SEC (87) 22 final, Brussels: European Commission

European Commission (1988), *The Future of Rural Society*, Luxembourg: European Commission

European Commission (1991), *Reflections on the Common Agricultural Policy*, Luxembourg: European Commission

European Commission (2003), *The Internal Market – Ten Years Without Frontiers*, Brussels: Commission of the European Communities

European Commission (2004a), *Area of Freedom, Security and Justice: Assessment of the Tampere Programme and Future Orientations*, Brussels: Commission of the European Union

European Commission (2004b), *Report on the Implementation of the Internal Market Strategy (2003–2006)*, COM (2004) 22 final, Brussels: Commission of the European Communities

European Commission (2006a), *A Citizens' Agenda: Delivering Results for Europe*, COM (2006) 211 final, Brussels: Commission of the European Communities

European Commission (2006b), *After Tampere 2006 – Priorities for the Area of Freedom, Security and Justice*, Brussels: Commission of the European Union

European Commission (2006c), *Implementing the Hague Programme: The Way Forward*, Brussels: Commission of the European Union

European Commission (2006d), *Public Consultation on a Future Single Market Policy: Summary of Responses*, SEC (2006) 1215/2, Brussels: Commission of the European Communities

European Commission (2007a), *A Single Market for Citizens: Interim Report to the 2007 Spring European Council*, COM (2007) 60 final, Brussels: Commission of the European Communities

European Commission (2007b), *Questions and Answers on the Protection of the Environment through Criminal Law*, Brussels: Commission of the European Union, Memo 07/50

European Parliament and European Council (2006), 'Directive 2006/123/EC of the European Parliament and of the Council on Services in the Internal Market', Official Journal of the European Union: http://eur-lex.europa.eu/LexUriServ/site/en/oj/2006/l_376/l_37620061227en00360068.pdf

Evans, A. (1999), *The EU Structural Funds*, Oxford: Oxford University Press

Fanning, R. (1978), *The Irish Department of Finance, 1922–58*, Dublin: Institute of Public Administration

Fink-Hafner, D. (2007), 'Ensuring Democratic Control over National Government in European Affairs – the Slovenian Experience', in G. Barrett (ed.), *National Parliaments and the European Union: The Constitutional Challenge for the Oireachtas and Other Member State Legislatures*, Dublin: Clarus Press, pp. 393–414

FitzGerald, G. (1973), *Irish Foreign Policy Statement to Dáil Éireann May 1973*, Dublin: Department of Foreign Affairs

FitzGerald, G. (1985), 'Ireland in Europe', Irish School of Ecumenics Lecture Series, 25 February

FitzGerald, G. (1998), 'Amsterdam Treaty Bears Stamp of Successful Irish Diplomacy', *The Irish Times*, 14 March

FitzGerald, G. (1999), 'The European Council', in J. Dooge and R. Barrington (eds.), *A Vital National Interest: Ireland in Europe 1973–1998*, Dublin: Institute of Public Administration, pp. 126–138

FitzGerald, G. (2000), 'People Entitled to Have Voting System Choice Put Before Them', *The Irish Times*, 26 February

Fitzgerald, M. (2000), *From Protectionism to Liberalisation: Ireland and the EEC, 1957–1966*, Aldershot: Ashgate Publishing

Fogarty, C. P. (1985), 'European Union: Implications for Ireland', *Administration*, vol. 33, no. 4, pp. 590–606

Foley, A. and M. Mulreany (eds.) (1990), *The Single European Market and the Irish Economy*, Dublin: Institute of Public Administration

Forfás (2000), *The Evolution of Economic Policies in the Republic of Ireland*, Dublin: Forfás

Forfás (2004), *Ahead of the Curve: Ireland's Place in the Global Economy*, Report of the Enterprise Strategy Group, Dublin: Forfás

Gallagher, M. (1988), 'The Single European Act Referendum', *Irish Political Studies*, vol. 3, pp. 77–82

Gelder, L. (1962), 'Ireland Ready for EEC Political and Defence Effects', *The Irish Times*, 4 October

Gilland, K. (2002), 'Ireland's (First) Referendum on the Treaty of Nice', *Journal of Common Market Studies*, vol. 40, no. 3, pp. 527–535

Gillespie, P. (2002), 'Ireland Must Not Shy Away from Debate on EU', *The Irish Times*, 30 November

Girvin, B. (1989), *Between Two Worlds – Politics and Economy in Independent Ireland*, Dublin: Gill & Macmillan

Girvin, B. and G. Roberts (eds.) (2000), *Ireland and the Second World War: Politics, Society and Remembrance*, Dublin: Four Courts Press

Giscard d'Estaing, V. (2002), 'Speech by Valéry Giscard d'Estaing, Chairman of the European Convention at the Opening of the Academic Year at the College of Europe', Bruges, 2 October

Government of Ireland (1958), *Programme for Economic Expansion*, Dublin: Stationery Office

Government of Ireland (1961), *European Economic Community: White Paper*, Dublin: Stationery Office

Government of Ireland (1972), *The Accession of Ireland to the European Communities*, White Paper, Dublin: Stationery Office

Government of Ireland (1986), *The Single European Act: An Explanatory Guide*, Dublin: Stationery Office

Government of Ireland (1992), *Treaty on European Union: White Paper*, Dublin: Stationery Office

Government of Ireland (1996), *Challenges and Opportunities Abroad: White Paper on Foreign Policy*, Dublin: Stationery Office

Government of Ireland (1998), *Treaty of Amsterdam: White Paper*, Dublin: Stationery Office

Government of Ireland (2002), *White Paper: The Treaty of Nice and Seville Declarations 2002*, Dublin: Stationery Office

Government of Ireland (2005), *The European Constitution: White Paper*, Dublin: Department of Foreign Affairs

Government of Ireland (2006), *White Paper on Irish Aid,* Dublin: Department of Foreign Affairs

Hartley, T. C. (1998), *The Foundations of European Community Law: An Introduction to the Constitutional and Administrative Law of the European Community*, Oxford: Oxford University Press

Hayes, F. (1984), 'The Role of COREPER in EEC Decision-Making', *Administration*, vol. 32, no. 2, pp. 177–200

Hayes-Renshaw, F. and H. Wallace (1997), *The Council of Ministers*, Basingstoke: Macmillan Press

Hayward, K. (2003), '"If at First You Don't Succeed…": The Second Referendum on the Treaty of Nice, 2002', *Irish Political Studies*, vol. 18, no. 1, pp. 120–132

Hederman, M. (1983), *The Road to Europe: Irish Attitudes 1948–61*, Dublin: Institute of Public Administration

Hederman O'Brien, M. (2000), 'The Way We Were', in R. O'Donnell (ed.), *Europe: The Irish Experience*, Dublin: Institute of European Affairs, pp. 6–17

Hill, C. (1993), 'The Capability–Expectations Gap, or Conceptualising Europe's International Role', *Journal of Common Market Studies*, vol. 31, no. 3, pp. 305–325

Holmes, M. (1993), 'The Maastricht Treaty Referendum of June 1992', *Irish Political Studies*, vol. 8, pp. 105–110

Holmes, M. (2005a), 'Irish Approaches to European Integration', in M. Holmes (ed.), *Ireland and the European Union: Nice, Enlargement and the Future of Europe*, Manchester: Manchester University Press, pp. 1–13

Holmes, M. (2005b), 'The Development of Opposition to European Integration in Ireland', in M. Holmes (ed.), *Ireland and the European Union: Nice, Enlargement and the Future of Europe*, Manchester: Manchester University Press, pp. 75–93

Holmes, M., N. Rees and B. Whelan (1993), *The Poor Relation: Irish Foreign Policy and the Third World*, Dublin: Trocaire/Gill & Macmillan

House of Lords, European Union Committee (2006a), *European Arrest Warrant – Recent Developments*, London: The Stationery Office

House of Lords, European Union Committee (2006b), *The Criminal Law Competence of the European Community*, London: The Stationery Office

Houses of the Oireachtas Commission (2006), *Statement of Estimates of the Amount of Moneys Required in Respect of Ongoing Expenditure for the Period Beginning on 1 January 2007 and Ending on 31 December 2007*, PRN A6/1673, October, published in accordance with Section 13 of the Houses of the Oireachtas Commission Act 2003

Houses of the Oireachtas Commission (2007a), *Annual Report 2006*, Dublin: Houses of the Oireachtas

Houses of the Oireachtas Commission (2007b), *Strategic Plan 2007–2009: Excellence in Parliamentary Service*, Dublin: Houses of the Oireachtas

Howe, G. (1986), 'Europe International', in J. Dooge (ed.), *Ireland in the Contemporary World: Essays in Honour of Garret FitzGerald*, Dublin: Gill & Macmillan, pp. 13–19

Irish Presidency (1996), *The European Union Today and Tomorrow: Adapting the European Union for the Benefit of Its Peoples and Preparing It for the Future – A General Outline for a Draft Revision of the Treaties (Dublin II)*, Brussels: Conference of the Representatives of the Governments of the Member States, CONF 2500/96

Jackson, J. (2005), 'The Effect of Human Rights on Criminal Evidentiary Processes: Towards Convergence, Divergence or Realignment', *Modern Law Review*, vol. 68, pp. 737–764

Joint Oireachtas Committee on European Affairs (2007a), *Annual Report 2006*, Dublin: Houses of the Oireachtas

Joint Oireachtas Committee on European Affairs (2007b), *Joint Oireachtas Committee on European Affairs: Work Programme 2007*, Dublin: Houses of the Oireachtas

Jones, D. (2005), 'UK Parliamentary Scrutiny of EU Legislation', London: Foreign Policy Centre, paper available at http://fpc.org.uk/fsblob/432.pdf

Kassim, H. (ed.) (2001), *The National Coordination of EU Policy: The European Level*, Oxford: Oxford University Press

Keatinge, P. (1973), *The Formulation of Irish Foreign Policy*, Dublin: Institute of Public Administration

Keatinge, P. (1984), *A Singular Stance: Irish Neutrality in the 1980s*, Dublin: Institute of Public Administration

Keatinge, P. (ed.) (1992), *Maastricht and Ireland: What the Treaty Means*, Studies in European Union Series, Dublin: Institute of European Affairs

Keatinge, P. (1996), *European Security: Ireland's Choices*, Dublin: Institute of European Affairs

Keatinge, P. and A. Murphy (1987), 'The European Council's Ad Hoc Committee on Institutional Affairs (1984–85)', in R. Pryce (ed.), *The Dynamics of European Union*, London: Croom Helm, pp. 217–237

Keatinge, P., B. Laffan and R. O'Donnell (1991), 'Weighing Up Gains and Losses', in P. Keatinge (ed.), *Ireland and EC Membership Evaluated*, London: Pinter, pp. 280–291

Kennedy, K. A., T. Giblin and D. McHugh (1988), *The Economic Development of Ireland in the Twentieth Century*, London: Routledge

Kennedy, M. and J. M. Skelly (2000), *Irish Foreign Policy, 1919–1966: From Independence to Internationalism*, Dublin: Four Courts Press

Keogh, D. (1994), *Twentieth-Century Ireland: Nation and State*, Dublin: Gill & Macmillan

Keogh, D. (2000), 'Irish Neutrality and the First Application for Membership of the EEC, 1961–3', in M. Kennedy and J. Morrison Skelly (eds.), *Irish Foreign Policy 1916–1966: From Independence to Internationalism*, Dublin: Four Courts Press, pp. 265–286

Komarek, J. (2007), 'European Constitutionalism and the European Arrest Warrant – In Search of the Contrapunctual Principles' Limits', *Common Market Law Review*, vol. 44, pp. 9–40, available at http://users.ox.ac.uk/~some2134/publ.html

Lacouture, J. (1991a), *De Gaulle: The Rebel, 1890–1944*, London: Harvill Press

Lacouture, J. (1991b), *De Gaulle: The Ruler, 1945–1970*, London: Harvill Press

Laffan, B. (1991), 'The Governance of the Union', in P. Keatinge (ed.), *Political Union*, Studies in European Union Series, Dublin: Institute of European Affairs, pp. 1–60

Laffan, B. (1997), *The Finances of the European Union*, Basingstoke: Palgrave Macmillan

Laffan, B. (2000), 'Rapid Adaptation and Light Co-ordination', in R. O'Donnell (ed.), *Europe: The Irish Experience*, Dublin: Institute of European Affairs, pp. 125–147

Laffan, B. (2001), *Organising for a Changing Europe: Irish Central Government and the European Union*, Dublin: The Policy Institute, Trinity College

Laffan, B. (2004), 'Lessons To Be Learnt from Presidency on Policy-Making and EU Relations', *The Irish Times*, 7 July

Laffan, B. (2005a), 'Ireland's Management of EU Business: The Impact of Nice', in M. Holmes (ed.), *Ireland and the European Union: Nice, Enlargement and the Future of Europe*, Manchester: Manchester University Press, pp. 171–188

Laffan, B. (2005b), 'National Parliaments and Domestic Core Executives', paper delivered at *Ireland, Europe and the Challenge of Democracy – Ensuring Democratic Control over Government in European Union Affairs*, conference held at Europe House, Dublin, Friday 20 May

Laffan, B. and E. Tannam (1998), 'The Rewards of Pragmatism', in K. Hanf and B. Soetendorp (eds.), *Adapting to European Integration: Small States and the European Union*, London: Longman, pp. 69–83

Lavenex, S. and W. Wallace (2005), 'Justice and Home Affairs', in H. Wallace, W. Wallace and M. Pollack (eds.), *Policy-Making in the European Union*, Oxford: Oxford University Press, pp. 457–480

Laver, M. (1998), 'TDs Have Not Thought Out Results of Changing PR System', *The Irish Times*, 2 July

Leczykiewicz, D. (2007), 'Constitutionalising the Third Pillar', available at http://cels.law.cam.ac.uk/events/Leczykiewicz.pdf

Lee, J. (1989), *Ireland 1912–1985: Politics and Society*, Cambridge: Cambridge University Press

Lee, J. (1990), 'Economic Development in Historical Perspective', in J. F. McCarthy (ed.), *Planning Ireland's Future: The Legacy of T. K. Whitaker*, Dublin: Glendale Press, pp. 112–125

Loader, I. (2002), 'Policing, Securitization and Democratization in Europe', *Criminal Justice*, vol. 2, no. 2, pp. 125–153

MacCarthaigh, M. (2005), *Accountability in Irish Parliamentary Politics*, Dublin: Institute of Public Administration

Mac Éinrí, P. (2002), 'The Implications for Ireland and the UK Arising from the Development of Recent European Union Policy on Migration', in NCCRI, *Migration Policy in Ireland: Reform and Harmonisation*, Dublin: National Consultative Committee on Racism and Interculturalism, pp. 38–51, available at www.nccri.ie/pdf/migration.pdf

MacSharry, R. (1999), 'Reform of the CAP', in J. Dooge and R. Barrington (eds.), *A Vital National Interest: Ireland in Europe 1973–1998*, Dublin: Institute of Public Administration, pp. 295–311

Maher, D. J. (1986), *The Tortuous Path: The Course of Ireland's Entry into the EEC, 1948–1973*, Dublin: Institute of Public Administration

Majone, G. (1994), 'The Rise of the Regulatory State in Europe', *West European Politics*, vol. 17, no. 3, pp. 77–101

Mansergh, L. (1999), 'Two Referendums and the Referendum Commission: The 1998 Experience', *Irish Political Studies*, vol. 14, pp. 123–131

Mathieson, T. (2006), '*Lex Vigilatoria* – Towards a Control System without a State?', in S. Armstrong and L. McAra (eds.), *Perspectives on Punishment: The Contours of Control*, Oxford: Oxford University Press, pp. 119–132

Matthews, A. (1988), 'Common Agricultural Policy, Reform and National Compensation Strategies', paper presented to the Statistical and Social Inquiry Society of Ireland

Matthews, A. (2001), *How Important is Agriculture and the AgriFood Sector in Ireland*, Trinity Economic Papers, no. 18 of 2001, Dublin: Trinity College

Maurer, A. (2007), 'National Parliaments in the Architecture of Europe in the Light of the Constitutional Treaty', in G. Barrett (ed.), *National Parliaments and the European Union: The Constitutional Challenge for the Oireachtas and Other Member State Legislatures*, Dublin: Clarus Press, pp. 47–103

McAleese, D. (2000), 'Twenty-Five Years "A Growing"', in R. O'Donnell (ed.), *Europe: The Irish Experience*, Dublin: Institute of European Affairs, pp. 79–110

McCreevy, C. (2005), 'EU Commissioner for Internal Market and Services, Speech to IBEC's Biennial lunch', Dublin, 15 April

McDonagh, B. (1998), *Original Sin in a Brave New World: The Paradox of Europe – An Account of the Negotiation of the Treaty of Amsterdam*, Dublin: Institute of European Affairs

McDonagh, B. (2007), 'The Intergovernmental Conference: How the Deal was Done', in G. Amato, H. Bribosia and B. de Witte (eds.), *Genesis and Destiny of the European Constitution*, Brussels: Bruylant, pp. 87–136

McNamara, T., R. Boyle, M. Callanan, M. Brady, M. MacCarthaigh, J. O'Riordan and S. Weir (2004), 'Review of Developments, Structure and Management in the Public Sector 2004', *Administration*, vol. 52, no. 4, pp. 3–48

Meenan, K. (1985), 'The Work of the Dooge Committee', *Administration*, vol. 33, no. 4, pp. 580–589

Meenan, K. (1999), '1984 – The End of Eurosclerosis', in J. Dooge and R. Barrington (eds.), *A Vital National Interest: Ireland in Europe 1973–1998*, Dublin: Institute of Public Administration, pp. 55–65

Meenan, K. (2007), 'What is the Role of a Committee on European Affairs?', in G. Barrett (ed.), *National Parliaments and the European Union: The Constitutional Challenge for the Oireachtas and other Member State Legislatures*, Dublin: Clarus Press, pp. 309–322

Mezey, M. (1979), *Comparative Legislatures*, Durham, North Carolina: Duke University Press

Milward, A. S. (1992), *The European Rescue of the Nation State*, London: Routledge

Mitsilegas, V. (2007), 'Police Co-operation: What are the Main Obstacles to Police Cooperation in the EU?', available at www.libertysecurity.org/article1379.html#nb10#nb10

Mitterrand, F. (1986), 'Ireland and Europe', in J. Dooge (ed.), *Ireland in the Contemporary World: Essays in Honour of Garret FitzGerald*, Dublin: Gill & Macmillan, pp. 1–8

Monar, J. (2000), 'Justice and Home Affairs in a Wider Europe: The Dynamics of Inclusion and Exclusion', *ESRC 'One Europe or Several?' Programme Working Paper 07/00*, available at www.one-europe.ac.uk/pdf/monarW7.PDF

Monnet, J. (1978), *Memoirs*, London: Collins

Monti, M. (1996), *The Single Market and Tomorrow's Europe: A Progress Report from the European Commission,* Luxembourg: Office for Official Publications of the European Communities

Moody, T. W. (1981), *Davitt and the Irish Revolution*, Oxford: Clarendon Press

Moravcsik, A. (1991), 'Negotiating the Single European Act: National Interests and Conventional Statecraft in the European Community', *International Organization*, vol. 45, no. 1, pp. 19–56

Murphy, G. (2005), 'From Economic Nationalism to European Union', in B. Girvin and G. Murphy (eds.), *The Lemass Era: Politics and Society in the Ireland of Seán Lemass*, Dublin: University College Dublin Press, pp. 28–48

National Forum on Europe (2003), *The 26th Plenary Session of the National Forum on Europe – Constitutional and Institutional Issues in the Convention on the Future of Europe*, Dublin: National Forum on Europe, available at www.forumoneurope.ie

National Forum on Europe (2004), *The 44th Plenary Session of the National Forum on Europe – IGC Agreement on the Constitutional Treaty for the European Union*, Dublin: National Forum on Europe, available at www.forumoneurope.ie

Neal, L. (2007), *The Economics of Europe and the European Union*, Cambridge: Cambridge University Press

Norman, P. (2005), *The Accidental Constitution: The Making of Europe's Constitutional Treaty*, Brussels: EuroComment

Norton, P. (1984), 'Parliament and Policy in Britain: The House of Commons as a Policy Influencer', *Teaching Politics*, vol. 13, p. 198–221

Nugent, N. (1999), *The Government and Politics of the European Union*, Basingstoke: Macmillan

Nuttall, S. (1992), *European Political Cooperation*, Oxford: Oxford University Press

O'Brennan, J. (2005), 'Ireland's European Discourse and the National Forum on Europe', in M. Holmes (ed.), *Ireland and the European Union: Nice, Enlargement and the Future of Europe*, Manchester: Manchester University Press, pp. 114–132

O'Donnell, R. (1992), 'Cohesion', in P. Keatinge (ed.), *Maastricht and Ireland: What the Treaty Means*, Studies in European Union Series, Dublin: Institute of European Affairs, pp. 50–55

O'Donnell, R. (2000), 'The New Ireland in the New Europe', in R. O'Donnell (ed.), *Europe: The Irish Experience*, Dublin: Institute of European Affairs, pp. 161–214

O'Halpin, E. (1999), *Defending Ireland: The Irish State and Its Enemies since 1922*, Oxford: Oxford University Press

O'Hara, P. (1998), *Partners in Production? Women, Farm and Family in Ireland*, Oxford: Berghahn Books

O'Hegarty, L. (2007), 'Parliamentary Scrutiny of European Affairs in Ireland – The European Affairs Committee, the Scrutiny Committee, and the European Union (Scrutiny) Act 2002', in G. Barrett (ed.), *National Parliaments and the European Union: The Constitutional Challenge for the Oireachtas and Other Member State Legislatures*, Dublin: Clarus Press, pp. 273–307

O'Mahony, J. (2001), '"Not so Nice": The Treaty of Nice, The International Criminal Court, The Abolition of the Death Penalty – The 2001 Referendum Experience', *Irish Political Studies*, vol. 16, pp. 201–213

O'Mahony, J. (2004), 'Ireland and the European Union: A Less Certain Relationship?', in N. Collins and T. Cradden (eds.), *Political Issues in Ireland Today*, Manchester: Manchester University Press, pp. 15–33

O'Mahony, P. (2000), 'The Impact of the Third Pillar on Irish Civil Liberties', in E. Regan (ed.), *The New Third Pillar – Cooperation against Crime in the European Union*, Dublin: Institute of European Affairs, pp. 157–176

O'Malley, E. (2004), 'Competitive Performance in Irish Industry', *Quarterly Economic Commentary*, Winter, pp. 66–87

OECD (1981), *Adapting Public Administration for Participating in Supranational Bodies*, Paris: Organisation for Economic Co-operation and Development

Offe, C. and U. Preuss (2006), *The Problem of Legitimacy in the European Polity. Is Democratization the Answer?*, Constitutionalism Webpapers, ConWEB, no. 6/2006, Belfast: Queen's University Belfast

Parlon, T. (2004), 'Speech by Tom Parlon TD, Minister of State, representing the Irish Presidency at the Third Cohesion Forum', Brussels, 10 May

Peterson, J. and M. Shackleton (eds.) (2002), *The Institutions of the European Union*, Oxford: Oxford University Press

Peyrefitte, A. (1994), *C'etait de Gaulle*, Paris: Editions Fallois-Fayard

Raunio, T. (2007), 'Ensuring Democratic Control over National Governments in European Affairs', in G. Barrett (ed.), *National Parliaments and the European Union: The Constitutional Challenge for the Oireachtas and Other Member State Legislatures*, Dublin: Clarus Press, pp. 3–27

Raunio, T. and M. Wiberg (2007), 'Too Little, Too Late? Comparing the Engagement of Nordic Parliaments in European Union Matters', in G. Barrett (ed.), *National Parliaments and the European Union: The Constitutional Challenge for the Oireachtas and Other Member State Legislatures*, Dublin: Clarus Press, pp. 379–391

Rees, N. (2000), 'The Kosovo Crisis, the International Response and Ireland', *Irish Studies in International Affairs*, vol. 11, pp. 55–70

Rees, N. (2005), 'The Irish Presidency: A Diplomatic Triumph', *Journal of Common Market Studies*, vol. 43, The European Union: Annual Review, pp. 55–58

Rees, N. and M. Holmes (2002), 'Capacity, Perceptions and Principles: Ireland's Changing Place in Europe', *Current Politics and Economics of Europe*, special edition, vol. 11, no. 1, pp. 49–60

Rettman, A. (2005), 'Iran Mujahidin to Challenge EU Terror List', *EU Observer*, 10 May

Robinson, M. T. (1979), 'Irish Parliamentary Scrutiny of EC Legislation', *Common Market Law Review*, vol. 16, pp. 9–30

Roche, D. (2003), *Appointment of President of Commission: Role of an Electoral College*, Brussels: The European Convention, CONV 496/03, available at http://european-convention.eu.int/

Rogers, J. (2001), 'Voters Should Not Be Blackmailed into Voting Yes to Avoid Giving Offence', *The Irish Times*, 19 May

Ryan, A. (2006), 'The European Evidence Warrant: The Emergence of a European Law of Evidence', *Irish Criminal Law Journal*, vol. 16, no. 4, pp. 8–14

Ryan, L. (2000), 'Strengthening Irish Identity through Openness', in R. O'Donnell (ed.), *Europe: The Irish Experience*, Dublin: Institute of European Affairs, pp. 55–68

Salmon, T. (1989), *Unneutral Ireland: An Ambivalent and Unique Security Policy*, Oxford: Clarendon Press

Savage, R. J. (1996), *Irish Television: The Political and Social Origins*, Cork: Cork University Press

Schmidt, V. (2006), *Democracy in Europe: The EU and National Polities*, Oxford: Oxford University Press

Scott, D. (1994), *Ireland's Contribution to the European Union*, Dublin: Institute of European Affairs

Scott, D. (1996), *Ireland and the IGC*, Dublin: Institute of European Affairs

Sharp, P. (1990), *Irish Foreign Policy and the European Community: A Study of the Impact of Interdependence on the Foreign Policy of a Small State*, Aldershot: Dartmouth

Shaw, J. (2000), *Law of the European Union*, Basingstoke: Palgrave

Sheehy, S. J. (1997), 'Towards Free Trade for Agriculture', in F. O Muircheartaigh (ed.), *Ireland in the Coming Times: Essays to Celebrate T. K. Whitaker's 80 Years*, Dublin: Institute of Public Administration, pp. 285–298

Sinnott, R. (2002), 'Cleavages, Parties and Referendums: Relationships between Representative and Direct Democracy in the Republic of Ireland', *European Journal of Political Research*, vol. 41, no. 6, pp. 811–826

Smyth, P. (1996), 'Little Ireland Can Take a Bow for a Presidency that Achieved Plenty and Was Widely Praised', *The Irish Times*, 16 December

Spring, D. (1997), 'Address by Tánaiste and Minister for Foreign Affairs Dick Spring to University College Cork Law Students', Cork, 7 February

Statewatch (2006), 'The "Principle of Availability"', available at www.statewatch.org/news/2006/dec/p-of-a-art.pdf

Staunton, D. (2004), 'Bertie and the Winning of the Constitution', *The Irish Times*, 3 July

Stewart, T. (2000), 'Foreword', in R. O'Donnell (ed.), *Europe: The Irish Experience*, Dublin: Institute of European Affairs

Sub-Committee on European Scrutiny of the Joint Oireachtas Committee on European Affairs (2007), *Fourth Annual Report on the Operation of the European Union (Scrutiny) Act 2002:1 January 2006 to 31 December 2006*, Dublin: Houses of the Oireachtas

Svensson, A. C. (2000), *In the Service of the European Union: The Role of the Presidency in Negotiating the Amsterdam Treaty 1995–97*, Uppsala: Acta Universitatis Upsaliensis

Tonra, B. (1997), 'The Politics of Justice', in G. Barrett (ed.), *Justice Cooperation in the European Union*, Dublin: Institute of European Affairs, pp. 49–58

Tonra, B. (2001), *The Europeanisation of National Foreign Policy: Dutch, Danish and Irish Foreign Policy in the European Union*, Aldershot: Ashgate

Tracy, M. (1982), *Agriculture in Western Europe: Challenge and Response 1880–1980*, London: Grenada

Urwin, D. W. (1991), *The Community of Europe: A History of European Integration since 1945*, London: Longman

Vaughan, B. and S. Kilcommins (2007), 'The Europeanization of Human Rights: An Obstacle to Authoritarian Policing in Ireland?', *European Journal of Criminology*, vol. 4, no. 4, pp. 437–460

Vergés Bausili, A. (2005), 'Ireland and the Convention on the Future of Europe', in M. Holmes (ed.), *Ireland and the European Union: Nice, Enlargement and the Future of Europe*, Manchester: Manchester University Press, pp. 133–150

Walsh, B. (1979), 'Economic Growth and Development, 1945–70', in J. Lee (ed.), *Ireland 1945–1970*, Dublin: Gill & Macmillan, pp. 27–37

Walsh, D. (2000), 'How the Third Pillar Works', in E. Regan (ed.), *The New Third Pillar – Cooperation against Crime in the European Union*, Dublin: Institute of European Affairs, pp. 23–58

Weatherill, S. (2003), *Cases and Materials on EU Law*, Oxford: Oxford University Press

Westlake, M. and D. Galloway (2004), *The Council of the European Union*, London: John Harper Publishing

Whitaker, T. K. (1958), *Economic Development*, Dublin: Stationery Office

Whitaker, T. K. (1983), *Interests*, Dublin: Institute of Public Administration

Whitaker, T. K. (1993), quoted in 'Whitaker Keen to Exclude NATO Option from EEC Talks', *The Irish Times*, 1 and 2 January

Whitaker, T. K. (2006), *Protection or Free Trade – The Final Battle*, Dublin: Institute of Public Administration

Young, J. W. (1984), *Britain, France and the Unity of Europe*, Leicester: Leicester University Press

Young, J. W. (2000), *Britain and European Unity, 1945–1999*, London: Macmillan

Index